Celebration
of Fools

Celebration
of Fools

An Inside Look
at the **Rise and Fall**
of JCPenney

Bill Hare

AMACOM

AMERICAN MANAGEMENT ASSOCIATION

New York • Atlanta • Brussels • Chicago • Mexico City • San Francisco
Shanghai • Tokyo • Toronto • Washington, D.C.

Special discounts on bulk quantities of AMACOM books are
available to corporations, professional associations, and other
organizations. For details, contact Special Sales Department,
AMACOM, a division of American Management Association,
1601 Broadway, New York, NY 10019.
Tel.: 212-903-8316. Fax: 212-903-8083.
Web site: www.amacombooks.org

This publication is designed to provide accurate and authoritative information
in regard to the subject matter covered. It is sold with the understanding that
the publisher is not engaged in rendering legal, accounting, or other professional
service. If legal advice or other expert assistance is required, the services of a
competent professional person should be sought.

Library of Congress Cataloging-in-Publication Data

Hare, Bill, 1934–
        Celebration of fools : an inside look at the rise and fall of JCPenney / Bill Hare.
        p.   cm.
    Includes index.
    ISBN 0-8144-7159-5 (hardcover)
        1. J.C. Penney Co.—History.   2. Stores, Retail—United States—History.   3.
Penney, J. C. (James Cash), 1875–1971.   4. Merchants—United States—
Biography.   I. Title.

    HF5465.U6P4519   2004
    381'.141'06573—dc22

                                                                                                2003027324

Printing number

10   9   8   7   6   5   4   3   2   1

FOR ELAINE

contents

Introduction   1

PART I—THE FOUNDER

1 America's Famous Old Man   7
2 Kemmerer   21
3 Bumpkins in the Big Apple   30
4 All Their Managers Are Like Masons   38
5 The Bailout   49

PART II—THE VISIONARY

6 Socratic Method   63
7 Their Own Thing   76
8 Batten's Ascent   85
9 The Common Touch   92
10 A Quiet Man   103
11 The Memo   112
12 The Transaction Recorder   119
13 Last of the Good Men   127

PART III—THE BETRAYER

14 New Blood   143

15 Bill Howell   156

16 The Taj MaHowell   163

17 The Designer   174

18 Showtime   189

19 The "Golden Crescent"   197

20 Onward and Upward   208

21 The Speech   219

22 Where Have All the Values Gone?   229

23 What If I Talk to W. R.?   238

PART IV—THE END

24 Jimmy-O the Farmer   247

25 There's Nothing There   254

26 Standing in His Underwear   267

27 The Funeral and HCSC   278

Acknowledgments   285

Index   287

JC Penney Stock Price Versus the S&P500, January 1998 to January 2001

(Weekly price change indexed from January 4, 1998)

Highest JCP price: $78.75 June 14, 1998; Lowest price: $8.69 October 8, 2000

JC Penney lost 80% of its value while the S&P500 gained 40%-60%.

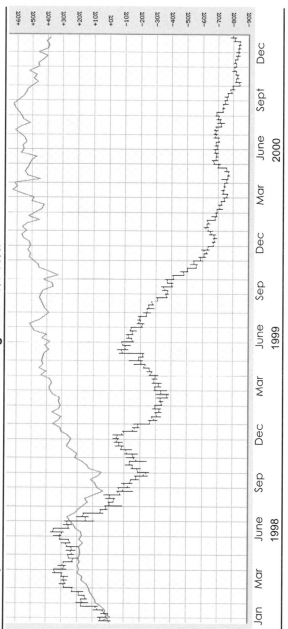

Source: Alternative Investment Advisors, LLC

introduction

"Change, of course, is the only constant, the future never assured. So to not plan for change and not invest in the future would be crazy—no matter what Wall Street says."

> —MIL BATTEN, legendary JCPenney Chairman/CEO
> and, after his Penney retirement, President/CEO of
> the New York Stock Exchange.

"I've seen top notch vice presidents who were promoted to president and performed poorly. The last rung is a leap. How will people react to power? I know of instances where the new CEO became a totally different person."

> —MIL BATTEN

ONCE UPON A TIME a retail chain grew from the humblest of Western origins. Its core value was the Golden Rule, and the first stores were actually known by that name. The company rewarded thrift and hard work by giving its store managers unusual partnership and control, provided they (and their "associates") performed significant community service. The company grew and prospered even during the Great Depression because America came to count on the chain's values and service as well as its good citizenship. Eventually, it anchored the malling of America, acquired other businesses, and became a giant enterprise. Clean as a whistle with deep pockets. What could possibly bring down such an icon of the American Dream? Yet down it came.

The subject of this book is the rise and fall of the J. C. Penney Company. It is not the present turnaround effort, which is being

well covered in the business press. These pages end with two incidents in the spring and fall of 2000, when the new administration
was just getting started. At that point in time the traditional J. C.
Penney operation was rapidly becoming a thing of the past.

To present a more engaging cautionary tale, this book is written as narrative nonfiction. That is, I have dramatized the resonant
moments that befell the company rather than simply lay out dry
facts. But, as explained later, all scenes are based upon the people
and events that gave shape and substance to Penney's remarkable
history. I have also occasionally compressed time to move the
story along (without bending the historical record, however).

Preparations were extensive. Research included a great deal of
archival material, interviews of all kinds, related reading, and investigative newspaper reports. Documentary materials such as
annual reports, company publications, videos, speech texts, presentations to Wall Street, court records, and a government investi-
gation were studied. Of particular interest were materials and
transcripts from Bob Pasch's Penney "Oral History" program
(which, consistent with the old Penney altruism, was "open to
view and use by the general public"). This presented reminiscences
dating from 1905. Also quite helpful was an essay about Penney
problems circulated casually by retired merchandise executives
Dave Binzen and Dave Fulcomer. And a special resource for information and fact checking was Mary Elizabeth Curry's Ph.D. disser-
tation, *Creating an American Institution: The Merchandising Genius of
J.C. Penney,* which was published by Garland Publishing in 1993.

The J. C. Penney Company was an odd duck in many ways.
One quirk involved its communications to outsiders. On the one
hand, historical material was generously available to almost anyone. On the other, the organization was traditionally tight with
any current internal information. As a rule, when a Penney executive spoke to an external audience, it was on a general topic like
textiles. In contrast to today's corporate blabbermouths, Penney
executives just hated to talk about internal affairs in public (which
made the speech described in Chapters 18 and 21 so unusual). The
only predictably forthcoming inside information would be obligatory reports to stockholders and the financial community, and
toward the end of the 1990s even these became artless obfusca-
tions.

Therefore, because of the Penney insularity, I could not even have considered this book without inside knowledge. The book's research associate, Michael Ponder, had 23 years with the company and provided a thorough understanding of the chain's history. He also provided important research and insights. The eyes, ears, and heart of the narrative grew out of my own 16-year experience as a speechwriter in Fortune 500 executive suites. Nearly half of that period was spent at J. C. Penney writing for top executives, including the last two CEOs of the twentieth century. Between Ponder and myself we thoroughly covered the company's present and past.

In order to dramatize early company events, I have created incidents and dialogue for company pioneers like Jim Penney and Earl Sams. This was necessary because, other than Sams's remembrance of Berta Penney, no record of such scenes apparently exists. This work was done, however, after careful study of the histories and personalities involved, and I am confident that the situations depicted are reasonable reflections of those days and people.

Later historical scenes were largely developed with the aid of the oral histories. Here, dialogue was mostly extrapolated or woven from specific remembrances caught in the transcripts. The contemporary scenes are reconstructions resulting from interviews, documentary materials (videos, newspaper reports, speeches, etc.), and firsthand observations. In all cases, I am confident of the accuracy and fairness of the representations.[1]

This book is not a comprehensive history of the J. C. Penney Company. For example, aside from a surprising cash register story, there is little about Penney's once-advanced information technology. There is little about the company's landmark real estate abilities either. Those two topics alone would be significant in any complete history. Instead, while historical contexts are present throughout, the book concentrates on the major events that drove the company up . . . and down.

Steve Rushin of *Sports Illustrated* devoted his column of September 23, 2002, to Johnny Unitas and the new and wonderful 1960s storytelling of NFL Films (Unitas lives mythically forever on film). When I read this fine piece, I found myself rereading the conclusion, first because it was so good, and then (in a humble appropri-

---

1. The reader is reminded, however, that a work like this requires drawing conclusions and making judgments.

ation) because it also seemed to summarize the ambitions for this book in a way that would never have occurred to me. Rushin quotes NFL Films founder Ed Sabol's favorite saying: "Tell me a fact and I'll learn. Tell me the truth and I'll believe. But tell me a story and it will live in my heart forever." So I hope that you learn and believe something here and that some of the stories in this book will live with you for a long time.

Bill Hare
Dallas, Texas
January 2004

part I

The Founder

chapter 1   America's Famous Old Man

AS FOUNDER OF the nation's best-known cash-and-carry business, James Cash Penney had never been amused that his own middle name described that which made his world go around. In fact, on all occasions he was quite serious about money, both in its prudent use and in assessing the value of things in trade.

Grapefruit, for example.

Gravity

Penney had been booked into the Great Southern Hotel in downtown Columbus, Ohio. He was not comfortable with such upscale accommodations on the road, but company travel people were often arbitrary, feeling that anything less was not in keeping with his elevated stature. So there he was now, in the rather elegant dining room ordering breakfast. "And about the grapefruit?"

"Yes, Mr. Penney?" said the waiter. Of course the dining room captain had quietly informed the waiter about their esteemed guest.

"Would you please serve me the bottom half?"

"Certainly, Mr. Penney." Then, just to be certain, the waiter added, "That was the bottom half, sir?"

Penney nodded, cupping both hands one atop the other as if surrounding a grapefruit. Then he straightened the lower hand into a knife and sliced the grapefruit in half, removing the upper part. "See?"

"Yes, the bottom half, then. Thank you, Mr. Penney."

In the kitchen, as the waiter placed hotel silver service on Penney's tray, he shouted at random, "Anybody know why the bottom half of a grapefruit is better?"

"Which is the bottom half?" someone said in passing.

"You tell me!"

And as the waiter, happily contemplating his gratuity, finally served the rich old man, he said, "There you go, Mr. Penney. The bottom half."

"Ah, yes. I can tell. Thank you very much."

"No problem at all, sir." He could not resist. "Oh, and excuse me, Mr. Penney?"

"Yes, what?"

"Well, the bottom half, sir? Exactly why did we order the bottom half?"

"Why?"

"I mean, as opposed to the top?"

"Oh," said Penney, seemingly relieved that there wasn't some larger issue. "It's the gravity." Again, his hands cupped an imaginary grapefruit. Now, as he grinned and his eyes twinkled, he raised and lowered his top hand as if pressing down on the fruit. Then he indicated the real grapefruit with pleasure. "More juice."

The old man finished his breakfast and checked his watch. J. C. Penney's district manager would be calling for him in the lobby, so it was time to inform the desk staff where he would be sitting in the lobby—as if the DM might somehow fail to identify one of the most famous old men in America. Penney was always early for everything but never wasted a minute. As he waited in the lobby, he would memorize notes prepared by the district manager's office about the first store they would visit that day (as it happened, the same store at which this book's eventual heroine, Gale Duff-Bloom, would begin her training three years later). Now, in the dining room, Penney rose, patted the suit pocket with his notes, and then reached into another pocket for something.

Soon it was time for the waiter to collect the anticipated generous tip. All waitstaff eyes were on the aged celebrity as he appeared to take out an old-fashioned twist-lock change purse. And, sure enough, a minute later the waiter looked around with dismay after stopping at the Penney table. Then he held up a dime between his thumb and index finger, swinging it around so that the size of the tip could be seen by all.

The date was November 1965. As he had for decades, Penney

was on the road visiting stores. He traveled alone, only receiving assistance as requested from stop to stop. He was 90 years old.

Two Quarters?

A year later in New York, Penney's president, Ray Jordan, was just returning from a difficult meeting with his boss, chairman Mil Batten. The two men oversaw Batten's baby, the great transformation of the J. C. Penney Company. Once America's Main Street merchant, the giant organization was becoming king of the malls with full-line department stores. The long-range business plan also included an expensive move into the mail order catalog business, which was soaking up money with no profit foreseen until the early 1970s. Consequently, dividends were down considerably. Wall Street, the financial press, and Penney stockholders were highly critical.

"Isn't it ironic?" Batten had said. "Now they complain bitterly because we didn't stay rooted in the past—"

"Yeah, but if we had," Jordan jumped in to straight-man the punch line, "and then started to founder like Wards—"[1]

"They'd scream bloody murder because we *stayed* rooted in the past!"

"Nobody said the job was easy."

"My, oh my, oh my."

"Maybe we should make this an ongoing educational project, instead of just saying something in the year-end letter. Send reports and 'progress' reports, and you give some talks on the Street."

"I hate speeches. Unlike our founder."

"Well, maybe we need to communicate better. 'Our future's at stake, we gotta keep on track and stay with the plan,' something like that."

"Maybe, I don't know. See what the others think."

"Will do," Jordan had said without much enthusiasm as he

---

1. The Penney Company had anticipated a recharged peacetime economy because of World War II and prepared for it (leading to its migration from Main Street to malls). But Wards did the opposite. Sewell Avery, head of Montgomery Ward, thought that wartime prosperity was setting up a postwar depression. Hence, the company was frozen and locked down to await the worst—and never realized its error until it was too late.

rose. Both men were tired of shouldering great responsibilities while fencing with myopic stockholders.

Jordan headed toward his office abstracted in thought when his secretary called, "Oh, Mr. Jordan, Mr. Penney wants you to call him."

"Oh, no," he breathed to himself, anticipating more pressure on the transformation. Might be catalog, he thought, since catalog was the whipping boy of the hour. He dialed the founder immediately.

"Mr. Jordan, I was wondering if, at your convenience, you might drop into my office for a moment."

"Certainly, Mr. Penney. I'll be right up."

"At your convenience, Mr. Jordan."

"It's convenient right now, sir."

"If you're sure."

On his way to the founder's office, Jordan shook his head with amusement. At his convenience! There was Mr. Penney, last of the mercantile royalty, still coming to the office at age 91 and still refusing to pull any historical rank. Why, they couldn't even get the old man to use a company car. Every morning he could be seen walking from his Park Avenue South apartment building to a bus stop!

Despite Batten's brilliance and Jordan's steady effectiveness, James Cash Penney was still the star of the company—ceremonially. He was by far the most popular corporate symbol in the United States, which represented a triumphant comeback from the humiliation of his financial failure and nervous breakdown suffered decades before. But while Penney had been trotted out for company conventions, store visits, and press opportunities, some New York insiders almost held the founder in contempt. The company had thrived without him and even despite him. And, once upon a time, hadn't several key Penney men actually bailed him out?

When Batten rose to power, his personal project had been the rehabilitation of the founder's reputation in the New York Office. In the field and to the public, Penney was a mercantile and moral god. So Batten set about promoting Penney's accomplishments, beliefs, and talents in the Big Apple. In time, Jordan joined in the effort.

Batten had long thought that Penney's self-improvement correspondence course for associates in the 1920s was a stroke of genius. He considered the founder's bold philanthropy, killed by the Great Depression, as uplifting and feasible in better times. And Batten had come to have an especially high regard for Penney's retail and personnel judgment.

Penney appreciated the renewed courtesies in New York. But he had never been bothered much by the remarks that he knew small men made behind his back. He ignored them, as he had learned to do the hard way long ago. Penney knew his role and had comfortably settled into it over the years. Today he was content to be only a public figure, to be an adviser only when prevailed upon, and to act as a conduit only when ardently summoned. It was in these roles, bolstered by the new respect of top management, that Penney happily lived out the rest of his life.

Jordan knew of the founder's desire generally to avoid anything but the ceremonial. But he also knew who *was* the J. C. Penney Company, and he knew it wasn't Batten or himself. He felt that Penney probably could not avoid being recruited for a cause, and therefore Jordan rapped quietly on the founder's door with more than a little apprehension.

"Thank you for dropping by, Mr. Jordan."

"No problem, sir."

"Actually, it's me. *I* have a little problem," he smiled.

"Catalog?"

"Catalog?"

"Well," Jordan said still warily, "it seems to be on everybody's mind these days."

"Not mine," Penney replied. "It's something else." The founder hesitated, as if unsure how to proceed.

"Anything I can do, Mr. Penney."

"It's about our barber."

Jordan hesitated. "Our barber? We have the same barber? I didn't know that."

"We do, and I have a problem."

"*We* have a problem, Mr. Penney," Jordan said with relief. "That man is a better storyteller than a barber, I'm afraid."

"He is?"

Jordan quickly regretted the comment. Clearly, he heard stories that the old man didn't. "Well, there's another problem, though?"

"Yes. What do you tip the man, Mr. Jordan?"

"Tip?" Jordan should have seen it coming, Penney being Penney. Still, it was all he could do to keep from grinning. "Oh, I don't know. Whatever loose change I have in my pocket. A couple of quarters."

"*Two* quarters?"

Jordan thought quickly and followed with, "If I'm feeling generous and he's somehow managed to give me a decent haircut. But I wouldn't worry about it anyway, Mr. Penney. After all, you're a celebrity, and when he's got you in his chair he's the star of that barber shop. He ought to pay *you*."

The old man chuckled. "I never thought of it that way."

"So, when do you and Mrs. Penney return to Arizona?"

"Tomorrow morning. I'm going to the apartment and pack soon. Right after my haircut," said Penney, now happily relaxed.

Blindsided

A month in the desert sun had elapsed when Penney got a call from Roy Johnson, the dynamo who had retired after running the huge Seattle store for years (and, in the generous Penney way, making as much money on profit sharing as the highest-ranking executives in New York). Johnson invited the founder to speak at an upcoming Los Angeles dinner for retired managers, field executives, and their wives. Penney agreed, thinking it was just a social affair.

The old man thrived in such situations. He still had a fabulous memory and would be able to thrill many retirees by calling them by name and remembering their stores. And he didn't have to think twice about what to say on such occasions. For 50 years Penney had been making speeches, and if you accepted his almost evangelical style, he was pretty good at it. In his mind was an encyclopedic file of phrases and statements he had used publicly over time, fail-safe material to select for any audience. And so, tonight in L.A. as he strode to the podium and everyone in the ballroom rose to their feet to cheer, he had decided to keep it simple, short, and inspirational. He smiled and bowed and raised his hands to quiet them:

"Thank you . . . thank you, my friends and fellow associates, thank you very much. Some today are expressing concern about the lower dividends of late due to the company's transformation for the future. This is natural and quite understandable. But I think that—in my old age—I might get away with some philosophizing instead of further comment on the company, per se."

He paused and looked around with a smile in such a way that the audience chuckled.

"Money, of course, can buy many things, but it can procure for us neither peace of mind nor well-being of soul. Therefore, the accumulation of wealth by itself is no measure of success, is it? No, we attain success only in proportion to the degree we are able to train ourselves to perform good deeds. Therein is the salvation of the soul. So things are of value only insofar as they serve to make us finer, more honorable, more cultured, more generous, more democratic, more influential and more faithful men and women. And as we likewise influence others. This I have seen and this I know from personal experience."

Again he looked around with a smile and again the people looked back with appreciation.

"Ladies and gentlemen, it's great being here and I am so pleased that Roy called to invite me. I look forward to speaking with as many of you as possible after dinner. Thank you."

Too short! He left them wanting more, and everyone got up and applauded—led by Roy Johnson, who returned to the podium with an odd, businesslike expression. "Thank you, Mr. Penney! As usual, wise words from our beloved founder!" Those two sentences served two purposes: They reestablished Johnson in control; he was the one talking now, the one in charge. And they set up Penney to be blindsided.

"Now, Mr. Penney, we have some business. I speak for everyone here and I speak for Penney retirees across the country when I say that it's now urgent to get something on the table." He looked around at the founder and spoke directly to him. "Mr. Penney," he continued, "Mil Batten is ruining the J. C. Penney Company! Please listen to what I have to say—listen to what our friends and associates here say after dinner—and then go back to New York for the next board meeting and have them fire Mil Batten before he kills our great company!"

Penney was stunned. Johnson went on at some length, saying that it was sheer folly to fix something that wasn't broken, that the Penney Company had been one of the most successful businesses in the nation, that it had always paid great dividends, and that it was now being driven to ruin by Batten's foolhardy attempt to start a catalog and turn Penney stores into mall anchors. Finally, the founder was asked to return to the podium for any comment. This time the audience was hushed.

"Thank you, Roy, but I have no comment at this time," Penney said. Then he added, "Your remarks were earnest and thought-provoking, and I have listened carefully and understand what you want. Now I must think about it, so I have nothing more to say at this time and will not for the rest of the evening."

A week later, back in New York for the board meeting, Penney waited for someone to bring up Johnson's complaint. He was now prepared to comment. But nothing was said on the subject, and the meeting was adjourned. Penney turned to Ray Jordan and Mil Batten. "Would you two please stay? I want to talk to you."

Penney reported the Los Angeles incident and then said, "When I returned to Camelback, I thought, 'Wait a minute. All of those managers in Los Angeles were retired. I wonder what the active managers think?' I decided to go out and visit as many stores as I could before flying East. I wanted to see the managers who are out there every day meeting the competition. And I managed to visit eight stores and asked the managers what they thought of the changes that were going on. Their attitude was entirely different. In every case they said that changes had to be made. They said that mistakes were bound to happen, but the worst mistake of all would be not making changes."

Jordan sighed, rolling his eyes to Batten. "And Roy Johnson was a friend of yours."

"Still is, I hope," said Batten. "This is just money talking. Or the lack of it."

"Mr. Batten," Penney said, "I just wanted you to know that you have my complete confidence. And I would like to celebrate that by taking both of you to dinner. Someplace special."

They went to an expensive restaurant and enjoyed an elegant

dinner. As they rose to leave, Batten looked at Jordan and nodded back at the table. The president then hung back and slipped some bills down beside the coins Penney had left.

Oh My, What a Judge of Character

Years later, Batten reflected on the founder's eccentricities with money. "He could give away millions, yet leaving a reasonable tip was just something Mr. Penney couldn't do. He had built his company on thrift, and waste was anathema to him—which blinded him to certain civilities. In the little day-to-day things he was very tight, some would say cheap.

"There are a lot of stories like this one I heard from Walt Neppl.[2] In 1952, when Neppl was first man at the big, new Denver store, Mr. Penney showed up early one morning for a program in his honor. He was carrying a satchel and said to Walt, 'They charge too much for laundry at the hotel. Where can I get this laundry done?' So, in the middle of this gleaming new Penney department store, they start honoring our founder as Walt sends somebody out with his laundry!

"But the big picture? Remember, Penney was the godfather of profit sharing. If you produced, you did very well. He was 'The Man with 1,000 Partners,' and they all got rich. So in the really important things he was completely open and very generous.

"And, oh my, what a judge of character. I've never known anyone who was more interested in people, really interested in learning about people than Mr. Penney. Nor have I known anyone I thought was a better judge of character than Mr. Penney. He almost seemed to have a sixth sense evaluating people."

But He Could Never Manage a Store for Me

As a rising star, Mil Batten had arrived at the New York Office in 1940 to upgrade the companywide training program. To his surprise, one day Penney's secretary called to arrange an appointment for her boss to visit. In Batten's office.

"Any time," said Batten. "I mean, he can drop in here any time he wishes, of course. After all, he only founded the company."

2. Penney president, 1977–1982.

"Oh, Mr. Batten, you certainly don't know Mr. Penney."

"What do you mean?"

"He would never just drop in informally."

"He's that formal?"

The secretary chuckled warmly. "Mr. Penney was born formal."

"But I'm nobody."

"Ah, Mr. Batten. Welcome to New York."

"Yes?"

"To Mr. Penney, everybody is somebody." Again she chuckled, now with a respectful edge. "Unless, of course, they prove otherwise."

The secretary made the appointment and Batten hung up in a reflective study. "That's interesting," he thought. "So Mr. Penney is still that choosy about people. I should be flattered," he concluded. "And careful."

The next day the founder showed up at the appointed time. The meeting was brief. "I have heard good things about you, Mr. Batten. If there is any way I can help you, please don't hesitate."

"Thank you, Mr. Penney."

"I mean it."

"I can tell, sir. And I won't hesitate."

"Good. Welcome to New York."

Batten found the chairman to be readily available and always helpful, a subtle savant with things to teach those who would closely observe. Ten years later, in 1950, while head of national personnel and assistant to president Al Hughes, Batten once again learned from the old man. Batten had always valued the founder's company and continued trying to carefully promote Penney's wisdom to top management. Hence, whenever possible he coordinated his store visits with the founder's own travel schedule. And there was another reason. As he recalled, "I had learned, of course, that this amazing man almost always had some lesson to impart. And he taught by case example. He didn't talk a lot like I do, with the notable exception of skillful small talk at stores and business functions. But he could make an indelible point by revealing something that we should have known but were somehow blinded to. I can cite a good example, a trip we took together to deal with a tricky manager situation in Pennsylvania.

"The town was growing and we were building a much larger store to replace the existing Main Street store. And this kind of a situation can present a personnel and public relations dilemma. Should the manager of the existing small store become the manager of the new, larger store? Is he ready? Or can he grow into the greater responsibility? Or should he be comfortably removed to somewhere else?

"Penney managers always have to be civic-minded, and this Pennsylvania manager we were about to meet had been very active in the community for years. He had many important friends locally, all of whom assumed he would be tapped to run the new store. Therefore, if we brought in someone else, they might think that the Penney Company had humiliated their friend.

"This could cause trouble. The newspaper could cover the store opening negatively, and an editorial could castigate the Penney bullies from New York. Bad publicity and word of mouth could mushroom. Citizens' committees could organize to boycott the new store. Key holdover personnel could begin quitting. Sales could nosedive, and the hand-picked new manager could suddenly be looking at an extra year to make up for this disaster.

"That would mean the hardest year in a manager's life— opening a store—would be rewarded by a low or nonexistent comp[3] check, so *he* could begin to crater. Meanwhile the cost of the money to open this store rises into the stratosphere. Since this isn't Neiman-Marcus and our margins are always thin, now it will be years before this store shows any kind of real profit. So what was the point? All that effort and expertise. All that time and money. Sheer futility. It could happen."

All this was on Batten's mind the next morning when the manager began showing them around the original Main Street store. First they were introduced to the store associates. The manager was not good with names, a Penney specialty, and several times the founder had to ask an associate, "And your name is?" Mid-morning, after shaking hands with several customers in women's ready-to-wear, Penney asked the manager what had caused the department head's injury. The manager looked around at the cast on the woman's foot and ankle and then shrugged and said, "Beats me." As they moved on, the founder looked around at Batten with a flat expression. Later the manager contradicted a number given

---

3. Penneyese for profit sharing, in those days relating to a manager's direct accomplishments.

by an associate at the hosiery bar. "Oh, no, no, no," he interrupted, turning to his guests. "We have to've done more than that because ever since the war when we couldn't get any, I've really stressed nylons." Just the slightest tightening of the hosiery lady's smile indicated that someone was wrong, and it wasn't she.

From department to department in the store, Mr. Penney continued to present the same expression to Batten—who was beginning to feel defensive, although the founder had yet to utter a word besides his effective small talk.

Just before noon, there was a session in the office during which the office manager and her assistant simply looked away as the manager pontificated about bookkeeping, inventory controls, and government forms. Then the manager took his guests to the Elks Club for lunch. On the way to their table, the manager seemed to wave at every other man in the room. After they were seated and had ordered their coffee or soft drinks, the manager rose, winked, and said, "Duty calls," and began working the room. As he approached his first targets, having no trouble with these names, his voice sounded a little too high and a little too much the hail-fellow-well-met, as though this were another performance for his guests. At every stop, the manager would always wave back at them, loudly making sure everybody in the room knew the identities of his distinguished guests.

Penney finally turned to Batten and quietly said, "I'd like to ask you something, Mr. Batten."

"Go ahead, sir."

"What do you think of this man?"

"You mean besides being an obtuse blowhard?" Penney smiled. "Okay, he's a calculated risk. And you're right, it wasn't an easy decision. We weighed all the factors, including his position in the community. On balance, we decided he should still get the job," Batten elaborated, keeping an eye on the manager glad-handing his way about the room.

Penney listened carefully and then quietly replied. "That's interesting, and I'm impressed with the thoroughness. But he could never manage a store for me."

"I accept that, Mr. Penney, but the man is going to be the manager here. The decision is made. At least until he proves otherwise."

"Well, I understand that, too. It's the way it has to be, of course." With flat eyes, the founder looked around at the sound of the manager's voice.

"And that was all Penney ever said about the matter," Batten remembered. "Nothing more. Not 'I told you so' or anything else. Because, you see, the manager did not work out at all. So it was a long time before that new store was in the black. Penney had none of the input we had in personnel. Yet he could make a gut decision that was superior to our sophisticated process back in New York."

Right off the Rack

Of course, Penney's store appearances, speeches, and press interviews were nothing more than well-meaning deceptions. As "the founder" and "honorary chairman" he was a respected and almost lovable symbol. As discussed, he had little to do with running the company any more. Even the suits on his back were a deception.

Penney's face was nearly as well known in America as Eisenhower's. In the last 25 years of his life he seemed ageless. Wispy hair, twinkling eyes, sagging jowls, full white mustache, and happy smile. The great-grandfather of ethical business success. It was important, therefore, that he look his best in public. This presented a problem for two reasons.

Penney was a hard fit, having become a pear-shaped elf in his old age. And for decades he had amiably bragged that he never wore anything that wasn't a well-made value right off the rack at Penney's—not the place for a man who needs a special fit. Yet in the photo section of this book, the reader will see a shot of the old man showing off the "Towncraft" label of his Penney suit. It's a candid photo, but the fit looks good.

It's a fake. For years the men's suit buyers had taken advantage of Penney's age (and diminished suspicions) to keep him looking right. They got his measurements on some pretext and then had a vendor build several suits as well made as those from Brooks Brothers. Penney would be taken later to a warehouse and shown various suits to pick out, all represented as heading directly for a Penney store rack until diverted, all with the Penney "Towncraft" label sewn in. Of course, they fit perfectly, and, as the photo clearly indicates, he never suspected.

James Cash Penney's favorite last promotional routine was also one of sweet deception. After his 90th birthday, his age always came up during interviews. His response was consistently something like, "Yes, I'm now 94 years old and I'm still so invigorated visiting our stores that I plan to live to be 100." Newspapers, magazines, and television sound bites spread the welcome words. Yet on February 12, 1971, while trying to recover from a fall, complications set in, and he left this mortal coil after only 95 years.

An enormous outpouring of sadness met the founder's passing. "Considering our insular little world of retail," Batten recalled, "the response was surprising. It was something like a national day of mourning." Penney's obituary ("Last of the Merchant Princes") was on the front page of every New York daily. His packed memorial service at Manhattan's St. James' Church was attended by government figures, business leaders, and other VIPs and was widely covered by all media.

There were thousands of messages of condolences. These included telegrams from the president and miscellaneous VIPs as well as notes from people of all walks of life throughout the nation. Every message that arrived at the Penney tower in Rockefeller Center was answered. This was accomplished by a team of secretaries under the supervision of Virginia Mowry, the founder's longtime executive secretary, who was becoming the first Penney archivist.

It was noted that many of the letters were from elderly men and women residing in small towns. In simple language they expressed gratitude for Penney's having enhanced their lives with quality goods that were sold with unfailing courtesy and honorable service at value prices. A few secretaries read feeble handwriting that told of a time when the stores had a different name. One read, "I am old! When I was a boy it was called 'The Golden Rule.' I think Penney was the junior partner of four older men. The chain was only five stores then. Imagine! Good-bye, Mr. Penney, and God Bless you."

Good-bye, indeed. How far the little giant had come in his long lifetime. How much his boundless energy and quick wits had accomplished with little more than ambition and integrity with which to start. How far and how much, an amazing journey from a cesspool of a Wyoming mining town to Rockefeller Center. And, as he would tearfully admit after he lost her, all because of an incredibly wonderful woman. Amazing.

chapter **2**   Kemmerer

ALL HIS LIFE it was agony for James Cash Penney to address *anyone* familiarly—including his beloved first wife, Berta. She was always "Mrs. Penney." Berta, however, always called her beloved husband "Jim" or "my Jim." This didn't mean, though, that she couldn't lace into him when angry. And the secret timidity, the lack of self-confidence she discovered in her new husband often made her furious. He was, she knew in her bones, far, far better than that.

The Self-Made Man

Berta Hess Penney pushed her husband toward rediscovery of himself. In later years when he was a larger-than-life heroic business figure, he would admit it. He would have been nothing without her. In Evanston, Wyoming, 1901, when they were living in one room with their infant son and Jim was working endless hours down the street at Johnson & Callahan's "Golden Rule" store, he would come home every night assailed with doubt. "I don't think I can do it," he would moan. "I'm afraid, Mrs. Penney." He would look at her beseechingly. "What am I? Just a clerk, that's all I am. That's all I've ever been, just a clerk."

"You owned a butcher shop!"

"And I failed!"

"Because you wouldn't pay bribes!"

"Because I'm stupid!"

"Because you're a moral man and I love you!"

Sometimes, at a point like this, Jim would start to cry. Or Berta would. Either way, they would end up in each other's arms holding on for dear life.

Guy Johnson and Tom Callahan had never seen a worker like Jim Penney, their new "first man" (assistant manager) in Evanston. They thought he was the best and most trustworthy young talent in their expanding small-town dry goods chain. Customers loved his energetic attention to detail, and he had the blood of a merchant in him. This was why he had received their coveted appointment to open the next Golden Rule store—in Ogden, Utah.

The problem was that Jim Penney was secretly terrified of Ogden, a large and prospering town whose size meant running one of the biggest stores in the chain. And when he was afraid, which was often, Penney covered it with what appeared to be a steely resolve. To Johnson and Callahan, he *behaved* like a man possessed. The illusion succeeded because, as an outgoing human working machine with a quick mind, Penney had their respect. Thus, when he said, "No, I will not open a store in Ogden," they had to listen. "I want to get my sea legs in a smaller venue." (Penney's vocabulary always amused the senior partners.)

"Such as?" Johnson asked.

"Kemmerer."

"*Kemmerer?* Are you sure?"

"Yes."

"But there's hardly a thousand people in Kemmerer."

"But enough to start."

"And it's a poor mining town."

"Not that poor."

"With a company store to fight."

"I am not afraid." (They believed this.)

"And growth? I heard it's peaked."

"No, no. Kemmerer will double, triple in size in the next few years."

"Well," said Johnson with disappointment, "I don't know, Jim. I'll have to talk to Tom about it."

"I trust he will understand. As I know you do, Mr. Johnson," said the seemingly cocky little man.

"You *are* our best man, Jim," Johnson said unhappily.

"Thank you," Penney replied. And then he went home and cried to his wife.

The next year, 1902, they opened a small store in Kemmerer. It was only 25 by 45 feet, and the Penneys lived in the attic with packing crates as furniture. But the store was loaded with merchandise, "rough corduroys and sheepskin-lined coats piled high on the center tables, with men's furnishings to one side, ladies' and babies' things to the other,"[1] and yard goods and shoes in back. The walls, shelves, and counters were also filled, and items such as notions and toys were tucked into corners (there were no cabinets or other fixtures because of the expense). Merchandise even hung from the ceiling. Guy Johnson, on his semiannual buying trip to the East, had bought well—a Golden Rule specialty. Other differences in a Golden Rule store were the absence of haggling (a single, written price for all customers) and the outstanding values. Also, exemplary service. And no credit: Every transaction was cash-and-carry.

Because the coal mine only paid once a month and the company store gave credit and accepted company "coupons," a cash business wasn't supposed to work in Kemmerer (Johnson and Penney couldn't get a loan at the local bank, despite the Golden Rule chain's excellent reputation). But Penney's store had more goods of better quality, and the "one price for all" was always lower than anything one could haggle at the company store. So the miners and their wives saved and bought. Word also spread to ranchers and farmers and railroad workers. Customers kept walking in the door, with Penney opening the store at 7 A.M. and not closing before midnight—during which time he seemed to be in perpetual motion, scurrying here and there making customers comfortable, making friends with them, explaining the quality goods, and making sales.

Still, every day Berta had to buck him up until he finally saw that he *had* succeeded and began to think he had done it all himself. This actually charmed his loving wife, who not only cooked, kept "house" in the attic, did the laundry by hand (hauling up water by rope and pulley), and did the mending, but also parked the baby's basket under a store counter and waited on customers for several hours a day.

At the end of their first year, "$28,898 of merchandise had been sold. Profits, to be divided three ways, were an impressive $8,514.

1. Mary Elizabeth Curry, *Creating an American Institution: The Merchandising Genius of J.C. Penney* (New York: Garland Publishing, 1993), p. 96.

Penney had succeeded in turning over his original inventory almost four times. . . ."[2] Johnson, Callahan, and Penney each had a third interest in the store, which was standard in the Golden Rule formula. Capitalization, mostly for inventory, had been $6,000, also split into thirds.[3] With the partners expensing his modest salary, after one year Penney was able to pay off his loan and deposit some $800 in the Kemmerer bank, making him one of its largest depositors. He was 26 years old.

A Simple, Great Formula

Tom Callahan had interests in some 20 Golden Rule stores in small Colorado and Wyoming towns located on railroads (a key ingredient). The chain was an amalgamation of partnerships that Callahan oversaw with practical ingenuity, installing several innovative concepts developed over many years as a dry goods merchant. One was no-haggle pricing. Another was cash-and-carry. Most important was astute buying by a small committee empowered to make wholesale purchases for all stores. Thus, on semiannual buying trips to the East, the "Golden Rule syndicate" became one of the most powerful wholesale shoppers and obtained excellent credit ratings from R. G. Dun's *Mercantile Reference Book* and *Bradstreet's Commercial Reports*. (The Kemmerer store, as a syndicate member, enjoyed a better rating than the mining company store!)

Callahan operated out of the syndicate's biggest store in Longmont, Colorado. Longmont had served as a training store, with head clerks ("first men") being tapped to open new stores in partnership with Callahan. Former first man Guy Johnson had been set up in Evanston (on the same basis that Johnson and Callahan would later set up Penney in Kemmerer). At about the time Johnson was getting his operation established in the corner of southwestern Wyoming, down the street from the Longmont Golden Rule, Jim Penney's butcher shop closed.[4] Broke, his savings gone, he applied for a job clerking for Tom Callahan. The merchant had

2. Ibid., p. 97.
3. Penney's funds came from new savings and a loan from his Missouri hometown bank (at a better rate than offered by Johnson and Callahan!).
4. Penney could no longer force himself to deliver a weekly quart of whiskey to the chef at Longmont's biggest hotel. He quickly lost the hotel's business and soon went belly-up.

been a customer of Penney's and had admired the young man's thoroughness and hustle. Penney was hired, and within a year he became a Callahan favorite. In the next year, Penney was on his way to Evanston. He would develop further under Johnson, be promoted to first man, and eventually be pointed at a likely new location by the senior partners. It was a great opportunity, and ordinarily Penney would have been thrilled with his new prospects. But two secrets held him down: his lack of self-confidence, which was an outgrowth of the failed butcher shop, and the fact that his girlfriend was pregnant.

Do Not Forsake Me

Petite and pretty, Berta Hess had endured a rotten and childless marriage in Detroit before divorcing her husband and heading as far west as her funds and contacts would take her. Staying with a relative in Longmont, she was hired as a butcher shop clerk by Jim Penney, her junior by two years. After closing time, Penney began walking Berta home before returning to work. When the shop failed and Penney began clerking for Tom Callahan, Berta found other employment and Penney continued their walks. In time, the evening strolls took longer and longer and it became harder and harder for the couple to part. Occasionally, Berta would only return at dawn to bathe at a basin and change. One such morning they arrived at the relative's front porch to find Berta's bags packed, her few newly acquired belongings neatly on top.

In Longmont, she had been able to hide her divorcée status and thus avoid the mean-spirited prejudices of the time. Now, as she took a room and the relative began gossiping, life in Longmont became difficult. She lost her job and took whatever temporary employment she could find, usually as a barmaid, where her "reputation" gave her a special allure. She hated her work, hated the gossip, and would have gladly moved on but for one complication. She was in love.

Life in Longmont got worse for Berta when her love moved 400 rail miles west-northwest to Evanston. Then she found out that she was pregnant.

Jim's duties were so demanding at the new Golden Rule that he was only able to see Berta once a month and for only half a day before getting back on the train for Evanston. She never said a word about her condition and Jim remained innocent—until she finally began to show and on his next trip he jumped up, aghast. "You're *pregnant?*"

"Yes, my Jim. But I'll manage."

"Pregnant?" he kept repeating, his eyes wide with fear.

Penney missed the next month's trip and failed to write. Berta thought the worst, that she had somehow misjudged Jim Penney and would never see him again. She was not sure what to do, where to turn. She knew returning to Detroit was out of the question; her reputation there—without a bastard child—was already in tatters. Night after night she pored over her address book, preparing one difficult letter after another to shirttail relatives. She had no real expectation that someone would extend a helping hand, and the letters piled up, sealed but not posted.

Never did she write a word to Penney, however, because she believed there was nothing about her feelings that he did not already know. And if he now chose to forget her, nothing in her power could change that.

Another month passed and there was a knock at her door. It was Jim, looking grave. Her heart sank. "I'm sorry, Miss Hess," he said. "I can't forgive myself." He stared at her. "I am so late. Here." He produced a small engagement ring. "I love you and want to marry you. Do you accept my proposal?" She nodded, extending her hand but unable to speak. Tears came. They were on the train within two hours, headed for Cheyenne and a simple, private marriage ceremony. Having never once allowed herself to cry when she was despairing alone in Longmont, now she cried all the way to Cheyenne. "I'm so happy," she said.

"I'm glad you told me," he grinned, holding her protectively. "You had me wondering."

They had a glorious if short honeymoon, enjoying each other and some of the Frontier Days festivities before heading due west across the breadth of Wyoming to Evanston, to the birth of their first child a few months later and to Jim's secret fears.

Mr. Sams, You Mark My Words!

As Penney had predicted, Kemmerer's population and commerce doubled and then tripled. In 1903, the growing Penney family could afford a tiny cottage as the store was doubled in size at a new Main Street location.

Now, let us stand back and take a look at this new store of "James" Penney's.[5] You can see by the signs that his neighbors had different agendas than the teetotaling Baptist. There, flanking the Golden Rule on both sides are the town's two busiest saloons. And look at those second-floor window signs right above: lawyers! Also overhead and accessible by the back stairs was Kemmerer's biggest brothel. But Penney never commented about the building's other businesses as he maintained his "regular" business hours. That meant staying open as long as anyone was on the street, and then remaining in the store for more hours of book and stock keeping. As a result, he was often the last person at work in the building—despite the nocturnal activities next door and up the back stairs. And in a short while those at work on or above Main Street, men and women alike, became James Penney's best customers, and he and his associates served them all with amiable courtesy and attention to the smallest detail of their needs.

In late 1903 Johnson and Callahan offered Penney a one-third interest in their Rock Springs Golden Rule store, an hour east on the Union Pacific. Recently established, the store had shown only mediocre results. But with Penney commuting to Rock Springs twice a month, he soon had his new store performing almost at the Kemmerer level. In the next year and on the same ownership basis, Penney opened another successful store in nearby Cumberland. By 1906, Penney's profits had been substantial enough for him to buy out Johnson and Callahan's interests in Rock Springs.

A year later, Johnson and Callahan had a falling out. But the former mentors had no quarrel with Penney, and they offered to sell him their interests in Kemmerer and Cumberland for $30,000 plus 8 percent interest. Their protégé gave them his personal note and paid the amount in full within two years. Although remaining friends with both men—and always, ardently grateful for the opportunities they had afforded him—Penney never again was a partner with either.

That same year, Penney hooked up with the most important man of his career, Earl Sams. Having seen how carefully Johnson

---

5. A more dignified name, he felt, in keeping with his elevated status in the community (but to Berta, he would always be "my Jim").

and Callahan had recruited talent, Penney made sure that *he* worked even harder at it. For every single hire, he would interview candidates at length, demand and check references, and then sleep on it for a while. Consequently, almost every clerk in Kemmerer, Rock Springs, and Cumberland was a candidate for a future store partnership. Despite Penney's exacting standards, word spread and applications mounted. He was, after all, a man who appeared to be going places.

Through a Denver employment agency, Penney heard from Sams, a 23-year-old Kansan with five years' retail experience and an eagerness to move ahead. They corresponded, Penney's final letter indicating an interest in meeting the young man. After boasting of his own accomplishments and ambitions, he acknowledged receipt of Sams's impressive reference letters and concluded in his language of the day:

> . . . I am corresponding with another very seemingly capable man. I have given you preference. This other party does not like Sunday work—we are looking for a man who is anxious to work any time of day—nights, Sundays, Holidays, or any other day—one who knows no hours, and is not particular about how much work he does. Only this kind of man I consider makes very rapid advancements. . . .

Sams and his wife, Lula, confidently arrived in Kemmerer with several bags. He was hired at the conclusion of the interview with Penney, and the Kansans never returned home. Earl Sams was a natural. No match for Penney's mental agility (almost no one ever was), Sams was quick enough and much more of a warm personality. Although a likable and diligent clerk, Penney was basically distant and formal. Probably not one person ever thought to offer him a drink (and not because he was a teetotaler, which few knew then). Everybody, on the other hand, wanted to buy Earl Sams a drink (and, when he could get away with it, he'd accept). But most important, Sams could work 100-hour weeks without complaint—one of those people (like Penney) who seemed fresh and spry at the end of the longest days. And Sams also had the heart of a merchant.

Sams started in Kemmerer; went to Cumberland as first man; and started a store in Eureka, Utah. By the time he joined Penney in the new one-room office in Salt Lake City in 1910, the company had 14 stores and was within a year of doing an astronomical $1 million in business. At that point, Earl Sams was the number-two man. And, utilizing the Penney formula and Penney himself as a financing partner, Sams had interests in three additional new stores.

In the sentence above is the phrase "the Penney formula." This, of course, is both a misnomer and a reflection of James Cash Penney's genius. It was Tom Callahan's concept, after all, that Penney was exploiting. He never originated a substantial idea in his entire business life, adopting and adapting the ideas of others and then *executing* brilliantly. That was Penney's game, execution. He would soon surpass the number of stores held by his mentors— eventually addressing Sams in his newly formal manner with, "Mr. Sams, you mark my words! One day we shall have a *hundred* stores!" Although Sams told Lula that night that the idea was daft, at the time he just nodded amiably in agreement.

chapter 3   Bumpkins in the Big Apple

FROM THE BEGINNING, three things were the most important in the Callahan-Johnson-Penney way of business:

1. Ethical behavior ("Golden Rule" was more than a clever slogan until much later)
2. A syndicate of stores buying skillfully in force
3. Partnership

Like Callahan's, the way Penney's syndicate bought gave it tremendous leverage over competition (and was even to lead to relief from a Penney banking dilemma). This meant that buying expertise was certainly the equal of the more celebrated partnership concept. But there was no question that partnership was the motor of the organization's rapid and then astounding growth.

The Chance of a Lifetime

At first, however, there was no competition between the buying and managing functions, as store partners and buyers were then one and the same. All the early store managers went on buying trips together. They got on a train in their small Western towns and traveled all the way to New York City with buying stops in Kansas City and St. Louis en route. Most of their buys, of course, were made as a group, but each manager also bought particulars for his own community.

It was a far less sophisticated procedure then because the first cluttered, chockablock stores presented mainly commodity items like basic shoes, yard goods, and work clothes. But James Cash Penney had also advertised "The Latest Fashions" from his first week in grungy Kemmerer. So he (or, later, Earl Sams) always accompanied the group to ensure that "fashion" at least had a token presence in every store. Managers who were not yet comfortable with style and fashion were thereby prevented from doing any damage to themselves.

From his first buying trip with Guy Johnson in 1903, Penney himself proved to be a major talent. Always a fastidious dresser who developed a keen sense of style, he was the original great company buyer. Despite the fact that New York City was at first virtually a foreign country to the Westerner Penney, as he placed ever-growing orders his sharp eye, knee-jerk parsimony, and abundance of backbone made him a highly respected player in the eyes of the trade.[1] They could see that Penney instinctively knew that buying led selling and that buying well meant selling well.

In time, when the number of stores made the traditional buying trips too unwieldy, Penney experimented. He formed a small group of full-time buyers and dispatched them to New York City, where, working out of a hotel (three to a room!), buys were made for the entire chain. Goods were shipped directly from factories to a Salt Lake City warehouse set up near the one-room company headquarters. But this concept failed because managers wished to continue buying at the source—which, of course, was impossible and ushered in the manager/buyer tension that dogged the company for most of the twentieth century.

Penney's answer was to establish a small buying office in New York's garment district, with invitations extended to all managers to visit "in season." This was basically continuing the former strategy with the addition of the psychological ploy of an established office and the invitation to visit. But it worked. "New York" attended company conventions at which managers now "bought." A full array of basic, quality goods was shown, with a minimal number of fashion, notion, and novelty items dressing out the presentation. Company brass stood ready to advise. Managers with particular community needs still occasionally traveled to New York, but the now formalized "buying department" fulfilled most of the store needs. In the years to come, the buying department's

---

1. Only in his old age did the discerning eye diminish.

major lines developed such leverage that the company became a leader in private brands.

But, again, it was the idea of partnership (and Penney's execution) that drove the organization's geometric growth. As he expanded from his base in Kemmerer, Penney refined Callahan's simple and powerful formula for success: Find ambitious men with admirable personal qualities and train them in the Penney ways of honor, value, thrift, and exceptional service. Then set them up in a new store in a growing small Western town located on or near a railroad.

Importantly, of course, every new manager also owned a piece, as did the previous manager who trained him. To review, ownership of a new store was typically split into thirds, one each for Penney, the old manager, and the new manager. In turn, the new manager selected a candidate for ownership of yet another new store and began training him as his "first man." Penney and established managers financed the new store owner-managers at affordable rates. Managers took little more than clerks' wages out of the cash flow, but they shared in year-end profits in direct proportion to their percentage of ownership.

Thus, as the West grew, the chain grew, driven by well-motivated quality men who would work anywhere for any number of hours per week with solicitous interest in any community's well-being. It was a revolutionary concept and a bonanza.

The Cold Hand

In 1910, Penney moved his family to Salt Lake City. He bought a new two-story, three-bedroom house in an upper-middle-class hillside neighborhood, paying $7,000 cash. Berta had become a full-time homemaker and was highly pleased with the move. Every bit as thrifty as Penney himself, she continued to do all the housekeeping chores, including sewing, mending, canning, and even repairs. Always a bundle of energy like her husband ("I never have time for aches and pains," she would say cheerfully), Berta was also active in church and community affairs and never failed to be available when "her Jim" needed to unburden himself of one or another business matter. The Penneys were immediately and solidly established in the city, and James Cash Penney was an admired and wealthy man at the age of 35.

Is there a difference between working endless hours—something that literally came with the territory in the Penney world—and becoming a workaholic? Penney no longer needed to put in as many hours as he had in the past. Earl Sams, in fact, had been urging him to scale back, to work less and reflect more. Now there were plenty of people (like Sams) to do "jobs," whereas Penney's greatest value was in dealing with issues and concepts. The founder agreed to cut down—after his next road trip scouting sites and visiting stores in the Northwest.

Penney scheduled a three-week trip that had him on the road during the Christmas holidays. Berta said that the boys would be disappointed but that they would manage. Then he sprung a surprise. The whole family was booked to Europe and the Holy Land, with departure in mid-January. It would be the Penneys' first real vacation. Berta was thrilled and began making preparations as her husband hit the road.

Because Berta suffered from asthma, her doctor recommended removal of her tonsils to lessen the risk of discomfort overseas. One day she walked two miles to have day surgery and, to save streetcar fare, again set off for home on foot after the procedure and a short rest. The weather had turned bad, a cold rain falling that turned to snow. Berta was soaked through and suffering chills by the time she arrived home. She caught a bad cold but continued her normal schedule until, a week later, she fainted in the kitchen and their eldest son raced to the pastor's nearby house for help.

Berta was diagnosed with the dread lobar pneumonia, an often fatal illness. Lula Sams began taking care of the Penney children, and Earl Sams looked in on Berta twice a day. The Penney physician brought in a specialist, but Berta's condition worsened, the pneumonia spreading and her fever rising. One evening when Sams arrived, both doctors and the pastor were bent together in a quiet discussion. The family physician turned to Sams and said, "It's not good. She wishes to see you."

Sams sat close by Berta's bed. "Did you contact him?" she asked, her voice little more than a whisper.

"I've sent telegrams everywhere," he said. "I expect something from Western Union . . . at any moment."

"Earl?" She smiled weakly.

"Yes, Berta?"

"Take my hand, please." He was shocked at how hot it was. Burning. "Earl? Promise me?"

"Yes, Berta."

"Please look after my Jim."

For the rest of his life, Sams never forgot any aspect of this moment—Berta's feverish hand, her pallor, her last attempt at a smile before her eyes closed. "I will," he managed. "I promise."

Penney arrived home a day later. Berta had slipped into a coma and never knew he had made it back. She died a few hours after his return. They had to pry his hand from hers long after it had turned cold.

Everything Penney had believed in all his life—God, hard work, "progress"—seemed to escape him. He felt "mocked by life"[2] and became extremely bitter. "Why?" he kept asking himself. One day after the big funeral, he was sitting like a zombie in the one-room company office when he suddenly screamed "Why?!" and burst into tears. Sams, who had quietly taken over day-to-day operation of the company, and their young accountant, J. I. H. Herbert, helped the founder from the room and drove him home in an automobile.

Enter: The Isaacs Brothers

Earl Sams did not officially become president until 1917, but with Penney's blessing he actually ran the company from the time of Berta's collapse in 1910. It was a job he had for the next 40 years. Once Penney more or less recovered from losing Berta, he belatedly followed Sams's advice and spent his time on issues and ideas—and on his once primary retailing interest: trying to keep the company's buying absolutely on top of the market.

1911. A major issue for Penney and Sams was incorporation of the stores. Another—since the name "Golden Rule" was not proprietary—was changing the company name to Penney's own. A third was major financing, a nettlesome problem. Only Eastern banks were capable of extending the lines of credit required for greater expansion. But they looked cross-eyed at the company's offbeat organization (disregarding Penney's sterling credit). The

---

2. Mary Elizabeth Curry, *Creating an American Institution: The Merchandising Genius of J.C. Penney* (New York: Garland Publishing, 1993), p. 125.

J. C. Penney Company was incorporated, yes, but there were so many classes of stock and different stipulations that the net effect remained an amalgamation of partnerships.

1913. One day in New York's garment district, Penney sat down with Moe Isaacs,[3] a wealthy supplier and business friend. These were two careful and strategic men. They also had high regard for each other's abilities and integrity.

"Making any progress on your paper?" Isaacs wondered.

Penney sighed and said, "Afraid not. The bankers here still have their doubts about the way we're organized." He smiled. "I think they detect a certain wildness of Western freedom."

"Mr. Penney, I have the highest regard for you and your company. *I* will buy your paper, then, my brother and I."

"*What?*" Penney laughed incredulously.

Isaacs grinned and wagged a finger. "And, with our lead, just watch. Markwell & Springer will start accepting your notes as well. Then, if you will only do two things, I guarantee you will be able to get all the money you want and you will never have occasion to have a sleepless night."

"Two things?"

"One, simplify your corporate structure—about which we will be happy to advise."

"And the second?"

"Move here, to New York City."

"*What?*" Penney laughed again. "New York? Come now, Mr. Isaacs. Why, we don't have a single store east of the Mississippi."

"Not yet, my friend. But you will. And believe me, with a new statement and a New York office, just watch how the banks here will swing open their doors for you. To say nothing about better buying and shipping."

The Great Watchwords

1914. In the most extraordinary migration in American business history, the bumpkins from the West got on trains and moved the J. C. Penney Company to offices seven walk-up flights above 34th

---

3. One of the unflattering oddities of the Penney Company was that it never employed a single Jew until Mil Batten hired Jack Behrend in 1963 to run Penney's Treasury discount stores. This was despite the Isaacs brothers' help.

Street. Before that historic event, but after the company stationery was redesigned to read:

J. C. Penney Company Incorporated
"36 BUSY STORES"

Penney had an important event to manage. It was the landmark 1913 convention in Salt Lake City's big Hotel Utah, which included the introduction of "The Body of Doctrine." Written by a colleague and later called "The Penney Idea," the founder introduced the precepts in a solemn and uplifting ceremony. Printed on fancy paper and distributed to every store manager-attendee, they were then narrated by Penney himself:

The Body of Doctrine

1. To serve the public, as nearly as we can, to its complete satisfaction.

2. To expect from the service we render a fair remuneration and not all the profits the traffic will bear.

3. To do all in our power to pack the customer's dollar full of value, quality and satisfaction.

4. To continue to train ourselves and our associates so that the service we give will be more and more intelligently performed.

5. To improve constantly the human factor in our business.

6. To reward the men and women of our organization through participation in what the business produces.

7. To test our every policy, method, and act in this wise: Does it square with what is right and just?

Finally, after the business of the convention had been concluded, Penney returned to the podium and, in his best preacher mode, added another written expression of values to the company lore. These were to balance The Penney Idea, framing the company's internal behavior. "Henceforth," he declared, "this company shall be in the embrace of another unshakable, everlasting tradition signified by four letters." He paused dramatically. "H—C—S—C." Another pause.

"I now ask each and every one of you to look beyond our business here and see your working life in light of four guiding principles. H—to stand for *Honor*, which bespeaks worth. C—to stand for *Confidence*, which begets trust. S—to stand for *Service*, which brings satisfaction. And C—to stand for *Cooperation*, which proves the quality of leadership.

"H. C. S. C. Honor, Confidence, Service, and Cooperation. Let *those* be our four watchwords from this day forward." He then asked each man to stand and affirm his dedication to those principles by saying, "I will."

Thirty-six men stood and thirty-six voices somberly replied, "I will."

Penney then concluded by saying, "Our company will be strong, but no stronger than we are as individuals; our company will be big, but no bigger than we are as individuals; and our company will be solid, but no more solid than we are as individuals. Then let us, you and I, be *strong* . . . be *big* . . . and be *solid!*"

In due course an "HCSC" lapel pin was designed. It was worn proudly by all initiates (eventually it was presented on the occasion of being vested in profit sharing). Thus, with The Penney Idea and HCSC, the J. C. Penney Company would grow into the only great American company whose business credo emphasized ethics.

Good-bye . . .

When the company began its historic move to New York, the founder lingered at Berta's grave so long that they had to hold the train. An automobile taxi was raced to the cemetery where everyone knew James Cash Penney would be found. Whispering urgently, men had to pull him away from the elegant grave marker.

Long after Salt Lake City, Earl Sams sadly reminisced from his Connecticut estate. "Some 18 years later, of course, was another bad time. But nothing like this. That was folly and to some extent fixable. This wasn't fixable at all. This was tragic. And there was guilt, of course. He was never really the same man after Berta died."

chapter 4   All Their Managers Are Like Masons

F. SCOTT FITZGERALD gave the "Roaring Twenties" a better name—the "Jazz Age." But there was no roaring success less jazzy than sober J. C. Penney's climb into the stratosphere of big business. It was sheer, brilliant pluck. Consider what was accomplished in an age without computers and Harvard MBA models. In 1924, for example, there were some 500 J. C. Penney stores. A year later, the chain had grown to 674—roughly a new store every two days! Imagine the travel involved, the expertise in real estate, financing, buying, and distribution required.

To say nothing of the personnel and training needed.

Mavericks

Because the company continued to offer a rare opportunity for young men without assets, there was never a lack of applicants. The average future manager in training was comparatively well educated, usually with a high school diploma (at a time when the academic rigors were much greater in American public schools). A few, like Latin scholar Al Hughes (a future CEO), even had college degrees.

The major common denominators, however, were modest family backgrounds and a willingness to work. Opportunities or not, in the early going nobody with a silver spoon in his mouth was likely to sign up for the overly long Penney workweeks.[1]

---

1. Interestingly, however, during the 1940s and 1950s there *were* several independently wealthy or previously self-made men serving as big store managers. Perhaps they were proving or reproving themselves. Also, a Penney manager (and especially those of the bigger stores) held a coveted and respected position in the community while receiving *very* good compensation.

Another aspect of the manager corps in the first half-century was their often colorful early backgrounds before joining J. C. Penney. Today, the most promising Penney trainees might be recruited out of retail curricula at schools like Texas A&M or the University of Florida (never the Ivy League!). In the past, they might have come out of the nose of a B-17 or from a stranded jazz band. Two J. C. Penney officers and directors, in fact, had been classically trained musicians who took "temporary" jobs at Penney stores just to get back on their feet. The legendary Homer Torrey was one.

Torrey opened the giant Denver store in 1936 and turned a profit in three months. He was a complete maverick who got results. They hated policing him from New York, but they loved his profits. Torrey became a wealthy man in Denver and had no inclination to "advance" to the New York executive suite (he did so finally as a lark and was not well received by Penney traditionalists). A highly creative manager, he was always up to "something." In addition to the usual Penney merchandise, he somehow obtained and sold impossible-to-get nylon hose in wartime 1942, scarce cigarettes in wartime '43 and '44, and a cute two-seater *airplane* immediately after the war.[2]

In 1987, long into retirement in La Jolla, California, Torrey explained his start with the company.

Q: You began in Hood River, Oregon. Why there?

TORREY: I was 18 and played three different instruments in a good band. We played pretty big dates and made good money, except our manager left with the payroll and I was stranded, owing money all over town. This small Penney store hired me for slave wages. A *lot* of work, too, but I had run up a bill at my hotel and the manager there had locked up my instruments. So I was there until I got my first check, and then it's gonna be adios, amigo.

2. A master at publicity, Torrey got wide coverage when the airplane was lifted (in pieces) into the store's fifth floor by means of a giant crane that blocked the whole street. Once, Earl Sams took a train all the way out to Denver to have it out with Torrey regarding his offbeat merchandising (including a Hammond organ played from a main floor balcony). But Sams saw the crowds lined up to get into Torrey's downtown store, and he meekly turned around and returned to New York without saying a word.

But the manager, who was a big man, dragged me down into the basement and said, "You lousy little jerk!" He looked like he was gonna lay some wood on me, so I said, "Well, Mr. Michael, maybe I can stay a little longer."

Q: You ended up liking Mr. Michael?

TORREY: A really good man, as most Penney managers were.

Q: How did you get to the next store?

TORREY: Mr. Michael recommended me for first man there, an opportunity. He let me go. That's where I met Mr. Penney. He was always on the road in those days, and one day he's there shaking my hand and then interviewing me in the manager's office.

Q: Did he ask if you smoked or drank?

TORREY: He did. And I said no, which was the truth—believe it or not, even as a musician. I could tell that he did believe me, and maybe that's why he remembered me later.

Q: Remembered?

TORREY: Mr. Penney was how I got to Lancaster, Pennsylvania, and really got ahead. New York had approved my transfer, but there was this little problem I had.

Q: Which was?

TORREY: I was really in hock to the store—$350, a huge amount. Talk about being overstocked, my closets were bulging at home. Also, a little short? Just put an IOU in the basket and run it up to the cashier and back comes your money. IOUs went into a shoe box, and I had half the whole store's. So what to do? A big opportunity in Lancaster, but I'm stuck.

Q: Somebody suggested you write Mr. Penney for a loan?

TORREY: Believe it or not. I'm this little nobody. But I do it and say I'd learned a lesson. And then here comes his check in the mail with a note for 6 percent.

Q: That was 1922?

TORREY: Yes. I was 24 years old. That was right when the company really began to take off. I took over Lancaster eventually and, believe me, I'd learned a lot. I never had a debt problem and I *never* had an overstock problem the rest of the way. Not personally, not in store inventory, not in airplanes.

Life of Leisure

Ironically, there actually was one irresponsible Jazz Age aspect to the J. C. Penney story. It involved the founder himself. Remember that for every new store that opened, James Cash Penney received (in effect) his cut. This translated into vast holdings of J. C. Penney stock, and the founder became a fabulously wealthy man. But no tragic Fitzgerald character ever spent more money with such reckless, self-absorbed abandon than Penney. Originally, of course, he had been quite thrifty and, in later life, he was well known for his parsimony. But now—without a drop of alcohol involved—his was a Jazz Age story to make one weep.

James Cash Penney was featured in newspaper and magazine articles. A best-seller was published about his career, *The Man with 1,000 Partners*. Because of the company's broad middle-class orientation, no other businessman approached Penney's popularity. And there was an egalitarian aspect to Penney's success as hundreds of other men—mainly store managers—also grew rich because of the opportunity he afforded them. Largely operating in small towns where they lived modestly, they retired quietly to places like Delray Beach, Florida, and only upon their deaths did anyone beside their bankers realize the size of their fortunes.

The national convention in 1925 would be the company's last (before year 2000) because of the organization's growing size. Henceforth, conventions would be held region by region, requiring senior management to be on the road for a month. This presaged another company redefinition on the horizon. It would take a while for this new identity to be fully defined, but the J. C. Penney Company had outgrown its status as a regional chain. It was well on its way to becoming America's Main Street merchant.

And Penney rode the gathering wave.

After an intense period in the early 1920s working on personnel and training, Penney himself spent less and less time with the company, having been seduced by the boom times and the power of his signature. With bankers eager to lend against his immense stock holdings, he began an attempt to build a second fortune through cattle breeding. (The barns at Penney Farms in upstate New York were designed by a renowned architect.) He built a country estate, a Florida mansion, and an entire village for retired ministers. He bought Missouri farms and great tracts of Florida land.

From art on the walls to jewels in the safe to entertaining opera stars and heads of state, the Penneys[3] led a celebrated life. In New York during the week, they resided in a 17-room Park Avenue South co-op with a live-in staff of five plus a full-time chauffeur. In addition to moving between residences, the Penneys traveled widely abroad with a retinue of servants. And, at all times, Penney directed greater and greater amounts of money toward more and more church-oriented charity. Consequently, toward the end of the 1920s, Penney's company activities had become limited to occasional speeches and ceremonies.

The Crash

In 1927, the company's 25th anniversary, sales reached $151 million from 892 stores. Penney predicted $1 billion in sales by the 50th anniversary (achieved on the 49th). The private label program became very successful as a pioneering testing center was built in New York to ensure quality. Stores were getting larger as well as more plentiful. In 1929, with 1,400 stores now (!), the Spokane, Washington, operation became the first to top $1 million in sales.

In light of such progress, Earl Sams initiated another historic step in becoming a national powerhouse. For the first time ever, shares in the J. C. Penney Company were sold publicly in the New York Stock Exchange.

The day that tickertapes across the country first carried the NYSE J. C. Penney Company symbol was October 23, 1929—six days before the great stock market crash.

On Black Tuesday, October 29, J. C. Penney stock closed at $13, down from a recent $120. As with so many others, the market collapse marked the founder's downfall. But historically even all-American icons such as John Wayne had to take their falls. The

---

3. Penney married Mary Kimball in 1919 and lost her to illness in 1923. He married Caroline Autenrieth in 1926 and remained contentedly with her until his death in 1971. There were children from both marriages.

story was in what happened next. With Wayne, you just knew that the big Duke would manage to get back on his feet, dust himself off, and glare ahead at the trouble now requiring immediate action.

But James Cash Penney as a resilient hero like Wayne? At a take, the idea is preposterous. Penney was more like the little loudmouth farmer who would be helplessly gunned down by the cattlemen's assassin in *Shane*. Look closer, though. In the company's first 20 years, Penney—the energetic pipsqueak who became an ageless, elfin statesman of the business world—actually was the living spirit of what became the Wayne myth. First of all, he was a true Westerner, an individualist if there ever was one. He was also a tough but fair competitor. He was a gutsy risk taker. He had standards that were hard to meet. And he stood for things; his word was utterly reliable. So to ride with Penney one had to be somebody special, and those who did formed a lifelong bond.

Unlike Wayne, however, when Penney took his real fall, he needed a hand up. And the story was in what happened next—because many Penney principals refused to help.

The J. C. Penney history is shot through with ironies and twists of fate, some of the best examples beginning with the distance that developed between the founder and many of the Penney high achievers several years before the crash. They saw Earl Sams running their company very successfully while Penney himself had entered the leisure class. After his zealous recruiting and training efforts in the early 1920s, Penney was now mainly concerned with living the good life, improving his prize-winning Guernsey herd, and guiding the vast J. C. Penney philanthropy. Penney was giving away great piles of money while his colleagues were still busy piling it up.

Then, for many, the stock market disaster produced the final cleavage. It turned out that Penney, of all people, had violated his most sacrosanct principle. He had been profligate. No matter that the impulse had been largely charitable, James Cash Penney had been a reckless spendthrift of gigantic proportions.

On borrowed money.

And now there was hell to pay. But among the many Penney managers and executives who had survived the financial calamity, few were willing to extend a hand. Their feeling of disrespect toward Penney was exacerbated by the times. When Penney hit rock bottom, so did much of the nation. Anywhere one looked, there were honest workers in dire need. And a survivor with means was not quick to sympathize with such a self-assured man who had lost so much so quickly and so recklessly.

Still there were some men who remained loyal, who had not disregarded the fact that the source of their power and money had been in the mind and strength of one man. However flawed the founder may have been, they revered the genius of Penney, the man who recognized and drove the simple brilliance of the manager-partner concept.

Earl Sams provided the quiet leadership in a fund-raising campaign to rehabilitate the founder. And Jack Maynard, the best store manager in Penney's Michigan-Ohio district, typified those in the field and in New York who needed no coaxing to contribute.

Birth of a Great Manager

In 1907 Jack Maynard had graduated from high school in San Francisco as a distinguished student and football captain. After two years working as a machinist and studying marine engineering by correspondence, he had nearly drowned when his ship foundered on the rocks just outside San Francisco harbor. Reconsidering a life at sea, Maynard took a job at the Levi Strauss overall factory. Ambitious and quick, he soon graduated from the factory floor to the office and what passed for management training. There he noticed something that captured his imagination.

Levi's biggest customer by far was a booming Western dry goods chain once quaintly known as the Golden Rule stores. Renamed and incorporated as the J. C. Penney Company, the chain was saturating the West and moving eastward. In two years alone—from 1915 to 1917—the company grew from 83 stores to 175. Maynard figured this was something he needed to be a part of, but the question was how.

There was also another, more troubling question. Eager to determine exactly what drove this new mercantile company's success, he made several discreet inquiries. All he managed to discover in San Francisco was that the Penney organization apparently had a special esprit de corps. One day an executive remarked with amusement, "All their managers are like Masons." Masons? Did this preclude Maynard, a Catholic, from any such future?

A good-looking young man with unusual presence and bearing, Maynard could also outthink his boss. Eventually, after some adroit questioning (having determined that questions rather than commentary often achieved greater results), Maynard asked the man how he might get a better inside feel for Levi's customers.

"Why," exclaimed his boss, pleased with his inspiration, "I shall put you on the road with a seasoned salesman, that's how!" A short time later Maynard had seen firsthand how unusually committed Penney personnel were. By deft, seemingly innocent questioning, he had further learned that there were no Jews in the Penney Company, but otherwise several faiths were represented, including Mormons and Catholics.

Finally, at the Walla Walla, Washington, Penney store, Maynard succeeded in pulling the manager aside and appealing for a job. The manager, Wilk Hyer, had interests in other Penney stores and was always looking for promising candidates to join the organization. He agreed to take on Maynard, sensing something special in the young man. A few weeks later, after giving his notice at Levi Strauss, Maynard and his new wife, Irene, moved their few belongings to Walla Walla, where Jack began as a basement stock boy.

It was 1916. In hardly more than a year, Hyer wrote Penney and Sams that he had an exceptional talent in Jack Maynard. Hyer wished to promote Maynard to first man—which would have represented a radically fast move up the ladder in any period of the company's history. But New York, not for the last time in Maynard's career, had other ideas. Hyer was advised to continue seasoning the young man; promotion to first man would follow in due course.

Hyer piled every kind of responsibility on Maynard's strong shoulders, often asking him to work 100 hours a week. Maynard always complied agreeably, and Hyer's sales increases were duly noted in New York. In 1920 Maynard moved to another store in which Hyer had an interest and became one of the organization's youngest first men. The store was located an hour down the road in Milton, Oregon, and its manager (and Hyer's partner), H. B. Hooper, was told by Hyer, "Just step aside and let this whizbang go." Hooper did, and a year later Hooper's sales were up nearly 25 percent. Hooper once remarked to Hyer that he didn't quite know how Maynard did it. He never seemed to give anyone instructions. His presence in the store was very strong, but all he seemed to do was engagingly ask associates and customers alike questions and more questions. Hyer responded that the same had been true in Walla Walla, where Maynard had unofficially run things although not receiving the first man designation until the move to Milton.

One day Penney visited the Milton store accompanied by Hyer, who now spent most of his time in St. Louis overseeing all of the company's shoe buying. Hyer, who filled many roles and would acquire great wealth, was also the founder's Northwest adviser before the district manager system became formalized. Everyone knew that Penney placed great stock in Hyer's word. Thus it was a shining moment when the founder shook Maynard's hand and said, "I hear good things about you, Jack. Keep up the good work."

In Milton, Maynard began his lifelong second career in civic affairs by serving as president of the chamber of commerce as well as by heading community fund-raising drives and serving on the school board. After two years in Milton, Maynard was given his own new store in Adrian, Michigan, a county seat located in a prosperous farming area in the southeastern part of the state.

Was it any surprise that Jack Maynard became the most popular and successful businessman and citizen in Lenawee County? Certainly not to Penney's management, which considered community service as important as floor sales and saw Maynard as one of a handful of national rising stars. In Adrian, Maynard ran the chamber of commerce, the community chest, the Rotary Club, the YMCA, and the Boy Scouts and served as a director of the bank. And his sales increased every year—even after the crash—making his store as profitable as any in the nation on a dollar-per-square-foot basis.

Efficiency, Success, and Sadness

In 1932, a time when most businesses were desperately retrenching or simply expiring, the J. C. Penney Company signed a favorable lease for a large space one block from the domed state capitol building in downtown Lansing. The corner building had five full narrow floors, a balcony overlooking the high-ceilinged first floor, and a large basement with alley access. Altogether, this would be a premiere "AAA" store, then one of Penney's largest. Because of the economic climate and the investment, there was considerable debate in the New York Office as to who should become this new store's manager. Jack Maynard got the crucial appointment and—despite later eccentricities—proved to be every bit as outstanding as management had hoped.

Not long after Maynard opened the Lansing store, he stopped his first man on the floor for some typically brief news. "Herb, a man from the paper will be here this afternoon, and there's a hectograph of my bio and a photo in the office." The first man—who had come from Adrian with Maynard and would continue on from Lansing for a long and solid Penney career—quickly picked up on this seemingly scant information (as Maynard fully expected him to). He nodded as both men then headed in different directions.

The *Lansing State Journal* reporter who appeared that afternoon was surprised on two counts. The first man, not the subject of the paper's article, was his host. And it was he, not the reporter, who asked most of the questions. Nevertheless, when the brief, pleasant tour and "interview" were completed, the reporter had Maynard's formal photo portrait and bio in addition to a full notebook.

Soon afterwards a large three-column feature on Maynard ran in the paper's first section. This was followed by half-serious joking in capitol corridors about the manager's political potential. No one could recall any other major state newspaper—not in Detroit, Grand Rapids, Flint, or Battle Creek—ever giving such coverage to a merchant. The article:[4]

J. M. Maynard Manager Here
Since Penney Opened Store
[SEE PHOTO SECTION FOR SHOT THAT ACCOMPANIED THIS PIECE]

Local Manager in Full Control

As manager of Lansing's J. C. Penney store, J. M. ("Jack") Maynard has total control, operating this unit in a manner that he feels is in the best interest of the customer, the community and the company. The Penney company believes that each of its stores is a distinct type of operation that can best be adjusted locally to meet the particular needs of its community.

Department store experts believe that this fact, coupled with the company's policy of "cutting-in" each manager for a

4. Reprinted by permission. © *Lansing State Journal*, 17 March 1937.

substantial share of the profits made in the individual store, is largely responsible for the success of the Penney organization.

[SEVERAL PARAGRAPHS ON THE COMPANY'S FULFILLED ASPI-RATIONS FOR LANSING AND MAYNARD'S BIOGRAPHY FOL-LOWED.] Mr. Maynard, who is also a business community and civic leader, feels that his plans for the store have been largely realized. Now, he is confident, the Penney store will reach new heights as a successful shopping center for the thousands of Penney customers in Lansing and the nearby trading areas.

Aside from its uniqueness, the *Journal*'s piece flagged three telling things at this stage of Maynard's career:

1. The Penney company success despite the egregiously bad economy

2. Maynard's own success

3. Maynard's growing influence in the community (making further good work more efficient)

Another interesting fact known only to the first man and the reporter was that Maynard succeeded in getting great ink while investing virtually none of his own time.

And so, as a self-made man rising (in bad times) to the pinnacle of his career, Jack Maynard would presently write a personal check and enclose it in the saddest posting of his life.

chapter 5   The Bailout

L ANSING, MICHIGAN, 1932.

Charity

Irene Maynard waited and then knocked on the library door. No response. She waited another moment, then carefully opened the door. Jack Maynard was at his desk, staring into space. A partly gone bottle of bootleg scotch was on the desk, a glass in his hand. Beside the bottle was a typewritten letter on the familiar J. C. Penney stationery. She recognized the signature even upside down. It was Earl Sams's, and she was concerned. So she focused on the scotch.

"You're drinking?"

Maynard looked around without speaking. He smiled, although he was far from happy.

"You were so quiet, I was wondering if everything is all right."

"No, everything is not all right. I'm going to send most of our savings to Mr. Penney."

"What?"

"That isn't the problem, dear. The problem is that he needs it."

"All of our savings?"

"Please, Irene."

"You want to be left alone?"

"Yes." He was only slightly drunk and still spoke clearly.

"Then I'll leave."

"Thank you."

She stepped back and drew the door shut with a bang. This was late one evening in 1932. Maynard was known to enjoy a social drink in the privacy of his own home. But his drinking alone late at night was unique in Irene Maynard's experience and so she hesitated just outside the closed door worrying about whatever was going on.

In the library, Maynard took another sip and then swirled the liquor in his glass. He looked away, once more into the past, to Walla Walla, to Milton, to Adrian, to the Lansing Grand Opening. He'd done well with J. C. Penney. And he was going to be a well-to-do man. Although the state and national economy was in the midst of the Great Depression, he was actually making a lot of money. The way things looked, he would easily recoup their donated savings with next year's comp check.

Maynard had made a solid impression in the right circles around town as well. Already he was being sought for club memberships and board seats. All of this, he thought again, was because of one and only one man: James Cash Penney.

Maynard was realistic. Upon reflection, he knew that even without the financial calamity, the founder would never have been lovable or even particularly well liked. He was just too formal, too distant, too fastidious and fussy to be cut much slack by most Penney people. Take away his energy and commentary, and he had the personal appeal of a 56-year-old bookkeeper. He was not close to being a man's man (like Earl Sams) and never would be. And, of course, Maynard had heard that Penney was oddly quiet and distant these days, just going through the motions. So he was not only broke but apparently now a little off his rocker—later confirmed when word of his Battle Creek stay got around.

But nevertheless—! Maynard pounded his desktop. Outside in the hallway Irene reacted, but managed to hold her tongue.

Maynard heaved a sigh and then whispered to himself. "Well, heal fast, Mr. Penney. And God bless you." He took a sip and then, becoming a little misty-eyed, put the scotch down and reached for the letter from Sams.

My Fellow Associates,

I am writing the identical letter to all of you who are listed below.

Our founder and friend, the man to whom we owe all that

we are, all that we have become, and all that we have, today needs our help. I wish to emphasize that I, personally, have undertaken this fund raising project and that it is a confidential matter known only to you and me and Marj, my loyal secretary. Mr. Penney knows nothing of this and will not know anything until money is in the bank and I am able to present a check to him from all of us. . . .

Maynard made out a check for $10,000. This was an amount that could purchase thousands of shares of Penney stock, or an amount with which the Penney family could live modestly for three years at their White Plains estate. He glanced at Sams's letter and made the check payable to "James Cash Penney Fund, C/O E. C. Sams."

He folded the check in a blank sheet and placed it in an envelope. He addressed the envelope to Sams at the New York Office, sealed it, and affixed a stamp. He slipped the envelope into his coat pocket, then he put both hands together on the desk top and shut his eyes.

In Denial

"Of course it's serious," Penney declared to his lead attorney one December morning in 1931. "But I really don't think it's a long-term problem. How could it be? It's just an adjustment after too much wild speculation."

"An adjustment, Mr. Penney?"

"The market is bound to come back. It has to."

"We certainly hope so, Mr. Penney. All of us here hope so. But we felt it was time to meet face-to-face because of the possibility of continued difficulties."

Penney's reply was quite amiable. "But how can you say that, sir? The market will rally, it has to. You mark my words."

"Perhaps," said the attorney, making the word sound as ominous as possible.

Penney knowingly held up a forefinger. "Or, my dear fellow, then at least as far as our own stock is concerned. After all, in no way does the current Penney price represent the real value of our company, the *real* value of our stock." In this, Penney was actually correct. Even in those disastrous times, the J. C. Penney Company remained well managed and financially strong. But, as the attorney knew only too well, Penney's bank loan collateral was prey to the market's capriciousness, no matter how sound the actual company happened to be. And this collateral represented the founder's entire holdings of common stock in his company.

Penney had paid for his stately lifestyle in cash, but he owed roughly $8 million[1] to five New York banks for expenditures primarily in agricultural and church-related philanthropy. Now the value of Penney's collateral was shrinking to that of his loans. With more negative movement, and with no foreseeable recourse on the part of the debtor, the banks would be empowered to sell him out.

"And let us not forget my personal reputation, sir," Penney continued. "I have no doubt that reason and loyalty will prevail at the banks until our price recovers."

"Mr. . . . Penney, I am loath to be so blunt, but good intentions have perhaps diminished with the value of your stock. And I am afraid that at the moment your bankers view the market's future as . . . tenuous." The attorney hesitated, hoping that the weight of his words would have some effect. There were two primary questions on his mind: How much in touch with reality was his client? And to what extent would Penney allow his affairs to be redirected?

Penney's reply was smugly beside the point. "You know, sir, there would be no J. C. Penney Company today if I had not taken risks and retained my faith in good men."

The attorney detested his artless reply, but it was the only thing he could think of: "Be that as it may, Mr. Penney, we feel that your personal situation is potentially rather grave. We recommend, therefore, that stern measures be taken. I know how difficult this must be for you."

With the most remarkable innocence, Penney pleasantly inquired, "What do you mean, 'stern'?"

"Here is a complete brief prepared jointly with your accountants." The attorney handed Penney a string-tied cardboard wallet. "In short, immediate and severe retrenchment. Assume that you shall lose all of your collateral—"

---

1. About $150 million in 2003 dollars.

"*All* of my common stock?" Penney interrupted, as though he had just heard the most preposterous story.

"—All of it, Mr. Penney. Therefore, you should immediately liquidate all of your Florida farms, your Missouri farms, your Florida land, all your commercial property and other holdings. All proceeds into federal government paper. And, importantly, cut the Penney Foundation back to a skeleton staff and severely curtail all activities so that—perhaps—it may remain a viable entity for some future better day."

"Are you quite certain . . . ?" was all Penney could say now.

"A defense must be prepared, principally because of Miami, Mr. Penney. What I have outlined will probably save your White Plains estate and your upstate farm and herd, as well as—perhaps—your charter position in Foremost Dairy. We can give no absolute assurances, but we are reasonably confident."

"Miami?" said Penney, as though he had heard no other word. "Yes. Troublesome."

"*Troublesome?*" thought the attorney, reflecting that he and his highly regarded firm had their hands full with their famous client. Penney's financial problems would stand out even in the cascade of calamity befalling America at the time. Yet when he had walked into the law offices that morning, his personal appearance had not shown any indication of distress. The attorney had observed the jauntiness, the perfectly tailored and appointed attire, the fine grooming and healthy color, the seemingly constant upturn of the mouth.

"I am afraid, Mr. Penney, it's a bit more complicated than that."

"Oh?"

And now Penney's countenance began changing right in front of the attorney. First the eyes went bad. They became oddly skewed, searching. It was as if there were suddenly two beings inhabiting Penney's body, the old upright Western tycoon along with some newly orphaned child.

"I am afraid that the Miami situation, Mr. Penney, is much worse than we had anticipated. We have just learned that the City Nation Bank will momentarily fall into federal receivership for insolvent national banks."

Penney was out of his chair with a loud, "*What?*"

"You are also the defendant in a suit brought by depositors in federal court because of, ah, banking irregularities."

"WHAT?"

"Mr. Penney, I am sorry."

Penney grabbed the edge of the desk and looked at his attorney with wide, wild eyes. "But I invested more than three million dollars to shore *up* the liquidity of that bank! To shore it *up!* Three million to shore it up!"

"I am sorry, Mr. Penney."

Penney sank back into the chair. The dapper merchant prince who had earlier breezed into the law firm suddenly seemed totally spent and haunted. This moment signaled the beginning of his physical and emotional decline.

Wiped Out

Over the next few months, Penney rejected the proposed emergency liquidation. In a daze, he maintained the agricultural and religious philanthropy until the last dollar was gone. Still, adroit maneuvering by his attorneys and accountants managed to protract his fall over another year, during which time, of course, the market and the economy sank lower and lower until there was no way for anyone to dodge reality. And the Hard Times resonated outwardly in ever-wider concentric circles of gloom. Unless you were a civil servant, a schoolteacher, or extremely lucky, the 1930s would mark your life forever.

The banks sold out Penney, his dividend income disappearing with his stock. Almost worse, the little stiff-backed formal man— that former paragon of rectitude and virtue—suffered severe damage to his personal reputation. The sensational Miami fiasco caused him to be cited for gross fiduciary negligence in bank matters, a federal court order eventually demanding that he make restitution in the amount of $1.5 million to the bank he once controlled for good works.[2] His misfortune was widely publicized, especially in New York, and the reactions were often sarcastic or even vicious. He was an easy target. One was likely to hear or see

---

2. "However well-intentioned, most of the bank's directors were 'mere dummies,'" said the court. Penney had loaded his board with like-minded religious and charity activists whose qualifying bank stock was actually owned by him. This put the bank in violation of national banking law requirements. The restitution was finally paid in 1943.

commentary like, "Where is Penney's 'Golden Rule' now?" or, "Does 'The Man with 1,000 Partners' have as many creditors today?" A tabloid screamed, "J. C. Penney: Deadbeat Do-Gooder!"

Now Penney was virtually broke, his spirit crushed. His bearing of polite but cool confidence changed to a look of dismay or pitiful humility. People averted their eyes when he approached.

Penney had lost their 17-room New York City co-op, the Belle Isle mansion in Miami, the farms, land, commercial property, and businesses. The great model farm cooperative in Florida disappeared, and the vast charitable endeavors ceased. The Penney family took up residence at Whitehaven, the small estate in White Plains where half the house was closed off to save expenses. Chickens were raised and vegetable gardens planted to further economize. To pay his attorneys, accountants, and modest household expenses, Penney cashed in his last available asset, an expensive insurance policy. So the possessions, position, and influence of the Penneys' former lifestyle came to an end, with trappings like cars, jewelry, servants, and club memberships vanishing into the sinkhole of the Great Depression.

The Helping Hand

Earl Sams survived the crash with prudent investing and was now particularly anguished over the founder's downfall. He could not help recalling the night when Berta Penney's burning hand had tightened on his as she whispered, "Promise me, Earl. Look after my Jim."

Well, he had—belatedly. Sams unreasonably held himself partially responsible for Penney's misfortune. Somehow, he felt, he should have been able to avert the founder's charitable extravagance. Failing that, he had now at least put together a plan for the founder's rehabilitation—albeit one fraught with danger.

The plan itself was sound. Sams knew that the bad publicity was largely centered in the East and would dissipate in time. Moreover, Penney's reputation and popularity remained intact in America's heartland, the heart of the company's constituency. So the plan was businesslike enough to dispel any aura of charity.

But Sams also knew better than anyone how stubborn Penney was, how willfully independent and proud. And so as he had proceeded with the plan, Sams had been flogged with apprehension.

And as the moment now approached, he continually reminded himself to approach the founder with the greatest tact. Otherwise, he feared, Penney was likely to blow up and collapse and perhaps never again regain his equilibrium.

The money had been deposited, and the time was at hand. Night had fallen. Other than the cleaning crew, the two men were alone in the 34th Street offices. They were meeting this late because Penney had not wished to be seen by anyone upon entering the building and making his way to Sams's office.

"Mr. Penney," Sams began. He, who could speak with ease at banquets, conventions, and congressional hearings, felt as if he could hardly breathe. "Many of the best men in this city are suffering terribly today."

"I know," said Penney, his dulled eyes lowered, his voice subdued. There had been no eye contact since Penney had slumped into the chair beside Sams's desk.

Penney! Once of the erect carriage, the firmest handshake, the most intense eyes! Sams recalled his first meeting with the little dynamo, in 1907. He was dazzled as he heard about the impossible number of men the founder would interview in order to fill a single post. Penney had said that he desired and demanded nothing less than the best men in the West—men who would then have to *prove* their worth by working long hours at low wages. And he, Earl Corder Sams, had been picked and had proven himself, and now he was one of the nation's most prominent businessmen. All because of the man seated beside his desk—the man he felt he had failed.

Sams looked at the disheveled and haunted Penney. With temples pounding, he again heard Berta's feverish voice. His throat felt parched. He took a swallow of water.

"Mr. Penney," he began, "I have a plan for us."

The founder stared at the floor as though at a movie newsreel of himself being stripped clean.

"Mr. Penney," Sams continued, "you are an incalculable asset to the great organization that you founded and built. As a spokesman and symbol for the *J. C. Penney* Company," he emphasized, "you would bring this company great publicity and attention and respect. With press-coordinated store visits and speaking engagements across Middle America—where you are respected and revered—there would be an avalanche of goodwill." Sams, believing everything he uttered, hoped that his words were not turning Penney off. "As such, at the maximum New York Office salary of $10,000 a year, you would be a bargain if you would resume your chairmanship of our board as well."

Sams tried to gauge Penney's reaction so far. But the founder had not stirred, his eyes still down. "I have something else to say and, Mr. Penney, I will ask you to please hear my words carefully on this." Fearful that at any minute Penney would come to life and walk out muttering scorn at even the *idea* of charity, Sams continued. "Many of your friends and colleagues have been in touch with me. These are men, like me, who are deeply indebted to you for providing them with the opportunity of a lifetime." He paused for effect. "Together, we want our chairman to again possess a significant share of his own company."

Sams took a deep breath and slid a check over to the edge of his desk. It was for $250,000, and Sams said, "They have contributed to a fund totaling that amount." Finally, Penney looked up. He stared blankly at the check seemingly without comprehension.

Now Sams managed a smile. "It was their wish, Mr. Penney, that you repurchase J. C. Penney stock. Our company is worth far more than its current stock price, and all of us are certain that the price will rise significantly in the years to come. And why is that? Because of you. Because of the Penney Idea and because, across the country, they will know that more than ever a Penney store is the place to look for the values so desperately needed in American households today. If we work carefully and diligently, Mr. Penney, these Hard Times can be good times for your company."

Sams took another breath and waited. He had done all he could to sell this moment. He braced himself. And then he slowly realized how much he had underestimated the distance the founder had fallen. Penney was a beaten man, every minute of his 56 years showing in the sag of his body and the pallor of his face. He looked at Sams with bloodshot eyes.

"Thank you" was all he could manage to whisper.

James Cash Penney was thus set back upon his feet. After three years he would cease taking the salary, and by 1940, when the company declared a dividend of $5 per share,[3] he owned 51,000 of them. But the going was rough at first.

---

3. A superlative dividend. In 1940 you could eat in the Plaza Hotel's Edwardian Room for $5—all day!

As Sams watched Penney perform his duties conscientiously but without spark, he and others in the New York Office waited for a change in the founder. They waited for the old spryness and twinkle to return. They waited for the return of the rapid gestures signaling the birth of some new strategy or his famously urging the use of a better idea from someone else. And they waited. The founder did not improve in these ways.

Brother, Come Join Us and Know Peace

One day in December 1932, Penney left the New York Office building and walked down 34th Street to the magnificent Penn Station, just blocks away. In better days the station had never failed to thrill Penney. When traveling with others, he would take particular pains to celebrate one of New York's architectural wonders, the breathtaking majesty of the steel and glass Penn train shed—its steel-ribbed and latticed pillars rising to the steel tracery of arches, vaults, and domes that supported acres of steel-framed glass over the tracks. But today he saw and felt nothing.

Penney entrained for a series of store visits. In an unhappy contrast to times past, nobody in the field was happy to see him. A few store managers even called New York, concerned about Penney's manner and appearance. He dragged through his rounds and, despite the cold weather, there was perspiration on his brow and his hands trembled noticeably. His face also showed the beginning of a rash. Sams heard this and did the only thing he could. Fearing that Penney was on the verge of a nervous collapse, he called ahead of Penney and spoke to Dr. Elmer Eggleston of the famed Kellogg Sanitarium in Battle Creek, Michigan.

About a third of the way through his itinerary, Penney stopped in Battle Creek at the sanitarium—as he had for years. The purpose was his annual checkup by the head staff physician and his boyhood friend, Dr. Eggleston. The doctor, once the smartest boy in western Missouri, had affected a jaunty breeziness since college to counterweight his IQ. And at every other checkup he had clapped Penney on the back and said, "Jimmy, you'll outlive us all! On your way, my friend!"

This time was different.

Eggleston set his stethoscope down thoughtfully as he smoothed his mustache. "Hey, Jimmy," he said in a measured voice, "guess what? You got a bad case of shingles, and that ain't all. You're suffering from severe mental depression, my dear friend. So whaddaya say we pop you in bed for a while and get this stuff fixed?"

With the diagnoses, something burst and Penney began sobbing uncontrollably. "I'm sorry, Elmer," he gasped, "I can't help it."

"I know, Jimmy, I know," said the doctor, holding Penney's hand. "And we're gonna get you glued back together, that I promise."

Days later, still unable to sleep well, Penney began shuffling about the sanitarium halls at night. Orderlies watched him carefully as he passed slowly along, mumbling to himself. They listened, occasionally picking out whole sentences. Eventually they knew the complete sad story: "I was in Washington and Oregon. Berta and the boys were going to have Christmas alone. I was too busy for Christmas. They would be alone. When she became ill, it was too late when I got home. Berta never knew I got back." Finally, exhausted, Penney would fall into an overstuffed chair, sometimes quietly sobbing under his breath. Then he would be led back to his room.

The little man was also suffering from a crisis of faith. By accident one night he heard people praying and softly singing hymns he recognized from his youth in Missouri. "God will take care of you," they sang. The sound drew him against his will into the small sanitarium chapel. There he defiantly said, "She never knew I made it back. She died without knowing." He had spoken to the backs of the tiny congregation. A woman turned around and extended her hand toward Penney, saying, "Brother, come join us and know peace."

These people also had problems, and there was compassion in the woman's voice. Penney spoke no more and found himself sitting in the pew beside her. He bowed his head. Moving his lips but uttering no sound, he said a bedtime prayer from his childhood.

In later years during his almost evangelical speeches across the country, he would say that what happened next was a miracle. Because at that moment in the chapel an enormous weight began to lift itself from his frail shoulders. It rose up through the ceiling plaster to the sanitarium roof, where it succeeded timber and tiles and ascended into the cold night and disappeared into the ether.

In that instant James Cash Penney began to recover. He hugged the woman and kissed her cheek, returning to his room with a strange, grateful glow. A week later, having regained much of his strength, he was breakfasting in the dining room on the sanitarium's health food, corn flakes. Dr. Eggleston approached with a medical record folder, which he rapped on Penney's table with a smile. "Hey, Jimmy, guess what? The record don't lie. You are greatly improved. So get yourself dressed and meet me in my office."

Eggleston strode away and Penney looked after him apprehensively.

But he was dressed and in the doctor's office within the hour. "Jimmy!" said Eggleston. "Didn't I tell you what we'd do? You're almost cured!" He laughed and then noticed the tender, tentative look in the little man's eyes. Eggleston touched Penney's shoulder and gently squeezed it. "Why don't you get outta here, Jimmy," he said softly. "Go home. All you gotta do now is rest up a while. Have them call your other stores and say you're postponing your trip. Better yet, I'll call Sams and ask him to do it. So all you gotta do is pack and get to the station."

The doctor put his arm around Penney and gently guided him toward the open door. "Go home now," he said. He gave Penney another squeeze and nudged him ahead. "Go home for Christmas, my friend."

At about the time Penney got on the eastbound train in Battle Creek, a young West Virginian received the first of three breaks that would define his J. C. Penney career. This same young man would eventually rise to a position that allowed him, as a personal project, to introduce full dignity into Mr. Penney's active old age.

part **II**

The Visionary

chapter 6   Socratic Method

THE MAIL HAD JUST BEEN PLACED on his desk. C. W. Coleman nodded his thanks and absently sorted through the delivery—then seized a particular business letter and rose to his feet. He held the envelope up to the light and then headed downstairs to the sales floor.

The Unlikely Move

Coleman found Mil Batten writing up the ticket after selling a suit.

"Mil?"

"Yes, Mr. Coleman?"

"New York," said Coleman, indicating the envelope.

"New York?" repeated Batten with the most tentative of smiles as the manager handed him the letter.

"Mind if I wait?"

"No, of course not," said Batten. He looked at the printed return address on the envelope:

> J. C. PENNEY COMPANY
> INCORPORATED
> 330 WEST 34TH STREET
> NEW YORK 1, NY

And the typed addressee and simply worded destination:

> MR. WILLIAM M. BATTEN
> C/O C. W. COLEMAN, MANAGER
> J. C. PENNEY COMPANY
> INCORPORATED
> PARKERSBURG, WEST VIRGINIA

He took a breath and held it, slowly tearing open the envelope.

Finally, perhaps, Mil Batten was getting on track. As he unfolded the stationery he thought of the irony. Named Most Likely to Succeed in his high school yearbook, Batten had been spinning in circles since he dropped out of graduate school two years before. He had worked and borrowed his way through Ohio State, where he earned a degree in economics with honors. He had also received scholarship offers to MBA programs at Harvard and the University of Chicago. This was in the teeth of the depression, 1931, and Batten chose Chicago because they offered $200 more than Harvard. But he never completed his first year. "MBAs weren't the credential they would become," he said decades later. "Also, while Chicago's a great school, I didn't think I was learning all that much more, and I was becoming anxious about my future."

Returning to Parkersburg, his home town, Batten's anxiety would not diminish until the arrival of the New York letter. Not that he couldn't find work. Unlike millions of men at the time, he was consistently employed and earned good enough money. "The problem," he said, "was that I was treading water. The jobs were either morally compromised or led nowhere. And I was in love and wanted to get married, which was out of the question until I could indicate some kind of future. But my prospects seemed as bleak as the economy."

So he finally made a very unlikely move.

One day Mil Batten stopped by the small Parkersburg J. C. Penney store—not exactly the place where one would expect to find even a Chicago MBA dropout. But Batten knew a great deal about the Penney Company: as a teenager, he had worked at the Penney store 25 hours during school weeks and 60 hours a week during the summer. He had so impressed the manager that he received a standing offer of full-time employment after college.

What he had not learned about the J. C. Penney Company from C. W. Coleman and from reading in Coleman's library of Penney materials, he had learned at (of all places) the University of Chicago. Bored with reexposure to economics and other subjects he already knew, he once spent a week in the business library studying the Penney Company and the retail industry in general. He was particularly struck by three things. The first: Of all the major businesses in the United States, only Penney was rooted in strong ethical core values. The second: Apparently the top men at J. C.

Penney were as highly regarded as anyone at General Motors or Standard Oil. And the third: While most J. C. Penney store employees suffered poor wages in return for fringe benefits, from the level of store manager on up the money could be *better* than at GM or Standard Oil.

Batten decided that he was willing to work long hours for low wages in Parkersburg—if, once under the company's wing, he would be free to look for career opportunities lying elsewhere in the Penney world. Coleman not only agreed; he immediately got a letter off to John Keys, a personnel executive in the New York Office. Announcing to Keys that he had reemployed Batten, Coleman then praised his work ethic; his touch; and, especially, his intelligence. He concluded:

> But Mil Batten is destined for greater things than we can offer
> him here in Parkersburg. In other words, John, here is a talent
> for the Company to cultivate. So I say with confidence: put
> this man in a big store under a progressive manager and watch
> him go.

Break number one.

John Keys turned out to be Batten's second break. The personnel man prided himself on being a talent scout; he also had unusual patience and a sense of humor. Batten was sent on interviews with managers of two prominent Ohio stores, both of whom offered him positions that he politely rejected. "I didn't feel either of those men had much to teach me," he remembered. "Which was hard to say tactfully to Mr. Keys. And this was a time of longer and longer breadlines. So add guilt to worries about any future."

Even a big operation like the Penney Company with its then 1,500 stores could offer precious few management-trainee jobs during the Depression. Batten continued in the small West Virginia store for nearly another year before the letter he now held in his hands arrived.

He looked up at Coleman with a smile. "It's good news." Keys had written:

> Dear Mr. Batten,
>   I believe that we have finally found a store and manager
> that will meet with your approval. . . .

This was the large downtown store in Lansing, the capital of Michigan, that was managed by the remarkable Jack Maynard. Break number three and the biggest of all.

Batten was hired at a salary of $70 a month, $15 less per month than he had made part-time in Parkersburg before college. "It's enough to live on until you prove you're worth more," he was pleasantly informed by Maynard. After collecting his things in Parkersburg and bidding a grateful good-bye to Coleman, Batten stopped by the Ohio home of his beloved (whom he had met in college). "I proposed to Kathryn after speaking with her father," he said. "I assured them both that by the next year I would be earning $100 a month."

Sophistication

The five-story Lansing store was one of the most productive in the whole chain. Only huge-for-the-time operations such as Seattle, San Francisco, and Denver were more profitable. This was doubly impressive because Lansing's automotive economy was quite depressed. "The reason for Lansing's success," Batten recalled, "was solely because of the manager. Jack Maynard—and I almost never use this word—was a genius with people."

Batten started in the shoe department, to the rear of the main floor. With the department manager looking on, Maynard sat him down on the first day and explained the job and what was expected. It was the only time Batten ever heard the boss give specific instructions.

Maynard finished with, "Mil, any problems, always feel free to talk to me. My office is always open to anyone here."

"Okay," said Batten.

"But say it's some sensitive issue. Say you're concerned but don't want to be associated personally with the problem. What then?"

Batten spoke too quickly: "I wouldn't be afraid to come to your office even then, Mr. Maynard."

The manager was still a good-looking man in middle age with a great smile and a mellow voice. He gave Batten an appraising look and then smiled and said, "You probably would. But let me explain what I tell every one of our associates."

"Of course, sir," said Batten.

"If you have any complaint, even if you don't like my tie or the shine on my shoes—anything—just write it down on a slip of paper. You don't have to sign your name. Just send it to the office in the tube." Maynard gestured at one of the old pneumatic tubes for sending sales slips and cash to and from the office. "The cashier puts the notes in a shoe box and we read them at the store meeting every Thursday morning."

"Is that difficult?" Batten asked.

Maynard smiled again and said, "No. I don't run the meeting, the first man does. But whatever the complaint, if it's reasonable, he corrects the situation."

"You don't attend the meetings, Mr. Maynard?"

"I'm there, but I stand in back."

Batten had wanted to say more but managed to restrain himself. Already, though, he understood that Maynard's methods were unusual. He quickly saw that the first man was completely in charge day to day. Maynard held him responsible for the operation of the store, its merchandising, most personnel, and everything else. But Batten saw as well that, somehow, Maynard's presence was everywhere, that his control was absolute without his seeming to exercise much authority at all. Fifty years later Batten looked back on his own career and said that Maynard's management techniques were the most sophisticated he ever encountered.

Ticket to Ashtabula

In early 1935, after a year in Lansing, when the manager of the shoe department was moved up, Batten got the job. He became the youngest department manager in J. C. Penney's Michigan-Ohio district, and shoe sales rose. Three months later Batten heard that Lloyd Rittenour, a 10-year veteran, was being transferred to a smaller store. Rittenour managed the Lansing store's main floor, the next-best job under that of the first man. The rumor puzzled Batten. He went up to Maynard's office on the balcony overlooking the main floor.

"Yes, Mil. What is it?"

"Mr. Maynard, I just heard that Ritt may be leaving. For Ashtabula? Is that right?"

"Yes, it is."

"Well, sir, I'm trying to learn everything I can, of course."

"And?" Maynard's question—particularly his sound and facial expression—was neither intimidating nor vague.

"I've been on the first floor for 15 months now, and I would have said that Ritt's a good man. If you don't mind a little interjection here." Batten managed a smile and waited as Maynard regarded the comments in his appreciative way.

"I don't mind, and you're right," Maynard said, indicating the floor below. "Mr. Rittenour is a good man and I think someday he will run a small store well. But he cannot stay here any longer."

"Why not?" The two words had tumbled out of Batten's mouth despite himself.

"Because I would have to give him instructions. And I never give people instructions." Maynard smiled. "Do I?"

"No, sir, you don't."

"Anything else?"

"No, sir."

"Well, I'm glad you came up on another count. Mr. Rittenour will be leaving in a month. And I'll be promoting you to take his place. Just keep it under your hat for a while."

Batten touched his chest and mouthed the word "Me?"

"Yes, and well deserved, I might add."

A month later Rittenour departed, and there was a small cake and punch party in celebration of Batten's newest promotion. Maynard (age 45) and first man Herb Steinmetz (age 38) said nice things about Batten (age 25), and the other associates crowded around with their own congratulations (smiles on the faces of some older men were a bit forced). In short order, Batten had the floor running better than before, to the surprise of many. This did not, however, mean that his work was outside the manager's unique scrutiny. Nobody's was.

Maynard was a floor-oriented manager, on the floor two to three hours a day observing everything and talking to customers and associates alike. One day he approached Batten and indicated the front of the store. "Mil, in women's accessories I noticed that you have women's gloves on the first table. I was wondering why you have that particular item on your best table."

"Well, because of its sales possibilities," Batten said, giving Maynard the rate of sale and projected sales for the gloves. "So, in my opinion, the sales justify that table."

"Fine," said Maynard. He added, with a smile, "You know, I'm not familiar enough with our merchandise to know what's selling and what isn't. But when I walked past the table I wondered, 'Now why is this item here?' I didn't think it justified such an important table." Maynard nodded and stepped away toward another interest with, "But now I can see that it does."

A typical encounter with the manager. Questions, never instructions, but always questions. Batten knew that if Maynard had heard him stumble, that if he had not had a sound reason for the gloves being on the prime table, the reply would still have been, "Fine." But in a different, thoughtful tone, his expression indicating the slightest shade of disappointment.

Maynard actually did not know much about merchandise and merchandising. He was not a merchant in that sense, which made him unlike the other star performers in the chain. He had a fundamental belief that people were the difference, that good people got good things done. Therefore he surrounded himself with the best people he could find, gave them responsibility, and consistently backed them up.

One day, for example, Maynard's wife, Irene, entered the store with two friends. Batten observed the ladies from across the store as Mrs. Maynard led them to the hosiery department. "Now you have to understand," he reflected years later, "that we had one of the outstanding hosiery departments in the whole company. Percentagewise, in fact, I think we were on top. A Mrs. Elsie built that business, a great associate. She was typical of a number of women in the store, real professionals who ran their departments and trained people like me. They provided the stability and know-how."

Mrs. Elsie and another woman were busy with several customers when Mrs. Maynard said, "Mrs. El-sie," in a loud, sing-song voice.

"Hello, Mrs. Maynard."

"We are wait-ting, Mrs. El-sie." Mrs. Maynard's friends stifled giggles.

"I'll be with you personally in just a minute, Mrs. Maynard," said the department manager. Her other customers scowled in the ladies' direction.

No more than 30 seconds went by before another "Mrs. El-sie."

"Yes, Mrs. Maynard. Just another minute."

The manager's wife's eyes narrowed. "That is *not* acceptable."

Mrs. Elsie looked desperately at her other customers and said, "I'm sorry," swallowing her voice. She abandoned those women and served Mrs. Maynard and friends with a tight face.

As the three ladies left the store with their new hosiery, Batten walked over to see Mrs. Elsie, who was too upset to face her unserved customers.

"Mrs. Elsie," he said, "I just wanted you to know how sorry I am that happened. I will see what I can do." The woman looked at Batten and then put her hand over her face and fled to the women's rest room.

Batten went directly up to the manager's office and related the incident.

"I'm terribly sorry that she did that. What do you think should be done?"

Batten only hesitated a second. He trusted the question and had thought about this while climbing the stairs. "I think you should go home and tell Mrs. Maynard not to come into the store for three months."

"You do?"

"Yes."

"All right, I'll do that." Maynard rose, put on his coat, and went directly home, where he waited for his wife to appear. After returning to the store, he also apologized to Mrs. Elsie, assuring her that such a thing would never occur again. Nobody saw Irene Maynard again for almost half a year, and when she returned to the store she was a model of deportment.

Some in the company thought Maynard's style was flawed. They felt that a good Penney manager should be more hands-on. In Batten's view, this was probably why Maynard never advanced out of Lansing—not that he ever wanted to. He loved his store, he loved his position in the community, and he loved his lifestyle.

Maynard had a beautiful summer home on Walloon Lake in the Petoskey resort region of northern Michigan. Every year just before Memorial Day he would leave for a summer of recreation and service as commodore of the Walloon Lake Yacht Club. He did not reappear in Lansing until after Labor Day. There was telephone contact, although it was rare. The Penney hierarchy was fully aware of this, and New York Office executives even occasionally spent a few days at the lake as his guest. "I have hay fever," he once told Batten, "and I'll kill the SOB who gives me a cure for it!"

The manager's sense of style extended well beyond his personal life, something that was underscored one day for Batten—indirectly, of course.

Romance the Trip

Jack Maynard had a heightened sense of a correct shopping environment. The moment Batten had set foot inside, he noticed that Maynard's store had a distinctly different appearance from any other J. C. Penney store he had seen. Substantial and very subtly stylish, it looked more like a city department store than the usually dowdy space one expected upon entering most Penney stores.

One afternoon after concluding some routine business, Batten turned to leave in the manager's office. "Mil," Maynard called, "hold on a sec." He caught Batten by the balcony railing that overlooked the main floor. "Just thought of something. I must be inspired today."

"You are?" Batten answered with a tentative smile.

"Well, since you attended the University of Chicago, for the longest time I've thought we ought to have a conversation." Batten had quickly learned to take almost nothing for granted about Jack Maynard, so the twinkle in the manager's eye was both exciting and perplexing. He knew he was about to learn something interesting, and he did not have the slightest idea what it would be.

"Okay" was all he could manage, making him feel a little unworthy.

"I'm going to point out something I normally confine to our visual people. Something that our other associates and our customers certainly feel, but something that most people don't really see, per se."

"Oh?" Batten replied, now unworthy without question.

"When you were at Chicago, which of the great Chicago stations did you happen to see?"

"Stations?" Batten repeated stupidly, hating himself further. He had no idea why the question hadn't been, "Which of the great Chicago department stores did you see?" But, as quickly, he knew that train depots—or at least the "great" ones—somehow figured into the way Maynard sold merchandise. "Only two," Batten answered. "Union Station was where I arrived, and I went up to Milwaukee one weekend from the Northwestern."

"Two of the best, perfect," said Maynard. "And why am I pleased?"

Batten still didn't have a clue, and said so. "I don't have the slightest. But they sure are spectacular buildings, outside and inside."

"Exactly," beamed Maynard. "To what purpose, though?"

Batten had to say something and gambled on logic. "I don't think you mean rich railroads splurging on fancy showplaces. So I'd say they celebrate traveling by train. They romance the trip."

"Yes, the perfect words," Maynard said, "'celebrate' and 'romance.' After all, as a practical matter what do you need for a city train station? Just a huge, nondescript barn, really. But those magnificent stations not only celebrate and romance travel, they do what? For the customer, the traveler?"

"Reassure?"

"Yes, but say there were two identical trains going to your destination, each for the same fare, each as convenient as the other. But one leaves from a big, dingy barn, the other from a great station. Which do you choose?"

"Obviously not the barn."

"Because?"

Batten glanced down at the first floor and had it. "The great station adds value to the trip?"

"Precisely." The manager had followed Batten's eyes. He delivered one of his grand smiles and waved at the store below with confirmation.

Batten played it out with confidence now. "So to sell dry goods and everyday apparel, all that's really needed is some clean, decently lighted space and some fixtures. Nothing more. And that's about all you get at the average Penney store. But this is not your average Penney store."

"Are we pretending we're something we're not, then?"

"No, we don't pretend we're Marshall Field's or Carson's. We sell value merchandise," Batten answered. "On the other hand, if the store looks better than it has to, in the customer's mind the values are enhanced. At the same time, the associate feels greater pride and renders better service. And the customer leaves happier than she might have otherwise, and she doesn't keep her feelings to herself."

Maynard beamed and clapped Batten on the shoulder, turning

back toward his office with, "Sometimes, Mil, I wonder if there's anything I can ever teach you."

I *Know* He Is!

As Lansing's civic and business leader, Jack Maynard had New York's respect. The Penney Company believed in community service and was probably the nation's best corporate citizen. Maynard was a frequent speaker at company meetings on this subject, always inspiring his audiences. In every speech he said, "A good store cannot exist in a bad community."

Maynard's civic involvement again concerned an Adrian-like spectrum of good works to which he added more politically specific duties like the governor's capitol building commission. He also included rather deft efforts in more practical areas. Late one afternoon, for example, he returned to the store and, needing to talk, waved for Batten as he ascended to his office.

"I've figured it out," he said, a glint in his eye. "Are you up on the anti-chain agitation these days?"

"I believe so," said Batten. He knew that a federal anti-chain law without much punch had been passed, and that Congressman Wright Patman was talking about introducing new legislation with more power to cripple chains. A worse problem for chains was the fact that laws had already been enacted in 39 states. Associations of independent merchants had successfully lobbied state legislators for severe discriminatory taxes on chains. The argument was unfair competition.

The anti-chain movement was building and now focused on Michigan, a key labor state that had not yet passed such a law. The thinking went that if Michigan did so, the remaining states would follow suit. Batten knew that this might put his career at risk. But the issue and political action were too removed from his personal everyday life to be little more than abstractions. Jack Maynard (whose radar was always on) suffered no such limitations, however. In fact, he had just succeeded in reducing the problem to a possible one-on-one solution.

"Well, the answer is Rouser."

"Yes, sir?"

"He's the one putting the bug in their ears."

Equidistant from the state capitol building and a block away on another corner was the C. J. Rouser Drug Store. Every day when the drugstore opened and every night when it finally closed, Batten passed by on his way to and from work. Even in the dire economy, he had sensed the independent druggist's prosperity and now he was filled in on Rouser's thriving prescription, sundries, and lunch-counter business as Maynard laid out his plan. The preponderance of the drugstore's customers were men ducking in from the capitol. And the druggist, a politicized and voluble man, patrolled his store and put the bead on influential legislators.

"Every day Rouser fills them with anti-chain propaganda. So stop him and Michigan doesn't pass the tax law."

"One man has such influence?"

"In this case, yes, believe it or not. That's how a lot of legislation gets done up there."

"Then how do you go about converting him?"

Answering with relish, the manager said, "Rouser's a decent sort, just misinformed. I'm going to become a very good friend of his. I'm going to give him all of our business. I'll drop in at all times. I'll find some reason to have a Coke. I'll have some reason to buy something. I'll even start having lunch there regularly." At that moment Batten knew the depth of his boss's commitment. Because Maynard loved nothing more than having lunch at his club as often as possible.

"And every time I walk in that drugstore," Maynard continued, "I'll find some reason to chat, and in the process he's going to learn a lot about chain stores. He doesn't know it yet, but I'm going to convert him."

It happened just like that. Following the anti-chain movement's failure in Michigan, the Supreme Court declared discriminatory taxes in Iowa unconstitutional. Other states repealed similar laws, the tougher federal tax proposed by Patman never passed, and the movement was over.

Months later Mil Batten happened to grab a quick bite at Rouser's lunch counter. The druggist was behind the counter talking to a customer about Michigan State football. When he finally started to walk away, Batten rose on impulse and reached out his right hand. "Hello, Mr. Rouser, I'm Mil Batten. I work for Jack Maynard."

"You do?" Rouser replied pleasantly. "Well, how do you do? And what you *really* mean is you spend all day answering Jack

Maynard's questions!" The druggist laughed. "Good heavens! He has to be the most inquisitive man on the face of this earth!"

"He may be at that, sir," Batten replied.

"I *know* he is!" The druggist laughed again as he returned to work.

chapter 7   Their Own Thing

AS SKILLFUL AS MAYNARD WAS, he could only push New York so far.

First man was the only major personnel decision not wholly vested with a Penney store manager. Because of the importance of the job, approval from above was required. When there was a stalemate between the store manager and the district manager, New York often simply dictated who the new man would be. This put Maynard in a bind. He could easily anticipate the knee-jerk objections to Mil Batten's first man candidacy—too young; not enough years of service; limited exposure to all store departments. To Maynard, however, Batten was clearly an exception to any rule in the personnel office. Therefore, the manager had planned a campaign. For over a year Maynard had carefully praised Mil Batten to his district manager and to New York. His theme was consistent: Batten, he said, was a fast-track candidate for advancement and must not be judged against normal Penney criteria.

Criteria Win—For a While

It was now early May 1936 and Batten had been in Lansing almost two and a half years. Maynard was finishing an airmail special delivery letter to New York. The topic was number one on his mental to-do list before heading north to Walloon Lake for the summer. He concluded with these words:

> I suggest that you recheck C. W. Coleman's letters from Parkersburg, John Keys' files in New York, and my own continu-

ing praise for Mr. Batten in correspondence from Lansing. Then you may more fully understand that Mil Batten's length of service should not weigh nearly as heavily as this fact: Here is a young man who can get more accomplished sitting on his porch in the evening than most men can by digging all day.

While broadly accurate, this was somewhat romanticized, as was Maynard's want. The truth was that Batten had neither a porch nor the time to sit on one. His ideas came when walking the few blocks between his one-room apartment and the store. Working 85-hour weeks, he usually only had time for a late supper with Kathryn (who was teaching school) before falling into bed.

Maynard put the letter aside as Batten entered the balcony office. "Ah, Mil, sit down for a minute."

"Anything wrong?"

"No. Right, actually. But I'm not sure I should tell you any of this."

"Oh?"

"Afraid you may be disappointed. Both of us might." Maynard regarded Batten and continued. "Steinmetz has been promoted. He gets the store in Upper Darby, Pennsylvania. Which leaves me short a first man." He paused to tease the moment, then produced his million dollar smile. "I'm putting in your name, of course."

"*Thank* you, Mr. Maynard."

"You deserve it." Then Maynard's expression changed. "The problem is New York. I'm afraid they're somewhat limited in imagination over there. You know, of course, that in the whole chain nobody has ever become first man at your age and with as little as your time here and in West Virginia. Nobody."

"Yes, I know."

"It'll be a tough sell."

"Yes."

"But if it can be done, I'm the one to do it."

Batten rose and reached to shake Maynard's hand. "Thank you, sir."

"No. Thank you for working out so well. Oh, and keep this to yourself until we see how it all shakes out, okay?"

It didn't shake out well.

Just before Maynard was scheduled to leave for the summer, he approached Batten on the main floor. The manager held out his hands, palms up. "Mil, I said we might be disappointed, and predictably, New York has other ideas."

"Well, thanks for trying, Mr. Maynard." Batten tried to hide his disappointment, to forget the fitful days and nights of waiting.

The manager chuckled dryly. "I don't know if they're trying to send me a message or what. But not only are they unable to see you quite yet as first man, they are sending me two first men instead."

"Two?"

"Believe it or not. I'm going to have to delay leaving for the lake in order to get them acclimated. But I'll be relying on you, Mil, for a smooth transition while I'm gone."

"Certainly."

"A bit awkward there, but I know you can handle it."

"Yes, sir."

"And, Mil?" Maynard produced a serious smile. "We just have to live with this. But on the positive side, both of these men have 12, 13 years of experience. Hmm?"

Batten answered with an obligatory nod. "They'll have things to teach me, I know."

"Yes, and between you and me I'm happy you have such a quick take on things." Maynard let it hang there.

"Thank you, sir. Because I'd better learn fast from these men?"

The manager cracked a smile and nodded once, his eyes asking for one more answer.

Batten returned the smile. "Because I imagine they won't be around for long?"

The co-first-men concept was, of course, doomed from the start. Batten managed to get along with both men and absorb much of their experience. The problem was that they couldn't get along with each other. Worse, both of them were totally flummoxed with Maynard's management style. "What do you mean?" one or the other would plead to the manager. "Please explain what you want." They were gone in a little less than a year.

Batten received a note via the pneumatic tube:

Please see me in first men's office.
—Maynard

He quickly went up to the balcony. The first men's office was between Maynard's and the room where the secretary and the cashier worked. Just outside, he had to step aside as two young men from the stockroom removed one of the twin desks. The manager was waiting inside with a big smile. "Congratulations to my new first man!" He gestured toward his own office. "I just got off the phone with Al Hughes, no less. Imagine. Paying long-distance rates at the Penney company!"

Batten was wearing a big grin as Maynard continued. "Mr. Hughes said, 'Jack, with great misgivings we are finally acceding to your request regarding Mr. Batten. I'm afraid if we didn't, you'd find some stratagem to get rid of whomever else we might send in.'"

1937. Mil Batten, age 27, now had a well-paying job for depression-torn Lansing. He would be making $250 a month, which was a good living. The Battens could now afford to rent a small house and buy a used automobile. But it was the attention that Maynard had forced New York to give him that mattered most. Misgivings or not, his name had been entered on the short list of Penney candidates for greater things. As he said much later, "I was with Jack Maynard for six years. I would never again learn so much so fast. I owed everything to him."

It's a Problem, Jack

Maynard returned from his summer at Walloon Lake tanned, relaxed, and fit as usual. But only a few weeks later he was in an uncharacteristically dark study. The problem was an especially bad Lansing economy. As the rest of the nation had inched somewhat out of the Depression, the automobile industry nose-dived, and the whole J. C. Penney district of Michigan-Ohio was affected. For the year, the district was down 23 percent, with Maynard's Lansing store down 7 percent.

"The automobile industry had its own private Depression that year," Batten recalled. "In Lansing we had Oldsmobile, REO, and Motorwheel and a lot of suppliers, and everybody was hurting. Business at the store was way off, but even so we were a lot better than the district numbers. Still, who loves a loss? And Maynard was very competitive. He just hated the idea of a loss on those comparison sheets in New York. So he was becoming more and more tense. Everybody could sense it."

After Batten oversaw taking inventory at the end of that year, he and the first-floor manager were talking in his office. They compared notes on how rough it was and what could be done about it. Adding gloomy emphasis to the discussion, Maynard appeared and just quietly hung by the door with a downcast expression. "It was the only time I ever saw him so discouraged," Batten recalled. "He was basically a very optimistic person. But now he was discouraged and terribly tense."

At his desk, Batten excused the floor manager and then rose looking at Maynard. "Oh, and Mr. Maynard?" Batten added, with formality because the dismissed associate was still within earshot.

"Yes, Mil?" the manager said distantly.

"On another matter, may I see you in your office?"

"Certainly," Maynard replied in a flat voice.

Batten closed Maynard's door. "What is it, Mil?"

"Jack, did you know you are very tense these days?"

"I do. And it worries me," Maynard said. "I'm afraid I might say or do something wrong because of all of the pressure we're under."

"Well, in my opinion what you ought to do is take a vacation."

"I was on vacation all summer."

"But I think you ought to take another vacation as well."

"You do?"

"Yes. The best thing that could happen for this store right now is for you to get out of here. Everybody knows your every breath, even when you're at Walloon Lake. And everybody sees how worried and tense you are, and now *they* are getting worried and tense."

"I see. I never thought of that."

Batten nodded. "It's a problem, Jack."

"Well, okay. If that's what you think, I'll get out."

"It would help."

"All right."

Maynard left that afternoon with his wife. They stayed at an American Plan resort hotel in Indiana, where, for two weeks, they canoed, hiked, enjoyed two-hour dinners, and spent evenings in the bar listening to a good combo.

When the manager returned, refreshed and in good humor, the staff's morale soared. The store soon returned to profit. "That was the only time I ever saw him close to changing his management style," Batten recalled. "And had he succumbed to giving direct instructions, we may not have survived."

Roses at J. C. Penney

While Jack Maynard rarely involved himself with merchandise per se, his personal tastes often found expression in his store (and caused displeasure in New York). For example, he loved to garden. In the spring and fall he worked the black dirt at his Lansing residence, and summers he did wonders with the sandy soil of northern Michigan. Raising roses was his specialty. One day in the spring Batten was called outside to the sidewalk, where, much to his surprise, a nurseryman was unloading balled rose bushes.

"Mr. Baton?" mispronounced the nurseryman, holding out a delivery slip. "You want these inside or what?"

"I have to check," said Batten. "Be right back." In a moment he was at the manager's door, poking his head inside. "Are we in the nursery business, Jack?"

"Ah, Mil," Maynard said, rising. "They're here? Did I get a little carried away? I thought a spring rose bush sale might make sense. That's excellent stock and the price is right, but if you don't like it I'll send them back."

"It isn't a matter of liking or disliking," Batten grinned. "It's the DM and New York having a conniption fit."

"Don't worry about them. What they don't know won't hurt them. But what do you think?"

Batten shrugged and said, "I don't know. I guess we could see how they sell."

This horticultural event became the second of four reasons that Mil Batten came to the active attention of Penney's eastern poohbahs. While a wag in the New York Office labeled it "The War of the Roses," hardly anyone else in Penney's hierarchy took this breach whimsically. The fundamental strengths of the chain lay in its core credo, its shoulder-to-shoulder uniformity, and economies of scale. J. C. Penney stores, with few exceptions, sold apparel, shoes, and soft goods, *period.* Only certain managers in the system ever challenged this limit on entrepreneurial imagination. Homer Torrey in Denver was the most notorious, but Jack Maynard frequently managed to be bothersome as well.

As one of the store managers who usually made as much or more money than the New York brass, Maynard had always felt a bit constricted and hemmed in by company policy in this regard. He never sold anything on the side for his own purse, always declaring inventory and revenue precisely every year. He just felt that even though he wasn't much of a merchandiser, the addition of a little spice and variation to the norm was healthy—and perhaps profitable. Over the years he continued to have his fun.

Hence, one of the front windows was dressed with rose bushes and signage, and a display of bushes was built near the shoe department at the rear of the first floor. Just inside the front entrance, Batten was placing an easel with a poster he had asked the store visual man to letter:

A rose by any other name will smell
as sweet in your own garden!

ROSE BUSH SALE: REAR

Maynard approached and said, "Ah, very nice, Mil." He nodded at the poster, saying, "Except the Bard may be spinning in his grave over the liberties you take."

"You know Shakespeare, then?"

Maynard held up his right hand like a hammy performer and raised his voice, reciting, "What's in a name? That which we call a rose by any other name would smell as sweet."

Batten began polite applause and was joined by Mrs. Elsie at the hosiery counter as customers looked on with unsure smiles. Maynard bowed and continued on his floor rounds.

An ad in the paper that afternoon completed the promotion. The next morning when Batten opened the store, a crowd was waiting. They ended up having to reorder from Maynard's contact several times. But while the spring rose bush sale was a smash hit, John Parker, the Penney district manager, made one of his unannounced visits and had the predictable reaction. A critical report went to New York, followed immediately by a telegram to Maynard from Bill Binzen, Penney's vice president and general merchandise manager:

JACK MAYNARD MANAGER
J C PENNEY CO
LANSING MICHIGAN

THE COMPANY DOES NOT
SELL ROSE BUSHES STOP

WHICH MEANS LANSING
STOP WHICH MEANS
CEASE AND DESIST STOP
IMMEDIATELY

BINZEN

Again, the manager asked his first man what he thought.

"Well, Jack, they're selling like crazy, and on this item alone we're making up for last year's loss."

"We are?" grinned Maynard.

"Easily."

"So what do you recommend?"

"Well, I say what the hell. Let's play this as long as we can."

Maynard just laughed and said, "Okay." Then he wadded up the telegram and tossed it over his shoulder. "Did you see a telegram around here?" he asked. "I think they must have misdelivered it somewhere else."

"Must have," said Batten.

Word of the continuing promotion, of course, got to Parker and he let New York know. Maynard received a registered, airmail, special delivery letter ordering him to dispatch *Batten* to a meeting of the Operating Committee so that they might be fully apprised of this intransigence.

A highly amused Maynard immediately put Mil Batten on a train. "The trouble with New York," he chuckled, "is they can't see the forest for the rules." It was Batten's first trip to New York and an otherwise unique moment. Never before in company history had a first man, one of perhaps 2,000, been called on the carpet in front of Penney senior management: CEO Earl Sams, COO Al Hughes, chairman Penney himself, Bill Binzen, and others. Corporations, even the great ones like this, sometimes do the silliest things.

"Well," smiled Batten upon returning two days later, "it was pretty much of a one-way conversation." Maynard was beaming and began to laugh under his breath. "They're really angry, Jack," Batten continued, unable to hide his own amusement. "Selling bushes . . ." He had to stop and catch his breath. "Selling bushes is against . . . company . . . *polisee* . . ."

Batten and then Maynard burst out laughing. Next door, the secretary and cashier were puzzled at the jovial racket, and even associates downstairs looked at one another quizzically. When the laughter subsided, Maynard managed to ask, "Well, what do you . . . want . . . to *do* . . . ?"

"I think . . . we'd better . . . *quit!*"

Again the secretary, cashier and people downstairs wondered what was so funny. And from the sound of it, they must have wished they had been in on the joke as well. In short order, the remaining stock was sold, the window dressing and display were struck, and the easeled poster was changed to read:

A rose by any other name will smell as sweet
in your own garden! But NOT here!
We are SOLD OUT! Sorry!

ROSE BUSH SALE: OVER

chapter **8**   Batten's Ascent

AYNARD WOULD HAVE his amicable revenge for the rose bush quash by failing to get New York approval on a far more important merchandising issue—thereby actually gaining it.

The Hidden Ball Trick

The third time the name of Batten was on New York lips was the result of a serious competitive problem suffered by all Penney stores, but especially those in larger urban areas. Maynard, among others, had complained about it for years. But more than one New York Office executive commented that only with the advent of Mil Batten in Lansing had a simple and easily implemented solution been forthcoming. The following letter arrived in New York addressed to the head man, Earl Sams. It was signed by Maynard, but everyone who read the letter thought that Mil Batten had probably written it.

> Dear Earl,
>   More than any other thing, of course, the autonomy of the J. C. Penney manager is what built this great company. Therefore, please note that in no way does the following proposal violate the cardinal rule of manager control. The plan proposed below is *voluntary* and could be canceled at any time.
>   To review, presently buyers must recommend fast-moving style merchandise on price lists from which managers then make their selections. At this point, our competitors in value

fashions are *already* selling what we have just selected—making J. C. Penney non-competitive.

Therefore, we propose that managers *voluntarily* assign a portion of their open-to-buy to the buyer of selected, fast-moving lines. The buyer is free to use this to buy and ship on the spot. If the manager dislikes the buyer's performance, the open-to-buy assignment is simply canceled.

Viewing this as a safe and progressive concept, we respectfully request its presentation to the Operating Committee.

Sincerely,
Jack

"But, oh, how they hated the idea in New York," Batten recalled. "Everybody was afraid that, over time, the sacred power of the Penney store manager would be compromised and eventually eliminated. They were afraid that this plan would be expanded and evolve into centralized merchandising. I always thought this was way overreacting. Without diminishing the managers' authority, in years to come the company would develop many ways to speed product to market. Anyway, at the time they rejected the idea.

"But can you imagine how we made up for the lost profit in rose bushes?" Batten chuckled. "We were used to being turned down in Lansing, so we had anticipated New York's reaction and prepared a second letter."

Dear Earl,

Of course, we accept the Operating Committee's decision regarding all store managers.

We wondered, however, if we in Lansing might adopt the plan for our own exclusive use? You could observe our results as a test case.

With that request, let me remind you that there is *no* other Penney store manager who values his autonomy and responsibility (and rewards) more than I do!

Sincerely,
Jack

"We knew it would be a burden for New York to allow that for just one store," remembered Batten. "But, I guess, in order to keep us quiet they agreed to do it, and from that time on Maynard was weeks ahead of any other Penney store in value fashions. But even though this resulted in a spike in Lansing profits, New York kept a lid on the idea."[1]

Who Wrote That, Jack?

Except for a few bad patches like the automotive bust, sales per square foot were nowhere greater than in Lansing. This was an especially strong accomplishment because, compared with larger operations like the huge new downtown Seattle store, Maynard's floors were too narrow and confined to be truly efficient. He made up for this in three ways. There was the outstanding shopping environment and a superior staff coaxed into outstanding performances by endless amiable questioning. And, of course, his value fashions were now in synch with the latest trends.

Maynard, therefore, was held in the highest regard by the New York brass. Despite the run-ins they had learned to anticipate, they appreciated his sales and respected his standing in the community. As a result, his presence and input at company meetings was always sought and appreciated. Maynard could make inspiring speeches on community service, but what really got everybody's motor running were his often trenchant comments on operations—in the chain *and* in the New York Office.

Consequently, at a Toledo, Ohio, regional meeting in mid-January of 1940, Jack Maynard's first out-loud remarks caused a stir in the ballroom. Rising from the floor to address the chair, CEO Earl Sams, he would imply that the emperor's clothes were a little drafty.

A corporate program, like CEO speeches, is often offered by the top executive as if it is of the executive's authorship. And, if not that, it is always clear that at least the executive's imprimatur is on it. This is only fitting, after all, since all programs reflect the CEO's mission and standards. Or they should. This was as true then as it is today.

1. Times and priorities change. As the consumer became more sophisticated, the merchandising talent and taste of Penney managers became suspect. After JCPenney's downfall, the first major project begun by the new management in 2000 was stripping managers of *any* buying authority. Instead, the buying function was centralized and strengthened with more expertise.

Earl Sams, the silver-haired picture of vigorous health, was watching Herb Schwamb, his personnel vice president, conclude a presentation of the new Penney Management Training Program. This material had been shipped to the stores months before. Its purpose was to prepare qualified young associates for store, district, regional, and New York management positions. The purpose of Schwamb's presentation today was to light a fire under store managers regarding the actual usage of the program.

When Schwamb concluded, thanking the audience to polite applause, Sams rose from his seat near the podium. He pointed a rolled-up meeting agenda at Schwamb and raised a fist in a token salute.

Sams stepped to the hotel ballroom podium and said, "Well! An excellent presentation, don't you think? Thanks, Herb. I think that was just great. Now, before we break for lunch, do any of you have any comments about what we've just heard?"

A DM and a manager offered successive favor-currying compliments on the program. Then Jack Maynard stood to speak.

"Nice job today, Earl."

"Thanks, Jack."

"Okay, let's see, let's see . . ." said Maynard, fishing in his coat pocket as if not quite sure of finding what he was looking for. "Ah, yes," he continued, pulling out five pages of handwriting.

"You see," said Mil Batten, again looking back in time, "when Maynard got anything from New York, he would always ask us to critique it. So in comes this training program, which he asked me to write a memorandum about. The next day I handed him five pages handwritten on a scratch pad. And what did I think? Not much, basically. It was too superficial, too narrow in scope, and not challenging enough. I just didn't like it. We had already developed our own training program, and it was quite superior. And I said as much—for Maynard's eyes only, I thought. It turned out that was the trigger that got me to New York."

"Well, gentlemen," Maynard said in the ballroom, "I know of at least one person who doesn't think much of that program. We all seem to like it, but he doesn't."

Murmurs arose in the room. "What do you mean, Jack?" asked Sams.

Maynard held up the pages. "I've got a memorandum here I'd like to read, if I may."

"Go ahead," said Sams evenly.

Maynard read the pages, his mellifluous voice heard clearly in every corner of the room. He finished and stuffed the pages back in his pocket with a smile and nod toward the podium.

There was a pause, and the murmurs grew louder.

In the life of any corporation, getting at the truth internally is always a major challenge for the leadership (or it should be). And there, in Toledo in 1940, was a demonstration of the Penney Company's traditional character: its ability to often cut through the crap and deal with the truth, to usually select the best available idea, no matter where it came from (give or take New York's teeth-gnashing over Maynard's creativity). While this trait would disappear in later years, it was as alive and well at this meeting as Sams himself.

"Who wrote that, Jack?" asked Sams. "I know you didn't, and I think I know who did, but tell us who did it."

"I'm not going to tell you," Maynard smiled. The murmurs peaked. "Not until you tell me what you're going to do to him."

"I'm not going to do anything to him."

"Is that a promise?" said Maynard, again with a smile.

"Jack," said Sams, "how long have we known each other?"

"Okay, Earl. Sorry. The author of that memo . . ." Maynard patted his pocket. "The author is Lansing's first man, Mil Batten."

Sams's face showed the slightest creases of a smile. "Why," he said, "am I not surprised?"

Brass Down the Hall

A few weeks after he read Batten's critique in Toledo, Maynard received a letter from Herb Schwamb, the personnel director, announcing his imminent arrival for a store visit. After two days of observations and interviews, Schwamb attended Lansing's own management training program, which Batten conducted. Afterward, Schwamb asked Batten if he might go home with him that evening to meet Kathryn and chat. Batten called home, and two hours later, after a light supper and a relaxed visit, the personnel man nodded approvingly at Kathryn and then said, "Mil, we'd like you to come to New York and work for me. On the training program. To fix it. What do you say?"

Batten, who was prepared for the offer, replied with his

thanks—and concern. "Herb," he said, "what if it doesn't work out? What if you end up not liking me, or I don't like New York?"

"If so," said Schwamb, "what would you want?"

"I'd want to return to a store I could run some day."

"Fair enough. A deal?"

"Deal," said Batten as Kathryn gave his arm a squeeze.

New York was overwhelming for the young couple. They coped by concentrating on work, Kathryn again teaching and Mil immersing himself in the training program problems. Initially, he traveled a lot, visiting many stores. He then began a writing and designing phase supported by a graphics budget and the aid of a secretary and a new assistant (those associated with the former program had been reassigned to the field). Batten worked on the 17th floor of the New York Office building on 34th Street. Down the hall from him were all the Penney brass.

Schwamb was highly pleased with Batten's progress and said so in a memo to Sams and the number-two man, Al Hughes. A couple of months later, Batten requested a brief meeting with Sams and Hughes and, as a courtesy, Schwamb. It was granted.

As the four men sat down, the three senior executives expected a discussion of personnel training matters. They had all come to appreciate the young hotshot's skill at advancing a point. Instead of explaining something, Batten often used a tactful and astute line of questioning. Answers usually led to almost painless accord, even among the older, more entrenched personalities.

Today, however, Batten had a surprise. "Gentlemen, since I've been here I've begun to wonder if in the future the fact that I've never been a store manager would be an impediment or an insurmountable obstacle to promotion. So could you please tell me now, because if that is the necessary stripe for advancement, then after my project is concluded I'd like to go back to a store and become a store manager."

Sams looked at Hughes, who looked at Schwamb, who looked at Sams with a shake of his head. "No," said the CEO, "it would not be an obstacle. Don't worry about that."

Good-bye, Earl

Earl Sams was 60 and had another 10 years to go. His life and remarkable reign at the top of J. C. Penney would end on a Sunday after a round of golf at his New Rochelle club. He would sit down heavily in the clubhouse, good naturedly complain of fatigue, smile at his friends, and slump in his chair. The next day in New York and across the whole chain, a cloud of true sadness enveloped the organization. The warm, approachable, and astute executive was immediately missed by all who had ever dealt with him, including his peers at Montgomery Ward and Sears Roebuck.

The company's public relations officer led a hastily called press conference on Monday morning. After announcing Sams's death, he introduced the chairman. James Cash Penney, five years Sams's senior, spoke briefly and without notes. Normally, there was no clearer and more appropriate extemporaneous speaker than Penney, but his grief would cause him to make a mistake that would unsettle him for a long time to come:

> My Friends—
> The steady hand of Mr. Sams had guided our business since 1917. As a testament to his ability, consider the vast reach and rock-solid financial strength of today's Penney Company. While Mr. Sams never sought credit for his many accomplishments—I now wish that it had been more generally understood how deeply grateful I have been for the assistance this fine man afforded me. I deeply and profoundly mourn his passing.

But nearly two decades had passed since Sams had engineered James Cash Penney's rehabilitation. Memories had dimmed or people had come along who had never known of Penney's difficulties. Therefore, to most of the media it sounded as if the chairman desired a wider appreciation—*not* for Sams's help in Penney's emotional and financial recovery—*but* for "the assistance this fine man afforded me" (presumably) in running the huge company! It sounded, in other words, as if the 75-year-old coot were using the somber occasion for self-aggrandizement.

This was instantly perceived by the PR pros. Because of some adroit defusing after the chairman left the room, little harm would come of it. Except to Penney himself, who eventually heard about his irrevocable faux pas and was distressed for years.

chapter 9   The Common Touch

BY THE YEAR 2000 and its 98th anniversary, there had been a total of seven J. C. Penney CEOs. All had spent virtually their entire adult lives with the company. But only one, Mil Batten, had never managed a store. A signal achievement, it also marked the beginning of the end of the company's historic flexibility.

By the time the administration of Jim Oesterreicher was canceled in September 2000, 17 years had passed since the company had been led by first-rate Penney people. Unlike Oesterreicher, who had the bad luck to preside over Penney's five-year fall (something not of his doing and beyond his grasp), the last of the really solid Penney leaders had been *very* lucky.

The reader will understand more about the Penney Company after being introduced to them.

Good fortune, of course, plays a part in every successful career. Think of the luck involved when Maynard connected with Wilk Hyer and Batten with Maynard. Of course, there are many other wrinkles leading to many kinds of success. Jack Maynard and Mil Batten, for example, would have succeeded almost anywhere. But Walt Neppl and Don Seibert needed the J. C. Penney Company to thrive. In a sense, Maynard and Batten found the company and made it their own, whereas the company found Neppl and Seibert and made them its own. This is because both were the Penney ideal: ordinary men with extraordinary ability. Back in 1917 when James Cash Penney began concentrating on personnel and went to even more exhaustive lengths to find the right men, he wasn't looking for a Maynard or a Batten. He was looking for a Neppl or a Seibert.

They were the salt, not the pillars, of the earth. They were the kind of men who are saluted as the backbone of America. You could line up 100 Harvard, Chicago, and Stanford MBAs and not find a single Neppl or Seibert. But you could easily see them rising to leadership positions in the Fire Department of New York. Over the years they would lose any rough edges and eventually move comfortably in the elite circle of top New York executives. But neither man ever lost the common touch.

Good Men

Neppl was exuberant and often mangled his syntax; Seibert was quiet and always correct. Together, they became fast friends and in due time a very effective two-man team at the top. And, throughout their careers, both men always tried to do the right thing. Ethical and financial disasters like Enron and WorldCom would simply have been incomprehensible to them.

Walt Neppl and Don Seibert were common men with good minds and steadfast character. They were unassuming. When they went back to work after the war, Neppl's ambition was to manage a Penney store like the one in his home town of Carroll, Iowa. Seibert's dream was to make a living heading a jazz band. Religious men without airs or complexity, both worked unusually hard to advance their careers. They willingly put in endless hours, endured the grind of the road, and continually uprooted their families. They believed in the Golden Rule and they believed in Honor, Confidence, Service, and Cooperation. They were perfect Penney people and the last of the outstanding men to run J. C. Penney in the twentieth century.

And they were lucky.

The Test

Walt Neppl was called up in early 1943.

The marine sergeant felt bad because Neppl was out on a technicality, flat feet. Otherwise, what a great-looking recruit: strong Nordic face, build of a farm kid, clear blue eyes that showed smarts. The sergeant nodded out the door, feeling the need to help. "Go across the hall to the Army Air Force.[1] They'll take you."

---

1. The U.S. Air Force was formed after World War II.

Young Walt had not hidden his disappointment. But he was respectful and polite. "Thank you, Sergeant."

The marine squinted, watching after Neppl as he headed across the hall. "Damn!" he thought to himself. "There goes the kind of smart hick we can do something with."

If he couldn't be a U.S. Marine, Neppl figured to try for the air cadets. But there was a problem with the Army Air Force as well. They gave a tough test. Neppl had been a top vocational student at Carroll High School, but the test he took was loaded with questions relating to physics and advanced math like calculus, subjects he knew nothing about. Another disappointed recruiter regarded him now, one who was also puzzled.

"You know, Neppl, you didn't miss the passing grade by much." He took the test papers and flipped to the last page. "See what the guy who graded this wrote at the end?" The recruiter ran a finger under the grader's scrawled note as he read, "'Who is this?!'" Then he looked at Neppl. "That's because you answered some of the hard questions and missed some of the easy ones. Strange."

"They were all hard to me," Neppl said with a flat laugh.

"What did you take in high school?"

"Practical stuff."

"Business?"

"Yeah."

"No science and higher math at all?"

"Just bookkeeping math."

"You took all vocational courses?"

"All they had."

"Why not anything academic?"

"Oh, we lost the farm." Neppl shrugged and smiled.

This was Iowa and the recruiter knew the story well. "Where do you work again?" he asked.

"J. C. Penney." Neppl was dressed in a suit. He looked good, his tie nicely knotted.

"Doing what?"

"Started in the stockroom right after graduation. Now I sell, do some ordering, help the manager and like that."

"Does your job have a title?"

"First man. It's like assistant manager."

"And you're how old?" The recruiter looked at the information sheet attached to the top of Neppl's test. "Twenty?"

"That's right," said Neppl, warily.

"I mean, you seem to have made quick progress."

"Oh. I like the manager, working there."

"Well, let me give you some advice, Neppl." He rolled up the test and shook it to emphasize each point. "Write down the kind of questions you missed on this. Go to the library and get the appropriate books. Get advice, see some high school teachers. Tell them the Air Force wants to test you again."

"You do?" said Neppl, brightening.

"Yes. So study for a couple months and come back and see me."

"Thank you, sir," said Neppl. "I can do that."

The recruiter felt that the young man would keep his word and would succeed, and he was right.

The Bombardier

The vastness of World War II and the transition in the United States have mostly been forgotten. But within *a year* of the attack on Pearl Harbor in December 1941, tens of millions of new industrial square feet had been created, and the "arsenal of democracy"[2] had begun producing previously unimaginable numbers of ships, bombers, fighters, tanks, trucks, jeeps, and artillery. Munitions, medicines, service clothing, and food rations likewise flowed from new or converted plants. There was an endless call for workers and managers in all areas and at all levels. Women went to work in defense plants. The dirt poor and dispossessed migrated by the millions to all points of the compass where new factories were eager to pay them high wages. And the Great Depression was over.

Almost everything was rationed for civilian use. Steak, butter, gasoline, rubber, and nylons became luxuries. Cigarettes were hard to find. New cars ceased to be made. A new nationwide speed limit of 35 mph was posted to preserve rubber and conserve gas.

The infrastructure for all-out war was equally immense. The best and the brightest from business, industry, agriculture, min-

2. From an FDR radio commentary.

ing, universities, and finance were recruited. The population and activity in Washington, D.C., grew exponentially. Some served as civilians; others were commissioned as officers.

Millions were in uniform, including thousands of J. C. Penney associates, all of whom were sent the new company magazine, *Pay Day*, along with $10 quarterly checks to supplement their military pay. Among those serving were 97 store managers and 390 New York Office associates, many seeing combat and many meeting death. Mil Batten was called to serve in Washington, D.C., in the Quartermaster Corps. By the end of the war he was a full colonel and was told that if he remained in uniform, it was wired for him to jump two ranks to major general and take over the whole corps—an incredible situation for a noncareer officer.

Walt Neppl had to wait a while to enter basic training because facilities construction, although massive, lagged behind the crush of new men to be trained. Finally, he reported to an infantry base in St. Louis (his first time out of Iowa), then went on to preflight college courses and initial flight training. Cadet school followed, then primary, bombardier training, and commissioning. Now with his bombardier wings, he was an officer and a gentleman in little more than 12 very demanding months.

Typically, for Walt Neppl the Army Air Force amounted to a crash course in human nature, in composure and focus. It also gave him an education in the personalities and geographic variety of young men. He learned leadership and teamwork. "You have to do that when people are shooting at you," he said. All of this would make a difference when he resumed his J. C. Penney career. Especially the shouldering of enormous responsibilities as a young officer.

"I became the wing's lead bombardier, 41 other B-17s bombing off my release. So it was important not to screw it up. That's the way it was the day I got my DFC. It was at Berlin. We hit Templehoff Airdrome and laid it in there." Neppl characteristically skips over the details of winning the Distinguished Flying Cross—which, in brief, involved coolness under fire, dexterous performance under terrible conditions, and outstanding leadership (the bombardier always flew the plane during the bomb run).

Neppl was offered inducements to remain in the service after completing his 30th mission. Because he vividly recalled every mission, including Berlin, and the fact that many bomber crews never survived the full mission quota, Neppl felt lucky to still be alive and declined the offer.

After a month's leave in Iowa during which he and his high school sweetheart, Marian Maher, were engaged, Walt was ordered back to Santa Ana and then to Midland, Texas, where he served as an instructor until he was mustered out a few months after Hiroshima. He briefly considered college on the GI Bill. However, as with many veterans who were products of the Depression, resuming a career and starting a family had the stronger allure for this now serious adult.

Mature Beyond His Years

Although Carroll was a much smaller store than Lansing, before entering the service Walt Neppl had made first man faster than Mil Batten. This, of course, required the joint campaigning of both the Carroll store manager Sören Kudsk and DM Roy Miller. Therefore, when the decorated 23-year-old Army Air Force captain came home, got married, and went back to work after a brief honeymoon, Miller and Kudsk saw nothing to discourage their admiration and respect for the young man. They began the traditional Penney Company nurturing of identified special talent.

Meanwhile, Neppl reacted to the town and store to which he had returned. They were virtually the same as when he had left in 1943 causing a momentary feeling of dislocation, as though experiencing a weird sort of time warp. Had he really been away? Did he really do all of that fast growing up? Neppl was nothing if not mentally tough, and he quickly forced himself to banish thoughts of the war and rejoice about being married and home. Now the town and store became reassuring and pleasurable.

Yes, Walt Neppl did return a changed man. Unlike many returning combat veterans, however, he was able to dive enthusiastically back into the civilian rhythms. If it was the same town, the same store, and the same company, *he* was different. Mature; stronger; wiser; well trained; and, yes, a survivor. All the better, then, for a renewed Penney person. So let's get going! Decades later he even maintained that he had never suffered nightmares because of his World War II experiences ("Nah!").

After his first days back in the Carroll store, Walt began to relish the familiar layout. As he put it, "Shoes were in the back, of course. Farther back, behind the stockroom, was the advertising room where I spent some time. The work clothes in the store were on the right, back of the counter, socks, gloves, shirts, and overalls. That's so, as you laid out that shirt and overall, you could pull over a pair of socks, another shirt, give them more than one to choose, work the counter, get the sales, make them feel good at the same time. Next we had men's dress shirts, underwear, ties, and a full men's department, and I mean full. We sold a lot of suits in those days. Then, across the front between the two doors, was the hosiery department. Then you had lingerie, piece goods, curtains, and draperies. Stairs nearby led up to the balcony, which was all ready-to-wear, the whole shebang. Quite a store, really, a lot going on there. A great place to be."

He wasn't there long.

In just over a year after Neppl's return, the attention of his manager and DM resulted in a New York–approved transfer to the Columbus, Nebraska, store. Therewith, the name of Walter J. Neppl was established in the minds of the men who mattered on 34th Street. While Kudsk was a born (in Sweden) merchant and saw the same bent in Neppl, the Columbus manager, Pete Lakers, was not. Instead, Lakers was an expert at cost control. Miller, the DM, thought Neppl could learn from Lakers. And, he thought, God knew that Lakers could use Neppl's merchandising touch.

So Mr. and Mrs. Walt Neppl moved to Columbus at the end of 1946 and began having their family on the road, as it were. Typical of upward-bound Penney people, they became uncomplaining nomads whose roots remained in Iowa but withered over the years. The company became their larger family, their permanent community, and it was always a stable and happy relationship.

My Kingdom for a Store!

Walt was clearly going places in J. C. Penney. And he was one of those unusual people whose success was enjoyed equally by those who abetted it and those who simply stood aside and watched him go. The only problem was that, despite rapid promotions, he felt unfulfilled. He wanted his own store with a passion. Yet his ascendancy up the ladder seemed to thwart this fondest hope. Walt Neppl learned the fine points of cost control from Pete Lakers in Columbus while—because of his merchandising eye, salesmanship and all-around exuberance—he caused the store's sales to rise significantly. In 1950, he (and Lakers) knew he was ready for his own small-town Main Street store. Instead, the company promoted him to first man of the big Colorado Springs operation. Run loosely by an independently wealthy man married to an opera singer, the Springs store made money but was far below its potential. Taking complete charge with the manager's blessing, Neppl achieved a total turnaround in one year. He improved the back office, controls, storewide personnel, training, efficiency, buying and merchandising, salesmanship, morale, and community relations. In his second year the store was humming so well that he felt certain of now qualifying to run a downtown store like this or perhaps one of the new suburban locations around the country.

Once again, however, he was promoted and assigned to someone else. The Neppls moved to Denver, where Walt was named manager of the giant downtown Penney store's main floor. This was a fast track, the floor being home to the company's number-one men's suit business, the number-one hosiery business (beating out Lansing), the number-one jewelry business, and even a large blouse bar that did $100,000 in expendable business.

"I really had to hustle," he recalled, "learning everything I could from the top notch people on that floor. And the first man, Earl Derby, was an exceptionally strong merchant, and he was also very good on details, which is a combination you don't see every day. Very good on promotions, too. He would write everything down. I learned a lot from Earl and we became good friends. We had some good times together, and then he got his first store in Chicago and I got his job."

This meant being responsible for what amounted to several Penney stores under one roof, which included keeping a rein on his boss. Paul Bass (who succeeded Homer Torrey) was a sales dynamo and another Penney manager who was unusually well off, having previously made money with Louisiana oil leases. "He was down on the floor all the time goosing everybody up," said Neppl. "I mean, Bass didn't get mad because he realized somebody's got to control the inventory. But he was also a merchant, let me tell you, with a lot to teach me. So we did a lot of business in Denver."

In another year Bass called Neppl into his office and said, "Walt, I know this isn't news, but you need your own store."

"You're right about that," Neppl said.

"Word to the wise, though. Just don't take any store. You gotta hold out for the *right* store, that's the ticket."

"How do I do that—as soon as possible?"

"Talk to the DM. He likes you and knows I do, too."

Neppl sighed. "I have already."

"Then *I'll* start talking. I'll talk to New York, everybody. You're gonna get a store, and you're gonna get the right one."

Albuquerque: Hello and Good-bye

Stores! Neppl was a store man,[3] and his career with J. C. Penney followed the curve of the company's growth in terms of stores. He served in nearly all of the historical store configurations except for the very first like Kemmerer and Cumberland. The stores in Carroll and Columbus were the classic Penney Main Street layouts that blanketed small-town America from the 1920s until the 1950s, when the company began a major transformation. He also worked in the big and really big operations in Colorado Springs and Denver, respectively. One of the new prototype suburban stores (finally) came his way, and later, in the company's move off Main Street, he would oversee opening strip-center full-line stores. Eventually, he was also to play a significant role in establishing the Penney anchor stores that led the malling of America.

So, for all of that, one would think that a few *years* of fulfillment as a model Penney store manager would grace his résumé. It never happened. Walt Neppl became held in such high regard by the company's upper management that no one wanted to isolate his talent and energy in a single store. Instead, they would see him saving or developing several stores at once. He just didn't know this for a while.

In 1953 Neppl was awarded a new Albuquerque suburban layout that was just being completed. He got to trim it, stock it, hire in his staff, shake it down, and open it. Told he probably wouldn't make a profit for several months, from day one the store had an 8

---

3. With a difference. Neppl understood the importance of the merchandise department function. In fact, he headed up the department in the late 1960s (a "developmental" move en route to the presidency). A retired merchandise executive wrote that Neppl "was a forceful executive who did an adequate job there"— high praise indeed considering the bitter rivalry between most of the New York merchandise department and the field (stores), whence Neppl had risen.

to 10 percent profit, outstanding for any Penney operation. Walt got a comp check for $3,800 covering just the last three months of 1953 (a *lot* of money then). And everyone on 34th Street and in the region and in the district was really watching Neppl now—as the Walt and Marian bought a house and a horse and made some lifelong friends.

And Walt remained unaware of the light that shone upon him.

Ten months after opening his store, Neppl saw New York executive Cece Wright standing on the sidewalk one morning—unannounced. "Mr. Wright, I wasn't expecting you. Good morning!"

"Well, I was headed from Tulsa to Phoenix and thought I should stop by and see how you do it."

"Then come on in and look around."

They toured the store, Wright hearing Neppl's staff enthusiastically describe what was selling. Then, summoning Marian, Wright took the Neppls to a good restaurant. In the middle of lunch, the executive cleared his throat and got right to the point. "We have something in mind, folks, something new. The upshot is that I'd like you to move to Pittsburgh."

"*Pittsburgh?*" said Neppl, looking around at Marian, who was speechless. "But we just got here, the store isn't opened a year yet."

"I know. It's a little fast. And we know how you love it here."

"What if Marian doesn't like Pittsburgh? We just bought a house."

"Well, we know we're asking a lot. But it's a good promotion, Walt."

"DM?"

"More like troubleshooter. We want you to work only on new stores, stores that are opening up out of Atlanta and in the Eastern zone. Then maybe fit in some problem stores as you can."

"I don't know, Mr. Wright."

"Cece."

"Well, Cece, is a DM gonna be happy when this young guy comes in from New Mexico to work his own district?"

"We'll make sure everybody's on the same page on that."

"A lot of travel, too."

"Yes, but I tell you what. If you and Marian don't like Pittsburgh—and I think you'll be surprised, but if you don't, and if you've done the job we think you will—then we'll move you back West in due time."

"I don't know," Neppl repeated, clearly crestfallen and not hiding it. "I finally get my store, and we're doing well, and not even a year goes by, and away we go."

Marian Neppl, still getting the family established in Albuquerque, was a trouper. "Walt, that's a fair offer."

"Consider yourselves flattered, too," Wright smiled. "The company thinks you're worth a lot more responsibility."

Marian squeezed Walt's hand as he replied, "Sure. Thanks. I appreciate it, of course."

They could put up with the Pittsburgh weather, but the house someone rented for them was a far cry from what they left behind in Albuquerque. They soldiered into the transfer, however, and Marian began reestablishing the family of six (including their new baby)—new schools, new dentist, new pediatrician, new household resources, new Penney and neighborhood and community networking, on and on. And Walt hit the road. He was gone early every Monday morning, returning late every Friday evening. After several months one of their neighbors approached Marian on a Monday morning and spoke sympathetically. "You know, Marian, Buddy and me like you guys, and we sure hope Walt gets lucky and gets a better job."

Although for some time he kept dreaming about it, Walt Neppl's store-managing days were over.

chapter 10   A Quiet Man

LUCK ALSO PLAYED an important part in Don Seibert's career, although his version was of the almost unnoticed Main Street workaday variety. But it did establish him in the mind of a Penney DM—a surprising development considering Seibert's invisibility at the time. Soft-spoken Don had been caught in the backwaters of the company, so far behind the dynamic and personable Walt Neppl that—*had* they known of Seibert—even the most imaginative Penney people would have never dreamt of making a comparison.

He was newly married, and his wife was expecting their first child when his jazz band was stranded at a third-rate resort in upstate New York. It was 1946. He had been out of the army for a year. Having worked for J. C. Penney part-time as a teenager, like Batten and Neppl, he went to work full-time selling shoes at Penney's. This was in Bradford, Pennsylvania, where his wife, Verna, had grown up and where they had been compelled to move in with her parents.

Unlike Batten and Neppl, Seibert disappeared for a while. His soaring ambition was to someday manage a shoe department (something, the reader will recall, Batten did almost immediately in Lansing). From another large, religious, Midwestern German family, Seibert was known as the wool-gathering poor relative who moved frequently, put in ungodly hours, and didn't seem to be getting anywhere during his first decade with Penney.

No one, least of all Seibert himself, would have guessed how far he would actually go.

The Life

Seibert walked a mile and a half to the store and got there at seven. He swept, made new signs, and restocked tables in order to be ready for customers when the store opened. Working in one department after another, he carried a brown bag and wrote orders in the stock room at lunch. Then he was back on the floor because that's how you made the district's "high ten list" (ten best floor sales). He always stayed after the store closed, sometimes getting home very late. He started in Bradford at $160 a month and there was no limit on his weekly hours. The plus was learning everything: the stockroom, ticketing merchandise, presentation (including trimming windows), and selling in every department. Eventually he learned costs; margins; office procedure; and, most important of all, what seemed to make people tick.

When spring came to Bradford, it brought floodwaters. So one night he was awakened by the screeching fire department siren. The first to arrive at the store, he pulled on his hip waders in the stockroom as the store manager and others slogged in. They put barricades up in front of the windows, then stood in the rising waters to ward off heavy flotsam carried by the annual spring flood. The waters receded by dawn and he walked home to shave, bathe, and dress. The store opened on time, half the mess already cleaned up as Seibert and his colleagues alternated mopping and sponging with serving customers.

Hitchcock and Hess

"Don," the manager said, "did you know that today is your fourth anniversary here?"

"Yes."

"Well, in recognition, Don, I'm going to promote you to oversee the balcony."

"Thank you, Mr. Klepper."

"Any questions?"

"No."

"Any ideas right off?"

"Yes."

". . . Ah, good, good. Then I'm sure you'll show me when you're ready."

"Yes, sir."

Seibert went up to the balcony, which had women's dresses, sportswear, and children's clothing. For years, the department had been run by two formidable women, Mrs. Hitchcock and Mrs. Hess. But almost from his first month in the store, Seibert had had ideas about improved merchandising. He had kept these to himself until given an opportunity to apply one or another. The first man and the manager had always been pleased with the results of his ideas, and now Seibert was confident that the balcony, his first major project, would bring similar success.

After walking around reviewing his thoughts, he addressed the two women during a lull. "Ladies, a moment of your time? Mr. Klepper has asked me to oversee ready-to-wear and I have some ideas that I think will make the balcony more attractive and generate more sales." He then led the ladies around the space explaining the changes. Finally, he asked for their reaction.

"Oh, Mr. Seibert, we're afraid none of that will work at all," said Mrs. Hitchcock.

"Yes, we are, Mr. Seibert," said Mrs. Hess. "Too bad, but it won't."

"I, uh, am sorry you feel that way, ladies."

"We have years of experience, Mr. Seibert," said Mrs. Hitchcock.

"Years," added Mrs. Hess.

"And I certainly respect that," Seibert said. "But I've been thinking about these for some time and I believe we should try them anyway."

"You do?" Mrs. Hitchcock said with a decided edge, looking at her partner.

"Do you?" Mrs. Hess said with a glare.

"Sorry, I'm afraid so."

That afternoon Seibert enlisted the stock boy's help and moved tables, fixtures, counters, and signage. The two women stood aside, claiming to be confused and unsure what to do. After rearranging all the merchandise, Seibert summoned the manager to inspect the new look.

"Very nice, I think. Quite nice, Don."

"Thank you, sir."

Mr. Klepper looked over at the unhappy women. "And you ladies? How do you like this arrangement?"

"Not very much," said Mrs. Hitchcock.

"Unfortunately," said Mrs. Hess, without the faintest charity in her voice.

"Yes, well," Mr. Klepper replied. "Ah, we'll just have to see how it works, now, won't we?"

It was a failure. In less than two weeks Seibert and the stock boy returned the balcony to its former appearance—the women still standing aside, now with gloating smiles.

Later, the manager stopped Seibert downstairs and nodded at the balcony. "What do you think, Don?"

"They just weren't going to let it work."

"That's right, they weren't."

"So I'm wrong even if I'm right?"

"Yes, because you didn't include them." Then Klepper smiled and thumbed the balcony. "And just watch. They'll probably sell more now than they did before your change."

Hitchcock and Hess did set a record, and Seibert learned a valuable lesson for future reference.

The Break

When Carl Potts, the DM, came into the Bradford store he was often pretty rough on everybody, always finding something wrong. But Seibert heard that Potts's favorite line of merchandise was suits. Potts was big on profits in women's dresses and hosiery, but his biggest passion was men's suits. So whenever the DM arrived, Seibert managed to engage him with new questions about suits and building the men's suits department. Whereupon, no matter what shape the store was in, they proceeded into a very positive discussion in which Seibert was taken to school on suits, Potts imparting his massive knowledge of the subject. As a result, the DM came to appreciate Seibert's potential. This led to Seibert's first break—something he later freely admitted is an important factor in how you move up.

There was a flurry of activity in Bradford as they prepared to reopen the remodeled store. Potts was there and he was sore. "Who the hell wrote these grand reopening ads?" he demanded. It was late and everybody was frazzled, especially the high-strung first man.

"I did. What's wrong with them?" asked the first man, teeth on edge.

"What's wrong with these? What's wrong is that they're piss poor, that's what!"

"If that's what you think, Mr. Potts, then why don't you take those ads and shove them!" After this very un-Penneyish remark, the first man stormed out of the store and nobody expected to see him again.

"Seibert!"

"Yes, Mr. Potts?"

"Can you redo these ads?"

"Sure he can," said Klepper.

Seibert added, "Come back in the morning and they'll be done."

They were. They were effective. Potts was happy. And when the first man did leave the company soon thereafter, the DM promoted Don Seibert into the job. This led to a position in the new Buffalo suburban store and more career momentum.

The House of Boxes

Buffalo was a tough go. The store was open from nine to nine, six days a week. Seibert, as a floor manager and then assistant manager, of course, arrived at seven in the morning and left no earlier than ten every night. Sundays the store was closed. But, during the week, the manager wanted everyone on the floor during store hours, so that left Sunday to catch up on paperwork and ordering.

At this time, the Seiberts had two little girls. For months, Don saw them awake only on Sundays before church. Then, twice a week, Verna began bringing picnic dinners to the store. They would go to the basement stockroom, where he had built a big walk-in dollhouse out of cardboard boxes. The girls played there happily as the adults ate. Then, as Don went back up to work, Verna ran and affixed tickets to merchandise he had to set out later. Family night ended an hour later when Don interrupted a sale to hug the girls and Verna good-bye.

Thirty months of progress in Buffalo, then Elmira, then Rochester, led to a special assignment. Seibert was sent to head a team of assistant managers (the new term) who were helping to open a big store in Staten Island. He was repeatedly praised by the manager, and his reputation grew.

After Staten Island he got his first store, the troubled Levittown, Pennsylvania, operation. Walt Neppl was the DM, although they had yet to meet. Levittown was on Neppl's rehab list for attention between new store openings. But by the time he was able to get there, Seibert had the situation well in hand. Neppl was amazed. The quiet man had done virtually everything Neppl would have proposed.

Overall, Seibert demonstrated a rare combination of attributes that Neppl quickly picked up on. First off, he had developed into an excellent merchandiser. He also had learned to be good with people as well as be detail oriented. And he was tough when it was required. Shrinkage,[1] for example, was a serious problem at Levittown. Seibert methodically eliminated possibilities until the finger of suspicion pointed at a popular and successful woman on the sales floor. He dove into the books and records, collected irrefutable evidence, called the woman into his office, and simply dismissed her. Losses were cut in half overnight, store morale rising as the shrinkage fell. With significantly improved merchandising, adroit buying, and careful planning, Seibert's store was moving into the black by the time Neppl arrived.

As the reader has learned, a Penney store manager was unique in his autonomy—the company championing the individual in charge (and his particular personality). Although both were highly successful managers, for example, Jack Maynard and Walt Neppl were polar opposites—the epitomes of hands-off and hands-on managers. Seibert, too, had his uniqueness. The job was in the details—and how the manager defined them—but no two Penney managers ever did it exactly the same way (until recently). This and a superb buying corps in New York built a strong and profitable organization.

Neppl and Seibert became admirers and then solid friends. "Don was a very low-key guy," Neppl reminisced, "but he ran a very fine store. He was a deep thinker and an excellent planner. Handled people well, too, a good listener. High standards and morals. I just liked and respected Don a lot. It was obvious that he was the kind of guy who'd be a good district manager, and I recommended him. Not too long after that they made him a DM, first out of the Twin Cities."

---

1. Employee theft, shoplifting, etc.

The Man Who Didn't Grow

Seibert finished checking out and correcting one store and then drove fast for hours in a straight line across the frozen prairie to make the next town and grab a late dinner. As he ate some of the bad meal, he reviewed the next store's records. In the morning he was at the store at seven. Nobody was there. He went across the street to a coffee shop and waited. Finally, the janitor arrived and let Seibert into the store. He went up to the manager's office, where he saw price lists (used in ordering) stacked on two tables. They were way past due. Orders should have been in New York three weeks earlier.

Back to the coffee shop. At length, he saw the manager arrive. He refilled his coffee cup. He was anxious to get started, but felt it necessary to allow the manager to settle into his day. In the store, finally, the manager came down and asked if Don would like to get some coffee. Sure. They went across the street for the ritual catch-up chat, Seibert careful to hide his coffee nerves. Back in the store, they went up to the manager's office—which was now spic and span, nothing on the tables. "I suppose you want to work with my assistant," said the manager.

"Right, be a good place to start," Seibert said.

The manager introduced Seibert and then left the very nervous assistant manager's office. The late price lists were now stacked on the young man's desk. With a wave, Seibert said, "So, I see you guys are running a little late with the price lists."

"Yes" is all the assistant could manage. He would not, of course, rat on his boss.

Seibert smiled reassuringly. "Well, I can help there. Why don't we get to work, okay?"

"Sure," said the young man with a shade of relief. And they worked out a plan to get the orders in, and then Seibert called New York with instructions to take care of this store and get the orders filled.

By late afternoon when Seibert said good-bye to the manager and his assistant and hit the road, he knew the problem well. The manager was a good merchant who had built up business to a point where he could not manage it anymore. He hadn't grown with the business; not an unusual problem. In a few weeks Seibert moved the man to a smaller store, and all were finally pleased.

Nobody Ever Told Me *That* Before

After another two years Seibert was running his third district—one of the most productive in the nation. He now worked out of Toledo. His visibility increased as several important new stores were opened in Ohio, with the New York brass continually dropping in.

One day Cece Wright called from New York. "Don, I have a special assignment for you. I want you to go out to Indianapolis and deal with Ted Allen."

"Allen?" repeated Seibert, immediately fearing this order.

"He's violating company policy. He's buying merchandise not authorized by the company and from some who are not even company vendors. I want you to get this straightened out."

"But Mr. Wright, are you sure I'm right for this?"

"Cece."

"I mean, does Ted Allen even know who I am?"

"Don, you're a hot young DM now running one of the most important districts. Ted Allen knows who you are. Get out there and call me when you're finished."

"Yes, sir." Seibert hung up with a heavy heart. Allen ran one of the company's six biggest stores, earning a very big comp check[2] every year. He was also of the Homer Torrey–Jack Maynard school, known for his maverick ways. Seibert was 36. Allen was 20 years older and a strong personality. The DM had no hopes for the assignment.

Seibert was in the manager's office a day later. "Well, I can't imagine why they sent you here," Allen said sarcastically in a gruff voice. "But I know where you've been, Don, and you've never been in a big store before."

"That's true."

"Furthermore, you have no idea what I'm up against here. Nobody seems to."

"Fine," said Seibert. "We need to understand it, so please. Tell

---

2. Penneyese for profit sharing. For a store manager, profit sharing wasn't systemwide but related specifically to his store. Managers got a generous cut (based on a formula relating to store size, market, etc.); the better the store did, the better the manager did. If you ran one of the giant stores well, you got a giant check each year.

me everything. Despite what you may think, I'm here to help, Mr. Allen."

There was some additional back-and-forth, and then the manager let loose, angrily at first, then reasonably and in a voice that belied the stress he was under.

Seibert then went down to look over the women's accessories area on the main floor. Next he shopped the downtown competition, noting that there were 30 or 40 accessory items at different prices compared to a mere 6 on the J. C. Penney price list. Allen had often tried Penney sources in hopes of finding items the company wasn't buying. Nothing. So, in order to compete, he was compelled to buy outside the company sphere.

Seibert shook Allen's hand late in the day and flew back to Toledo, where he outlined his report. First thing the next morning, he called Wright in New York.

"Hello, Don. How'd it go?"

"Pretty good, Mr. Wright."

"Cece."

"But—Cece—I have a surprise. I'm about to type up a report that says, yes, Ted Allen is violating policy, but he's right and we're wrong."

"Huh?"

"We are. The company needs to send a buyer out there and work with Allen to figure out a way to offer the stuff that he needs."

After a pause, Wright said, "Well, nobody ever told me *that* before." But Wright took the advice.

chapter **11**   The Memo

AMERICA CHANGED IN THE 1950S. There was a migration from towns to cities and, with many collars changing from blue to white, from cities to the new suburbs. Tastes and interests were changing as well, with people making more money and spending more money. With all this, shopping obviously changed. By 1957 Mil Batten was vice president, a board member, and vice chairman under Al Hughes (the former Latin scholar). Batten saw the changing demographics with a clarity perhaps unmatched in the retail industry. His response was to write "The Memo."

It summarized the Penney business at the time. It accurately forecast the future. It concluded that vast changes had to occur in the company. It provided a plan for doing so. It became the most famous communication in Penney history beyond The Body of Doctrine (The Penney Idea). And it hastened Batten's appointment the next year to president/CEO as Hughes, past retirement age, remained as chairman.

Leading Up to an Emotional Vote

The Memo made these points: The Penney Company profile was basically a soft goods store primarily in small and medium-sized towns selling for cash. This was largely a shrinking market.

It concluded that capital should be concentrated in metropolitan suburbs and other growth areas. As opposed to the old pinpointing, the company should also serve an increasingly widespread and increasingly demanding consumer with an increasingly expanded assortment of merchandise in increasingly convenient locations. This was a transformation of such scope that it would require special verve, imagination, and controls. Plus adroit use of "other people's money," particularly in new store development.[1]

If all this seems somewhat routine today, it was absolutely revolutionary at the time. And four revolutionary implementations had to accompany the plan:

1. New, bigger, and newly located stores. Batten identified the emerging shopping-center moguls—the DeBartolos and Simons—and figured they might be interested in an anchor-store partner whose leases they could take to the bank. It became a marriage made in heaven.

2. Committing to the expensive and protracted project of starting a catalog. Batten bought a small catalog operation, the General Merchandise Company of Milwaukee, primarily because of its technology. Its fully automated warehouse made anything at Sears and Wards look archaic.

3. Even farther out was developing a way to recover data at the point of sale in the new stores. Nobody else had ever thought about doing it. Not Federated, not IBM, not anyone—and therein lies a story (coming up).

4. Emotionally at least, the most seismic change of them all: consumer credit. The Penney Company had sold for cash and cash only since its inception in 1902. The founder, in his eighties and still quite active, was a *devout* believer in cash. Next to God, he feared the ravages of debt that credit portended (for good reason).

But The Memo anticipated moving to the suburbs, where consumers *consumed*—including expensive hardlines like appliances and electronics ("brown goods")—and there the operational sine qua non was selling on credit. Every other major retailer sold on credit. Nevertheless, Mr. Penney actually became ill and had to go home when he heard what was afoot.

The credit issue came down to a boardroom vote. The special

---

1. Penney had deep pockets, a conservative balance sheet and still paid real dividends in dollars. But *nobody* had the kind of capital needed to pay for everything in the new plan.

occasion called for tallying all directors plus some key Penney executives who were not on the board. Twenty votes in all. Batten, with mixed feelings, laid the appropriate groundwork. To every director he sent a new, cogent, and convincing brief reaffirming the need for sales on credit. A copy went to Mr. Penney, of course, to which Batten added a handwritten note:

Dear Mr. Penney,
    I know how egregious this development must seem to you.
It does appear, however, to be the prudent way to go.

—Mil

Batten began the meeting by changing the rules. He looked around the table as he spoke. "Gentlemen, given the importance of the issue at hand, I will ask each of you to state your vote, yea or nay, and then add your reason for it. In order that Mr. Penney have the last word, I will start and then ask that we go around clockwise." He drew a loop in the air with his forefinger, starting with the man on his immediate left and ending with the founder on his immediate right. Then he continued briefly.

"All of you I trust have read the brief I mailed to you, which sums up my feelings. I vote yea." He nodded left and the next man rose. When it was time for Mr. Penney to speak, 19 yea votes had been cast.

"I congratulate you," said the old man. "Serving as representatives of our shareholders, you have voted wisely as you must." There was a hitch in his voice as he continued. "For myself, on the other hand, I must respond at a different level—token as my vote will be. I am opposed to the move for fear that credit would impose hardships upon our customers." He hesitated again, looking from man to man. Many averted their eyes, knowing what was coming. "You see, I knew the hardships of debt firsthand, and I would not wish the company to contribute to this state in any fashion. For those reasons, I am compelled to vote against the proposal." He waited for a breath, said "Nay" and "Thank you," and sat down.

The Troubleshooter

Without guts, character, and an other-worldly ability to focus, you do not win the Distinguished Flying Cross by taking control of the lead bomber in bad weather and having to improvise a new approach to the target while sighting the run as a maelstrom of flak tears holes in your airplane and kills the left two engines and shouts explode from every intercom station. So, once again, Walt Neppl came through, doing what was expected of him. All over the East and Southeast, he got new stores up and running and he got bad stores turned around.

"The biggest thing with new stores was new people, and with the big push there just weren't enough experienced people to plug into new stores. Sometimes I'd get a store opened right and nothing would happen. The reason was that the manager didn't emphasize organization and training, didn't get good people going, and that's deadly. So I'd have to go back in and fix it.

"I was all over the place opening stores. I cut across district lines—Toledo; Dayton; Carlisle, Pennsylvania; Philadelphia; Frederick, Maryland; Washington; Newport News; Richmond; New England; all over there. Opening stores and working with trouble spots like downtown Norfolk and New Haven, which were duds. I didn't open them, but they were problems.

"At first, the situations weren't too friendly, either. The word in the districts and the big stores was, 'Oh, I see, they're sending in the kid from out West.' But I worked with the people on the floor and got their respect, and we held good and exciting meetings. So that changed."

I Want Cedar Rapids

Neppl worked for three years without ever spending more than a few hours a week in his Pittsburgh office. He loved most of the Penney people with whom he worked, but he loved his family more and hated life on the road. He was also very successful. The Neppl family built a house on a cul de sac and came to thrive in Pittsburgh. "The people were wonderful," Walt said. "We made some good friends."

Again, he finally set his sights on a store—as he became vested in the company,[2] raising his right hand, taking the oath, and re-

---

2. After a minimum number of years with the company and achieving a certain level of responsibility (those great women on the floor with so much experience never got the pin).

ceiving his HCSC pin. But, again, New York needed him to deal with *stores*. In 1957 he was made DM of a key district with an office also in Pittsburgh. "District 12, which was just fine, I guess, a real opportunity," he said. "Had that about four years. Sixty stores." Visiting most of which, of course, meant hitting the road.

"On the typical visit I'd be there about 7:30 and spend some time with the manager and assistant manager—the 'first man' we used to say. Then I'd go over the whole store, then review all the records. I'd look at the organization, the staffing, just review the whole operation of the store."

In 1961 Neppl told New York that he was fed up with travel, that seven years was enough. He was determined not to go to New York, however. When they asked him what he wanted, he was prepared. He said, "I want Cedar Rapids, Iowa." It was a big store that he would have loved, and he knew the manager was retiring soon. New York replied, "Oh, we'll have to talk to Cece Wright about that." A little while later, Bill Marshall walked into Walt's Pittsburgh office. Marshall had been made head of stores when Wright shifted over to run merchandise.

Marshall shut the door and shook Neppl's hand, saying, "Walt—I was coming through and thought I'd better stop."

Neppl laughed and said, "It's funny how people are always happening by. Cece Wright did that in Albuquerque."

Marshall returned the laugh and said, "You really get right to it, don't you?"

Neppl grinned and said, "What can I do for you, Bill?"

Marshall replied in kind. "Come to New York and work for me."

". . . New York?"

"It's not as bad as you think. You'd get used to it. And Walt?" Marshall nodded seriously. "For a man of your ability, it's the place to be now."

Neppl sighed and said, "Okay, Bill, what's the deal?"

Marshall nodded again, with, "All right, think of all these new strip stores—you've opened how many yourself?"

"Couple dozen, maybe."

"And where was the manual, the pro forma?"

Neppl pointed to his head and said, "Here." But he said it warily, sensing what was coming next.

"Right. Physically, they're all about the same. But the markets are different, the people are different, the merchandise mix will be different, et cetera, et cetera. You have to keep all that in your head because there is no standardized approach to all this. Every department knows what they're doing, but there's no overall coordination."

"And you want me to do that?"

"Yes. And you know why—especially? Know what's going to happen in the next 10 years?"

Neppl spread his hands. "New stores."

"Four *kinds* of new stores, all bigger and bigger for bigger and bigger markets. In time there'll be indoor shopping centers with J. C. Penney anchoring down one end."

"Oh, boy," Neppl said quietly, feeling it coming.

"And we need an overall plan, get everybody on the same team. Rather than having a meeting with departments and guessing for this one, guessing for that one, I want a book on the whole program. I want every store element for every type store, and stores by market size, projected profit, et cetera. A five-year plan with every department signed off and pulling together. It's the only way we can get this thing going right. And this thing *will* get going. So, what I'm talking about is important."

"Yeah, I bet," Neppl said without enthusiasm.

"I need someone who can get this done. You'd be on special assignment. You can put together a team, anyone you want. You're the only one I ever considered, Walt."

"Yeah. Thanks." He looked at Marshall with a weak smile. "Yeah, okay."

The Prophecy

Walt Neppl had one last DM trip before pulling up stakes for the Big Apple. One night he managed to have dinner with his friend Don Seibert, a fellow DM now with the important adjoining Ohio-Michigan district. They had done this before when their routes had swung close and it wasn't difficult to meet somewhere in between. Now they compared notes and talked about their families, and Seibert commiserated with Neppl over the New York move.

"Well, my friend, look at the bright side."

"Which is what?"

"Well, there's more to J. C. Penney than running a big store."

"There is?"

"Seriously."

"Okay, what?"

"If you do this thing right—and you will—you're in a good position on the New York Office staff. Not such a bad thing."

"In whose opinion?"

Seibert talked his friend through the frustrations of changed plans and the dread of working in New York. Neppl, in turn, had good DM advice for *his* friend—and then a last laugh.

"Y'know, Don, they have their eye on you, too. Keep doing the job you're doing and guess what? *You'll* get sentenced to New York!"

Two years later (1963) the Neppl prophecy would come true and Seibert would join his friend in New York as head of planning and research. His reward for doing a good job there would be another promotion in 1966: taking over the catalog division, which, to stockholders, analysts, and associates alike, was a profit-less black hole.

chapter 12   The Transaction Recorder

A S WALT NEPPL WENT to New York and, in a year's time, put "The Book" together,[1] Mil Batten pressed ahead on the four main implementations of "The Memo." By 1964, a credit division was in full operation, the giant upgrading of stores was progressing (thanks, in part, to Marshall and Neppl), and the cash-hemorrhaging catalog division was at least still showing long-term promise. Now Batten turned his attention to the point-of-sale data dilemma. It would be a real test.

As he recalled, "We had made a total systems study and come to the conclusion that the vital key for us was something that was not in existence. We had to be able to gather essential data at the point of sale. We couldn't do it with the cash register. There was nothing else. We asked around outside the company and nobody was even thinking along those lines. Nobody."

The Great Idea

Trying to get something going, Batten formed a technical team to develop a set of specifications for what was labeled the "transaction recorder." The next step was to find a manufacturer who would be interested in making such a product. Batten thought that

1. Considering the departmental sprawl of J. C. Penney, it was a striking accomplishment for Neppl's team (abetted by several senior execs). "The Book" included every level of market, store type and size, merchandise assortment, and profit projection. Every major department was represented, including stores, merchandise, planning and research, real estate, personnel, and accounting. It became the company's operational bible, whose computerized cousin was in use decades later.

with Penney behind the concept, somebody would jump quickly. And the logical place to start was National Cash Register, supplier of all Penney cash registers. Batten called Bob Oelman, NCR's chairman.

Batten exchanged hellos with Oelman and then added with a chuckle, "But the reason I called could be a little unsettling." Oelman responded with forced humor and Batten continued with, "Well, what I have in mind is of such import, I wonder if you and a couple of your other top people might come down to New York and meet with me? It's along the lines of an advanced product we need."

Oelman tried to push for more, but Batten parried with, "Bob, it's a big concept. I need to show you tentative specs and speak in some depth. It would be unfair to tell you anything more on the phone."

The top three NCR executives were in Batten's office the next week. After brief pleasantries, their host dove right in. "Well, gentlemen, we've been doing some thinking about your primary product." Batten opened a big file on the conference room table. "And we have come to the conclusion that the cash register, per se, will be obsolete within the decade." He had wanted to get Oelman's attention, and he had it. The NCR people were clearly shocked.

Batten handed out tentative specs as he began describing the Penney concept to the numb execs. "Gentlemen, here is a rough work-up of specifications for what we have given the working name of 'transaction recorder.' In plain words, it's a cash register that also captures all relevant data at the point of sale. We believe it's the wave of the future and will mean the death of the simple cash register—at least as far as J. C. Penney is concerned. We wanted NCR, of course, to hear this first and respond."

The response of the men from Dayton was not very positive. They were immediately skeptical about the need for such a product, irrespective of Penney's interest. Still, they agreed to form a joint venture to develop a prototype. NCR would provide the technical know-how, and Penney would work on the requirements and full specifications. It was a handshake agreement that Batten felt uneasy about. And, sure enough, before the lawyers had anything ready to sign and before much had transpired in NCR's research facility, Bob Oelman was on the phone to Batten. He very apologetically backed out of the project, citing two main reasons:

1. The idea didn't seem feasible.

2. NCR couldn't find a single additional retailer interested in such a device.

Batten next tried Singer, which was making a bold move into computers from their sewing machine concentration. But not that bold.

Then Control Data called. They had heard that NCR might be working on an automated cash register for "X" customer. They immediately went to a close contact at Sears for more information. Sears knew nothing about any such device, had no interest in the idea, and suggested that Control Data contact J. C. Penney. As Batten recalled, "Sears said that, in terms of automation, the most technically advanced retailer was us. So Control Data called and discovered that we were the culprits in back of the whole thing. They came in, and we explained the idea and asked if they would have any interest. A small computer? It was obvious at the end of this first conversation that they either didn't understand what we were talking about or didn't have any interest in it. Control Data at the time was focused on large mainframe computers to compete with IBM. They never came back."

Batten next tried AT&T, on whose board he sat. There was lukewarm interest at the top of the telephone monopoly, but then the Western Electric division got in touch. They were highly excited about the concept, could see its future applications across the entire retail industry, and quickly bought into the joint venture. It just had to be run through AT&T legal. Where it was killed. At the time AT&T was operating under a consent decree with the Department of Justice that prohibited its getting into anything but the telephone business. Nobody had thought to check first.

The Worst Decision IBM Ever Made

The next attempt had to be with IBM—a company Penney was reluctant to call because, as Batten put it, "They were then a high-price, high-cost operation. Their prices usually were not too competitive. We wondered if they could sell the equipment at the kind of price we'd be willing to pay. Assuming they would be interested.

"But we were running out of candidates. So we got in touch and, surprisingly, IBM was interested, even after my repeated concerns about price. We formed a joint venture almost exactly like the one with NCR." And then Batten received an unexpected phone call.

"Of all people, Bob Oelman was on the line. He wanted back in." Batten explained about IBM, saying that IBM would have to agree to NCR rejoining the project. If that happened, he said, then they would have to establish two separate task forces going in different directions, IBM and NCR, with a Chinese Wall between them so no proprietary information could be exchanged. "And that's what was done," Batten recalled. "But after initial work had begun, Oelman called again and said they'd soured on the project. They were out for the second time."

Penney proceeded with IBM, and a prototype was developed. The venture rented and secured a warehouse where a mock store floor was built. In secrecy, the IBM and Penney people performed simulations of transactions and collected data. Basically, the device worked—although, not surprisingly, extensive refinements were called for. Everyone at the testing and technical levels wanted to go ahead.

In Manhattan, however, Batten received a call from an IBM officer.[2] They agreed to meet the next day at J. C. Penney. After the project was reviewed, the officer said, "Mil, we had a policy committee meeting yesterday and we've decided to drop the project."

"Really? I'm surprised. Would you mind telling me why?"

"Three reasons. We've already spent about $20 million in research, development, and machine tooling. It's an expensive project, Mil."

"Yes. Which we both knew going in."

"And if that was the only thing, we're still in it."

"So your second reason?"

"Market research. We cannot find anyone else out there who is even slightly interested in this. And as much as we like the Penney

---

2. Twenty years later Batten could not recall the man's name.

Company, we can't afford to make this equipment just for you at the price you're willing to pay."

"And the third?" wondered Batten. He was stumped. He had anticipated the first two objections (he had seen figures), but a third problem eluded him.

"It's the biggie," said the IBM officer. "What you're doing, really, is asking us to develop a small computer. These specifications are really a small computer."

"We understand that."

"But you're not in the computer business. We are." IBM practically owned the mainframe business, and mainframes *were* the computer business at the time. "So we would naturally look to spin off some of the development costs elsewhere if possible— look for other markets for a small computer."

"Of course."

"But, Mil, we've drawn a total blank."

"There's *no* other market out there?"

"One. Small businesses. The problem is that almost nobody there could afford it. Bottom line? There will never be a small computer."

". . . All right," said Batten. "We have to accept your decision, but I'm not going to do it gracefully." But he was smiling and his voice was pleasant, putting the officer at ease.

"Okay."

"So I have to say that I think your committee made the wrong decision, one that someday you'll regret. In fact, I would suggest that you circle yesterday's date on your calendar and keep the calendar."

"Yesterday?"

"Your policy committee meeting." Batten was actually chuckling, as though what he said next was a joke for both of them to share. "Someday you're going to look at that date and remember the worst decision IBM ever made."

The officer chuckled himself, agreeably saying, "Okay."

Some time later Batten called Fred Borch, chairman of General Electric, checking out a small news item. He had read that Federated Department Stores and General Electric had worked together on a proprietary project that had been dropped. No further details. Borch explained that Ralph Lazarus, Federated's chairman and a GE board member, had approached GE to help develop a successor to the cash register. GE went ahead. "But they ran into too many problems," Batten remembered. "Everybody became exasperated and both sides agreed to erase the partnership. Hearing that, I told Fred that we had the same interest, but we had made some progress. Would GE possibly be interested in continuing with J. C. Penney? Almost immediately, he said yes."

It soon became clear to the Batten team, however, that GE's approach was problematic. At the time, GE was in the computer business with mainframes. They wanted to use one to cover a region, with transactions fed into the computer by telephone line and data fed back to the store. Penney argued against the approach, but GE was convinced that small in-store computers were not feasible. "So we went ahead with misgivings," said Batten. "We had no other place to go. And maybe we'd learn something. So GE set up a regional center in Phoenix with lines feeding in from 44 Penney stores in California and Arizona.

"But then there was a serendipitous occurrence that began to turn the tale."

NCR was having a board meeting in London during the week when GE and Penney finally announced their joint venture "to develop electronic equipment." It happened that the next week Citibank, on whose board Batten sat, had a board meeting in Gleneagle, Scotland. Mil Batten arrived at a Gleneagle hotel the afternoon before the meeting. Going down in the elevator that evening, who should get on but Bob Oelman, the NCR chairman, who was also a Citibank director. Oelman looked at Batten as though he had just lost his last friend.

"Of all people," smiled Batten.

"Mil," said Oelman gravely, "we read the article. What does this mean with you and GE?"

"What do you mean, Bob?"

"I mean as regards our long-term relationship with J. C. Penney? Mil, I have to tell you that the news virtually ruined our board meeting in London. We have to talk."

"Certainly," said Batten. He pleasantly added, "But don't forget, you were the ones who pulled out, Bob. Twice."

"But GE? NCR has no better customer than J. C. Penney, Mil."

Oelman became emotional, and when the elevator opened at the lobby his eyes were moist. "Bob, hold on," said Batten. "Let's go over and sit." He led Oelman to a secluded couch and then assured him that the news release meant nothing more than the fact of the joint venture. The Penney-NCR relationship had not dissolved. "But," he felt compelled to gently add, "we had to go with GE because there was no one left after NCR kept walking."

"We made a mistake."

"Yes, and you were our first choice. We thought we'd click together."

"Mil," said Oelman, his voice unsteady, "is it too late for us to try again?"

Batten hesitated, then delivered a reassuring smile and said, "We're not married to any particular company and we have no commitment unless something is developed."

"You'll let us back in?"

"If you're willing to work with us while we work with GE, fine, we can do the same thing that we did with IBM."

"Then let's do it. It's a deal?"

"Deal."

As it soon developed, the GE/Penney mainframe venture in Phoenix was dropped, the telephone linkage proving too unreliable. "All that work just confirmed our original thinking," Batten remembered. "The equipment had to be in the store."

Now NCR had a clear run at developing the transaction recorder. This time they came through. The NCR 280 was the world's first point-of-sale data-gathering device. "By 1968 we were finally ready," said Batten. "To introduce the equipment, it was installed in the new Parkersburg, West Virginia, store, the town where I began as a part-time and then full-time associate. Bob Oelman and I met there to celebrate. He was just as happy as I was."

Years later Batten was asked to assess the value of being so far ahead. "Not as much as you would think," he answered surprisingly. "These things can be duplicated and they don't remain proprietary for very long. And even though we had this big lead, we also had all the hassle and extra expense. So it evens out.

"One might ask, then, 'Why bother to innovate?' In my view, a business cannot afford to ever sit back. That can often hurt you more than plunging ahead, perhaps even be fatal. Examples come to mind. A majority of the dominant retail companies of 1940 have disappeared. They sat back and died. But at Penney, we always felt it was important to identify what we needed for the future and then go out and get it, regardless of what the others were or were not doing, and regardless of what Wall Street thought. It's a cultural decision, having to do with your values. Importantly, too, you establish a reputation for being innovative, for being a leader, and that does something for your people. They feel like they're part of a progressive organization on the cutting edge of things. Which is of no small value."

The Grocery Bag

Soon after taking over catalog in 1966, Seibert went to Atlanta to inspect the world's largest, most highly automated warehouse. The building was just being completed, and his driver suggested a sight-seeing approach. Before the warehouse came into view, they turned up a hill and stopped, the young man motioning and saying, "Right up there, Mr. Seibert, for the sight of sights."

"Kid's a romantic," Seibert thought as he walked toward the hilltop, the driver several steps behind. A very wide rectangle of flat industrial roof came into Seibert's view. With each step he took, the rectangle of roof grew in depth . . . and grew . . . and grew. Seibert finally stood at the top of the hill in total awe, looking down at *50 acres* of warehouse roof. The sight made him tremble, a chill running down his spine. Never had the challenge of running catalog been more dramatically apparent than at this moment.

Five years later on a winter Saturday in 1971, Ralph Henderson called Seibert and said, "Don, you've got to come over." Henderson was a tough catalog expert brought in from the outside. He lived in New Jersey, 15 minutes from Seibert. By his kitchen phone, he showed Seibert the back of a grocery bag on which he had scrawled a column of numbers—the final P&L for the year on catalog. At the bottom was a $3.2 million black number.

Henderson gave Seibert the bag, which was framed and hung in his office. Catalog was profitable from that day until the company staggered in the late 1990s.

chapter 13   Last of the Good Men

T HE COMPANY GAVE SEIBERT a couple of years' vacation running things in Italy, Spain, and Belgium, where Penney was phasing out its European experiment.[1] Then the board passed over president Jack Jackson and made Don Seibert J. C. Penney's fifth CEO on the recommendation of retiring Mil Batten.[2] When Jackson retired (and became a prominent Dallas banker), the board made Neppl president, and the two friends began their close collaboration.

Most friendships would have been bruised by one man rising above the other. Not these two. Seibert said years later, "I was as surprised I got it as I was surprised Walt didn't, because everything he did in New York was outstanding. And I told him that right away." Neppl added, "No problem. I always thought Don was someone special. I would have voted for him over me, too. Because then I get to heckle him."

Pull It Together

Hal Eddins was a vice president and administrative assistant during Mil Batten's last years in charge. He then served Don Seibert's entire chairmanship and Bill Howell's first few years at the top. He had this to say about what Seibert faced at the end of Batten's reign:

   1. The problems included corruption in the sunny countries and suffocating regulation on the North Sea.
   2. Batten was not pleased with the widely known fact that Jackson had a mistress (on the payroll). Although admiring both Neppl and Seibert (and their solid families), Walt was probably a little too exuberant for Batten.

Batten was the visionary, responsible for more new ideas and programs than anybody. Most, like dominating the malls, were great successes. Others were not so successful. Some, like trying to expand into Europe, were flat-out losers. When he retired and went on to run the New York Stock Exchange, he left a very successful but scattered company. So now it was up to Don Seibert to sort things out and pull the company together. Not the easiest of assignments. People say, "Don Seibert was such a quiet and thoughtful man." Well, yes. What they don't realize, though, is that Don *had* to be more of the stable, healer type. The time for flamboyance was over. But he also had a passion for the company and, in particular, this overarching desire to create a mechanism to perpetuate what was best about JCPenney.[3] Sounds noble, but it doesn't sound easy, which certainly proved to be true.

The Women

In Seibert's time with the company, the staff of the average Penney store was 75 percent women. These women were mostly married and middle-aged, and many could teach the male executives everything about their departments. While retail doesn't pay well (and pays women less than men), most women liked working at Penney's for two reasons. Despite the double standard, there was dignity in the job and it didn't cost them much to wear different dresses every day. Also, the additional discounts they got off sale and clearance things meant real bargains for their families.

But Seibert kept imagining his Verna working there behind a counter, his dear wife earning less than her male counterparts for doing as much or more work. The unfairness contributed to his efforts as chairman (1974–1983) to improve the status of women[4] and minorities. Juanita Kreps joined the board. When she became secretary of the treasury under Jimmy Carter, Jane Pfeiffer from

---

3. At about this time the company began to be known as "JCPenney," having had several appellations over the century from "The Golden Rule" to "Penney's" and beyond. For the rest of this book, "JCPenney" will often be used. However, when appropriate, I will also designate "Penney" and "J. C. Penney," as well as sometimes affixing the formal "Company."

4. Seibert served on the first board at Catalyst, the nonprofit women-in-business advocate, which is discussed in a later chapter.

CBS replaced her and remains on the board to this day. Minorities also appeared in the Penney catalog for the first time (bringing hate mail), and minority suppliers became a significant source of merchandise.

The Kicker

"After spending our lives selling sheets and shoes, why did we ever think we could sell brown goods?"

Seibert smiled at Neppl and said, "It seemed like a good idea at the time."

In the late 1970s the two men were presiding over the beginning of the end of the "all everything" full-line store, the place where one could get a lube job while picking out a wedding gown and a bowling ball. One-stop shopping made sense in the 1960s when America was under-stored. But now the sell-through on appliances, electronics, paint and hardware, sporting goods, and automotive just wasn't competitive with Penney's traditional soft goods—merchandise the company *did* know how to buy and sell better than anyone. And the consumer was signaling a swing to specialty merchandise with deep assortments. Penney research finally identified this as a wave to catch in the future. It would take years, but "America's department store" would jettison most hardlines and return to an improved concentration on apparel, underwear, and soft home furnishings.

And it was decided that the repositioning to soft needed a kicker, something to make the change seem like a new era for Penney.

"Anyway," Neppl said, "Hoagy and some guys are working on this, working on a kicker."

"Before you tell me, do you like it?"

"It's different."

"Okay. So what is it?"

"Fashion."

"Fashion?"

"Fashion." Both men were working to keep a straight face.

"You've got to be kidding."

"It's something we should look at."

"Fashion?"

"Fashion."

"Uh, Walt," Seibert said quietly with a grin, "have you been in outer space?" Without saying it, he easily referred to the fact that Penney sold more polyester leisure suits and other unfashionable apparel than any three competitors combined.

"No, we should be getting into wool."

"Botany and Hart Marx would never sell to us."

"Then we develop our own brands."[5]

"We know nothing about wool."

"So what? We'll learn. We may not know brown goods, but apparel's in our blood."

"You're really serious."

"Just for a look."

Seibert, at heart, was as much of a merchant as Neppl, as much of an innovator. In Elmira he remodeled a basement room, sourced fabric and hardware, and developed a thriving drapery business at a time when the company offered no such merchandise. In Rochester, long on snow blowers at winter's end, he built a mass display near the entrance with prominent signage that said, "We Over-Bought! Long On Snow Blowers! LOOK! →" The arrow pointed at the price (in the largest type). It was actually the normal markup, but they sold out in days. In the Levittown infant department, Seibert dressed a sales associate in nurse's whites and offered special layette packages made up from regular counter merchandise; the department set records.

So Seibert eventually bit on fashion.

But the world outside 1301 6th Avenue had its doubts. In 1977, McCaffrey-McCall became Penney's new advertising agency. Fashion specialists, McCaffrey-McCall, and account executive Peggy McMahon[6] tried to get the company to change its name. Seibert heard about this from executive Jack Rhiel, head of fashion promotion. "They lead up to it," Rhiel said, "and then Peggy hits it hard. We gotta change our name. I say, 'Sorry, Peggy, we can't do that, millions trust that name and we can't.' She then goes on and on about how McCaffrey-McCall spells fashion and how chal-

---

5. Penney did develop its own comparatively upscale brands for men and women, an arduous process that finally succeeded and caused the quality national brands to rethink JCPenney and sell to the company. ("JCPenney" was the retailer's new designation.)

6. Long before the prefix became derogatory, they were known as the "McAgency" at watercoolers.

lenged they are. But that JCPenney spells polyester and commodity goods—"

"Which is true," said Seibert.

"—and we need a new name to make this thing work. 'Sorry, again, Peggy.' 'But, Jack,' she says, 'you need a new image.' '*Yes*,' I tell her. '*But*.' 'Okay,' she finally says. 'I think this is a mistake, but, okay. We'll make the best of it.'" Rhiel lowered his voice. "Should we drop them, Don?"

"No, they're just doing their job," said Seibert, a bit disquieted. "Tell her that. Tell her the name's just worth more than the fashion program."

Later, despite McCaffrey-McCall's good work, the business world remained skeptical.

Business Week made the question a cover story:

CAN JCPENNEY MAKE THE TRANSITION?

The photo showed a woman's legs from the knee down—skirt of a silver sequined evening gown, silver pumps. But instead of hose, she wears white sweat socks.

The fashion program was an obviously slow sell (and to this day, fashion remains a challenge with the new Penney leadership as they centralize buying and improve the presentation of trendier apparel). Seibert finally left it to Neppl and the others. In his last two years before retiring, he became quietly obsessed with a problem that he saw as central to the company's very survival.

Symptoms

> "I always felt that despite the bother and expense, big meetings were good for the company's soul. The basic idea, of course, is to impart wisdom and sell programs to the troops. But there are other equally important values. Management gets to look at the whole organization. A convention teaches an executive, if he's smart enough to look and listen. You shake hands and listen and get a feel for things."
>
> —MIL BATTEN

J. C. Dunn rose fast, moving from store to district to region and then on to a sequence of accomplishments in the New York Office. In 1980 he was put in charge of orchestrating the December district managers' meeting, the most important event on the

Penney calendar. Every district manager and key executives from the regions and New York—hundreds of management associates—would convene for a week at a Lakeland, Florida, resort.

On the last day of the convention, everyone would board buses for a banquet in Sarasota, followed by a full evening's entertainment at the Barnum & Bailey Circus's nearby winter home. Otherwise, it would largely be a working week spent entirely on the resort grounds. Afternoons were free for the associates to enjoy golf and other amenities (where most of the conversation would be about Penney business). But starting early every morning, there was a general meeting followed by a dozen breakout sessions to be attended in rotation. Presentations were scheduled for every lunch and dinner as well, with the company's top executives setting forth their vision for the coming year and with every division, department, and region following with multiple programs for the DMs to achieve those visions. (From experience, DMs arrived with an empty suitcase with which they could lug home all the handouts and practical mementos they were bound to collect.)

Altogether, it was a fairly typical corporate sales-type convention. But J. C. Dunn had a worry that was hard to define.

The coordination responsibilities that he and his staff shouldered were not the problem. Dunn was a cool and effective operator and was excited by the meeting's demands. What bothered him was something he sensed, something that he wished Seibert could address at this convention. Yet because he didn't really have a handle on the problem, the young man felt constrained to say nothing despite continued contact with Seibert leading up to and through the meeting week.

As it happened, however, the chairman had already been distracted by the same vague feeling. Seibert's difficulty, too, was a lack of definition—his disciplined mind telling him that he was brooding over symptoms, not the real problem. Then, on the first morning at Lakeland as he faced the convention for his keynote speech, he received a jolt that would cement his uneasiness.

The year 1979 had been good for the company, a comeback over the past year. Seibert told Dunn the tone of the DM convention should be as relaxed and enjoyable as possible, a reward for the year's accomplishments. Hence, a December conclave in Florida with the circus wrap and professional entertainment for every preceding evening.

Seibert monitored one of Dunn's early meetings to plan the event, pointedly standing in back and staying out of the flow of ideas. At one point, Dunn said, "Since this convention will be more relaxed, what about the dress code?" He was referring to the fact that unless told otherwise, a Penney person would show up on a desert island wearing a suit.

"How far do we go?" came a quick reply. To an outside observer, the discussion that ensued would have been quite amusing. Nobody knew exactly what "casual" meant—not wanting to go *too* far. Finally, Dunn said, "Well, why not compromise with something like a blue blazer and gray slacks?"

"Problem solved," someone said, and agreement was reached. Soon word was deliberately leaked to the district managers. But Dunn took care to stress "something like" blazers, clearly granting leeway for any lightweight sport coat from brass-button navy to khaki to seersucker. Nevertheless, in another part of the JCPenney world a menswear buyer soon noticed an odd spike in blue blazer sales, a curiosity for this time of the year. What could possibly be the cause? He would never have guessed that the reason was what would become known as "The Blue Blazer Convention."

Blue Blazers and Haute Couture

On the first morning of the convention, Seibert entered the green room before his keynote address. Always distracted before a speech, he sat at a table and leafed through his text making a few margin notes. The speech was titled "Highwire Act" in the printed convention agenda, and the chairman would be playing on the metaphor regarding the skill and courage required of every Penney DM.

Before Seibert knew it, a small entourage of upper-middle managers had spontaneously gathered around him—something he always hated but was too Penney-polite to quash. Then, making things worse, he remembered something and made a quick suggestion that elicited the following agreement:

"Good idea, Don."

"Yeah, really, Don."

"Why didn't we think of that?" There was forced laughter as Seibert heard the beginning of his introduction from the wall speaker and rose. He nodded and smiled as he rolled up his text and then realized, much to his further dismay, that all of the other men wore blue blazers and gray slacks—as he himself did.

Seibert could and often did easily act and think in two separate directions at once. Now, hesitating at the edge of the stage with a benign expression, he angrily thought, "Doesn't *anyone* in this company think for himself anymore?"

"And so without further ado . . . let me present: The Boss!" said the man at the podium, milking the moment. "*Donnn . . . Seibert!*"

The Boss strode to the podium with hands raised and a well-faked smile on his face. They were giving him a standing ovation—and nobody had a clue that he was secretly shocked. Not at the standing O, which he could endure. But because he now faced a ballroom *filled* with men in blue blazers and gray slacks!

Seibert was followed by the head men's buyer, who introduced Lee Wright, a promising young fashion designer who had just signed on to produce an exclusive line of young men's apparel for JCPenney. His remarks were brief and lively, and then he cued a carefully choreographed men's fashion show. J. C. Dunn looked out from the wings with mixed feelings. He thought the Lee Wright line was good for the company, but he now regarded the whole scene in front of him without much confidence. Gaunt young models coached to show attitude with no smiles were strutting to loud, edgy music in front of a room full of middle-aged men in blazers. *Those* were the people who would take JCPenney "fashion forward"?

The Future?

As Don Seibert was suffering his blue blazer angst, two more incidents added to his malaise. Dave Miller, a senior stores executive, told him that before the convention he had complimented a store manager about his Christmas village display. After Lakeland, Miller was back visiting a string of stores. "Get this, Don," he said upon returning to 6th Avenue. "The word was out and *every* store now had a Christmas village display! I mean every *one*."

"Good Lord," Seibert said with a flat laugh. "I guess you could compliment them on getting the things up fast."

"I guess."

Seibert himself then went off to visit some stores. Sure enough: Christmas villages at every one. But this was now actually less dismaying than what occurred during his last stop. The store manager had indicated a direction and—with the company's grand future showing in his eyes—had proudly said, "Mr. Seibert, you *have* to meet a special young man."

Seibert was led to a clean-cut and supposedly eager new associate who had been put in charge of the men's underwear section. The chairman noticed a neat, well-merchandised area, with all the signage perfectly in place and all of the inventory displayed by color. But the special young man stood by apprehensively.

"How are sales?" Seibert asked.

The young man shook his head with frustration. "Not good," he said, with an embarrassed glance at the store manager. "And I'm doing everything by the book, sir."

"If he says so, he is," said the store manager, a little too quickly.

"Mind if I look around a minute?" Seibert asked. Almost immediately he saw that all of the stock was in extra-large and extra-small sizes. Not a small, medium, or large to be seen. He pleasantly pointed this out, and the young associate looked even more frustrated.

"I *know* that, Mr. Seibert," said the young man. "But every time I reorder, the stuff comes prepackaged in all sizes. Then the popular sizes go fast and I'm stuck with that." He waved disconsolately at his remaining underwear stock.

The chairman managed a smile as he drew a breath. Then he patiently explained how to special order and bring the inventory back into line.

The store manager punctuated Seibert's teaching with, "Yes, yes, of course, of course." Seibert merely managed another smile, said good-bye to the young man, and changed the subject. Still, he kept *thinking* about what had just occurred and, as he completed the store tour, began making a mental list that he would review again and again:

1. This store was a major mall anchor, the manager supposedly among the company's elite.

2. Yet the manager was clearly not on top of things and his protégé was incompetent, seemingly incapable of thinking for himself.

3. The manager could build a Christmas village virtually overnight, but he couldn't train a dull young man to keep underwear inventory in balance.

4. And these people were the *future?*

The Revelation

That night Seibert sat alone in the CEO's office on the 43rd floor
of the J. C. Penney tower. Regrettably, his friend and closest colleague, President Walt Neppl, was out of town. The problem Seibert was wrestling with was just the kind that Walt would respond
to. Together, they might spark an idea, an approach to an answer.
Theirs was an unusually harmonious partnership at the top. Each
man covered the other's weaknesses, each man's strengths com-
plementing the other's. Neppl would be back tomorrow afternoon. He could be reached at a hotel tonight, but the telephone
wasn't the way to get into this. They needed to be together in the
same room, connecting as they always did in person. Seibert
would have to wait, trying to think through the parameters in the
meantime. He had known immediately that the three incidents
that triggered his concern were just symptoms—and seemingly
innocuous ones at that. He thought that most (if not all) of his
other senior colleagues would dismiss the incidents as nothing
more than anecdotal corporate silliness. Yet he was certain—and
certain that Neppl would agree with him—that the real problem
lying beneath the symptoms could have grave consequences for
JCPenney.

He got up from his couch and walked to a window. Below
was 6th Avenue, and immediately beyond, the original Rockefeller
Center buildings were ablaze in light. He smiled wryly to himself.
Here he was, one of the most important business leaders in the
country, looking at the most imposing symbol of American capi-
talism. And what lofty thoughts possessed Don Seibert, captain
of industry, at this moment? Blue blazers, Christmas villages, and
underwear! But people not thinking for themselves was just a
damned symptom! He shook his head and turned from the window. He had felt that the view would invigorate him. Instead, tonight, it made him feel insignificant and helpless.

He chose an easy chair. Shutting his eyes, he tried to concentrate. A wave of fatigue washed over him. He had not been sleeping well lately, and he never got enough sleep as it was. Maybe that was the reason he couldn't focus. But he had always been a disciplined and trenchant thinker, even when he'd had little or no rest. So it had to be—what?

It wasn't the company's overall health because after a flat 1979, things were going better in 1980. JCPenney was king of the malls, with hundreds of smart-looking (for Penney) and profitable anchor stores. The repositioning from full-line to primarily soft goods had begun slowly but effectively—even the fashion edge was beginning to be taken somewhat seriously. Aside from closing the Treasury discount stores, the other businesses like catalog were doing well.

So why was it so hard to probe deeper now? Why did he keep returning to the blue blazer, Christmas village, and underwear incidents? He didn't know. He kept seeing the Lakeland convention and JCPenney stores. Stores . . . His mind was wandering. "Would I ever have guessed?" thought the former jazz bandleader. "I've lived a life of stores."

Seibert's eyelids were growing heavy. He felt too tired to think anymore, too tired to—

Suddenly he was on his feet, his eyes widening and a cold sweat beginning to bead on his forehead. "Good Lord," he thought. "Good *Lord!*"

Now he knew. And the answer was so simple. It had been right there under their noses all along. The J. C. Penney Company's huge size wasn't the problem. That was an easy answer leading nowhere. The subtle and truly scary thing—the cause of those symptomatic problems—was that somehow over the years the company had lost its rugged, thoughtful individualism. Historically, the best men in the company had always been independent and self-reliant. The wonder of the organization was that they were also bound to square their work with what was right and just, to be honorably confident and render service cooperatively.

Today, however, the true Penney person who built the company was becoming extinct. As never before, Seibert realized that most associates had become stultifying conformists. And people like Seibert and Neppl—exceptions, as there always were exceptions—had simply missed it. They had been too busy to really notice.

So it was with a weird sense of relief that Seibert got into his Pontiac in the parking garage and headed home to New Jersey. At least he now understood. So all he and Walt had to do was come up with some answers before this monster irreversibly killed their beloved company.

A Plan

"My God, Don," Neppl said the next day. "How did we miss it? It's only the all-time personnel problem."

"Any ideas offhand?"

"No. We've got some thinking to do." But they were dry for several weeks until the tris scare.

One day a news report tied every major retailer in knots. Penney, thanks to Seibert, shook it off much faster than its competition. The bad news was that tris, a flame-retardant chemical used to treat children's clothes (a big Penney profit center), was discovered to be a potential carcinogen. The day the story broke, journalists all over the country asked retailers what they intended to do about it.

Seibert immediately called an ad hoc committee together. It contained managers from public relations, the head children's buyers, the distribution and inventory control groups, legal, and consumer affairs. After a hasty report on the potential impact, senior merchandise executive Bob Gill said, "Well, there's really no issue. We have to yank the goods." After details were discussed, the committee members went back to their various departments and got to work. By that afternoon the company had begun to pull all tris-treated merchandise from its shelves. The Penney action was communicated to customers weeks before any of the other large chains had even framed a response.

This experience provided the germ of an answer to the larger question that had come to haunt Seibert and Neppl. A big company could be just as responsive as a small one if it could be organized into a broad array of smaller, fully empowered operating groups led by *individuals*. Strategic thought would come by cross-departmental working groups led by responsible *individuals*. Tactical decisions would be made at the level where they were to be implemented by empowered *individuals*. Such an organization would never suffer from bureaucratic paralysis, instead encouraging associates to think through issues and *act*, rather than waiting for new directives or procedures to trickle down from above.

From concept to workable plan *was*, in Neppl's original words, the "all-time personnel problem." However, both men knew it was a doable deal. Then Walt Neppl retired in 1982, soon to be followed by Seibert. Their plan was taking shape but required skillful development for another year or two. But this was one of the reasons Bill Howell had been chosen as the next CEO. Howell was young, in his late forties. He would be able to follow through with the former administration's plans (a Penney tradition) and still have ample time left in which to set his own course.

And so Seibert retired with misguided confidence in the plan's future.[7]

7. Ironically, the plan was a diametric opposite of the consensus management style that peaked during the reign of Howell's successor, Jim Oesterreicher. Assumption of responsibility and action, not consensus conformity, was the backbone of the Seibert/Neppl plan.

part III

The Betrayer

chapter **14**   New Blood

I N THE EARLY 1980S, the company issued a positioning statement. This attempted to define how JCPenney would become the value-fashion "Department Store of the '80s." Gale Duff-Bloom, about whom much more will be heard in subsequent chapters, was excited by this. She had finished her stint managing a big Bay Area anchor and was headed across the continent to the New York Office. She believed in the company's direction and was eager to help create this national department store.

But the positioning statement dodged the big problem of gaining fashion credibility, which had gotten no easier. High-end women's designers had joined the better men's wool brands like Botany 500 and Hart Schaffner & Marx in refusing to do business with huge but humble JCPenney. Most feared getting toasted by association with the old commodity merchant. And for the few inclined to sell out, there was a production quandary. Penney had 1,600 stores at the time. Macy's, in contrast, had a solid reputation but only 13 stores in 1982. Putting 20 designer pieces into each Macy's meant a production run of 260. For Penney, it would mean 32,000. And the flip side of meeting the production challenge, of course, seemed to be turning the designer brand into a commodity. So a big Penney contract did not seem to be worth it to the majority of upscale suppliers. It was a lose-lose situation.

Vertical Integration!

Still, there were some victories. In addition to men's designer Lee Wright's signing, Halston, who was fading in stature but still well known, agreed to design a women's line for Penney. Also, the company's developing private brand expertise in wool was revved up further. If more big names wouldn't sign on, Penney would produce and promote more private brand apparel.

Fashion—even value fashion—would never be easy for JCPenney. Nevertheless, soft goods played to Penney's strength, and fashion provided an edge. It was worth the struggle.

Before Neppl and Seibert were fully out the door, the "new blood" waiting in the wings was given full rein to develop a radical change in an old organizational structure. This was to give the "fashion forward" program more teeth. It turned out to be a serious mistake, although the idea initially looked great on paper and got the nod from Neppl and Seibert.

But first, a little clarification for the lay reader. The retail industry has needed a better vocabulary for a long time. The word spelled "merchandise," for example, has *two* distinctively different meanings. One, pronounced "mer-chan-*dice*," means goods for sale. The other, pronounced "mer-chan-*dize*," always means the presentation of goods for sale, and sometimes means the selection of those goods ("buying") as well. And a derivative word, "merchandising," represents the *combined* meanings of "merchandise."

Merchandise, merchandising, and marketing had formerly been separate departments. Now six "merchandising divisions" had been created, a grab-bag term relating to multiple functions and not just actual "merchandising" per se. Each division contained three general areas along with support functions: merchandise (buying), merchandising (presentation), and marketing (promotion). The idea was that vertically integrated divisions—women's, men's, children's, home, home improvement, and automotive—would spawn faster, more focused results. Overall plans would still come from the executive suite, but important day-to-day moves would be decided much closer to the action.

Bill Howell, the former field leader who had been handpicked by Seibert over the other finalists, Bob Gill and Dave Miller, immediately praised this new arrangement (to which he had contributed). He would back its further development in the next few years. And he added a wrinkle. For a more intense companywide merchandising effort, he made the divisions competitive among themselves. Another benefit of the change was to further isolate merchandising areas in order to more easily attack and obliterate the people and merchandise in conflict with the soft goods and fashion swing.

Indeed, as the worry beads came out, by the end of Howell's second CEO year, automotive, home improvement, cameras, electronics, and major appliances were gone. Although the decisive heavy lifting for soft/fashion had been led by Seibert and Neppl, Howell was credited with a courageous follow-through. The company was walking away from over $1 billion in annual business, while another billion had to be committed for remodeling the store space freed up by the dearly departed.

Bipolar Disorder

Before continuing with the seemingly powerful concept of competitive, integrated merchandising divisions, it is important to first present a short history of antagonism.

Among the several reasons for the success of the J. C. Penney Company covered in this book, two stand out. These were the company's concept of retail partnerships and the evolved power and expertise of its wholesale buyers.

The buying and retailing functions, of course, were the guts of Penney's business. They were also competitive bipolar antagonists. The following, simply put, compares these functions and their politics over the years. Conclusions are then drawn regarding company defects that grew out of these politics.

No question, the most celebrated concept in the company's growth was "partnership." From the beginning, this meant unique autonomy for the store manager—including doing his own buying. Except for the earliest years, however, that was "buying" in quotation marks. Buyers in New York did the actual buying. After district and region input, they selected the assortments from which managers then chose. Naturally, managers resented the buyers' leverage over them while buyers scorned the managers' lack of street sophistication. But what the buyers hated most was a store manager's status in the organization.

But it all begins with obtaining goods from manufacturers at wholesale for reselling to the public. The business begins with a buy. For most of the century, this was accomplished by the Penney merchandise department, whose buyers were a different breed from Penney store and field personnel. They were, first of all, sequestered in New York City and worked in their own esoteric world. Well dressed, they had an easy and off-putting arrogance, epitomized by the familiar street slogans "Wholesale leads retail" and "Hard to buy, easy to sell."

The trick, of course, was keeping the bipolar buying and selling functions in practical balance. For decades this had been diligently achieved, the New York Office (including buyers) and the stores playing in tenuous harmony. The tone began to shift in favor of the field in the 1960s and became a store solo in the 1980s.

While the Penney store manager had traditionally been a first-rate individual, the increasing political clout of the Penney field was largely due to the great rise in an average store's size. As the company moved from Main Street to anchoring malls, the influence of the field overtook New York's. Store managers and regional executives felt that they, not the Manhattanites, should call all of the merchandise shots. Then ex–field executives came to dominate the company's senior management, and total merchandise control passed to the stores. The weakened company that resulted can be explained by two sets of comparisons.

In the stores the concentration on merchandise was necessarily broad and shallow. In buying it was the opposite—narrow and deep. A good store associate knew something about a lot of lines. A good buyer knew a lot about one line. Consequently, executives from either camp were always seeing merchandise from opposing points of view. But the real merchandise expertise and contacts clearly resided in New York.

There was another difference.

Buyers had to stay closely in touch with the likes of fiber producers, textile mills, and manufacturers. Hence, of necessity, buyers were aware of (and often influential regarding) what was going to happen in the future. Store executives, of necessity, were focused on what was happening right now.

JCPenney became, therefore, a right-now organization with little focus on the future and diminished depth of merchandise knowledge. This, in turn, led to the good old all-American corruption of executives getting into bed with vendors. Elise Greenberg had been one of the three senior buyers in the men's division before she resigned in disgust in early 1999. "I couldn't deal with the unethical business practices," she said—having gone to her boss again and again with ways to save the company a bundle, only to be scolded because she was targeting a favored supplier.[1]

Previously, merchandise and values mattered while professionalism and integrity glued it all together. The customer had been the total reason for being. Profits took care of themselves. But now perquisites, getting ahead, and declaring dividends were the names of the game. And the customer? Shuffled off to Buffalo. These, then, formed the beginnings of deep-seated troubles that would eventually bring down the once-proud organization after nearly a century of success.

Bonehead Moves and Other Mistakes

Back to the competitive, integrated merchandising divisions originated in the early 1980s. Were they as good as the plan had promised? Not exactly. In their practical application serious flaws began to surface—particularly among those who understood the importance of maintaining the delicate balance between merchandise and store influences.

Here were the problems:

➤ Competitive merchandising divisions operating in silos knocked the second "C" out of HCSC in the company's basic business. Merchandising was JCPenney's raison d'être. Eliminating internal cooperation has to rank high on the Edsel list of bonehead moves in corporate America.

➤ It also tended to muffle the grapevine. Why did this matter? Because the grapevine almost always helps keep the executive suite more responsive to customer concerns *and* those of the rank and file. However indirectly, the grapevine speaks to management. It also helps keep a company alive and vital. One has to care to complain and gossip.

➤ Top executives became more isolated. In the executive suite, a war party from silo number one coming across one from silo number two promoted anxiety, not camaraderie. Hence, the reflex to limit access.

1. From "Penney Pinched," a November 25, 1999, *Dallas Observer* article by Miriam Rozen; used with permission.

➤ The abilities of senior management diminished. A new idea from one silo would be torpedoed by another. Since ideas have authors, and because such people were now largely seen as threats, they were represented less and less among company officers. This contributed to the infection of mediocrity that eventually overcame company leadership.

➤ Combined with Howell's insistence that second thoughts and mind changing were counterproductive, limited access to the top also contributed to the lockstep bureaucracy that increasingly enveloped the company.

➤ In a divide-and-conquer foreshadowing of the Dallas move, splitting up the merchandise department hastened the stores' total triumph.

➤ The management of most new merchandising divisions was from—where else?—the stores!

Wild Horses

In the early 1980s, fashion credibility remained an issue. Seeking an answer, management came up with a marketing ploy disguised as "sourcing." If most name American designers remained hesitant to hostile, Penney would recruit foreign designers eager to expand into the giant U.S. market. Thus, in 1984, the company launched its first major international promotion, "A Salute to Italy." For a limited period, Penney stores would feature second-tier Italian designer clothes while celebrating the Italian culture. Any strong-selling labels could then continue as part of the regular JCPenney assortment. Results were mixed. None of the Italian labels fared particularly well. Research could not pinpoint the culprit. Was it unsophisticated Penney shoppers or designer/manufacturers who were unsophisticated in selling to Penney shoppers?

Still, changes in the market were going Howell's way—and were an affirmation of Seibert and Neppl's original wisdom (moving from the "all-everything" store to more Penney-traditional assortments). The trend signaled in the 1970s had become the wave of the future in the early 1980s. Customers were in fact showing increased preference for more specialized stores with deep assortments.

(Also during this time, as Seibert monitored Howell from the retirement sideline and saw him at board meetings, he realized that the Seibert/Neppl concept for recapturing individualism had been set aside with disinterest by the new CEO.)

The international salute for 1985 featured designs from Great Britain. In a publicity coup, arrangements were made through the British consulate to have Princess Diana visit a JCPenney store near Washington, D.C. Since she was a world-class fashion icon, the press gave the story wide coverage. The night of the visit, Johnny Carson mentioned it in his monologue, adding that "Nancy Reagan was supposed to accompany Princess Di to JCPenney, but nobody could find a team of wild horses."

And fashion credibility remained an issue. In a short two years, however, the biggest company event since 1914 would have a far greater effect on merchandising than any sort of fashion twist.

Certainly No Way

"Before the company moved to the 6th Avenue building, there was some thinking about Westchester or Connecticut or even Dallas, with a campus and trees and lakes. A strong case was made regarding the numbers, the premium we paid to remain in New York City, etcetera. Well, nobody loves natural beauty more than I do, but, I'm sorry, New York is where it's at. I strongly felt that our business was too dynamic, too ever-changing to be headquartered anywhere but New York. I thought our people should draw from the city's energy, be stimulated by the maelstrom, be in the center of it all, the activity, the gossip, the rumors, the tension, be in the midst of the battle. New York is tough. Not for nothing do you always hear that if you can make it here, you can make it anywhere. I think that's good for us, as well as our being only minutes away from some late breaking item on Seventh Avenue."

—MIL BATTEN (1986)

In 1986, rumors of a move from New York to Dallas began to seep through the company. Such rumors were not new. They had surfaced sporadically since Batten's days. As Batten explained, a Dallas move would make a lot of sense from a financial and operational perspective. The Penney tower needed costly refurbishing. Manhattan was very expensive and space was limited, with Penney now renting several floors in two other buildings.

There were other arguments as well. Getting to work in Texas would be remarkably easier, thereby conserving associates' time and energy for the tasks at hand. Then there were time zone communications, an often critical issue in national retailing. At 5 P.M., when many New York Office associates had to leave to catch their commuter trains, an afternoon of action still remained in Los Angeles. In the central time zone—especially with everyone driving to work and able to arrive earlier and stay later—communications within the whole company would be much easier and greatly improved.

Travel would also be easier and more efficient. Dallas had an outstanding airport and was an airline hub fairly near the geographic center of the United States. And it would be far, far easier getting to flights in Dallas. Associates could fly out of Dallas in the morning and still do at least a generous half-day's business anywhere in the country, usually with lower fares as well.

And then there was the easier and much less expensive lifestyle—an aspect that had grown to paradisiacal proportions to those commuting to Manhattan.

Also not new were rejections of Dallas. Although never publicized, through the grapevine the rank and file knew that three Dallas proposals had been killed in Don Seibert's administration alone. He had recommended against them, and the board had voted the motions down. Although the arguments had been the same, Seibert had echoed Batten in citing the serious intangible costs—as well as the loss of experienced personnel—that such a move would inevitably cause.

Therefore, since Howell said he wished to be careful and certain, late in 1986 an external group was contracted to evaluate the move. The work was done in secrecy because of the fear of unwanted press coverage before any decision was reached. There was a substantial antimove faction at the top, and at this point they assumed two things would come out of this evaluation:

1. The bare numbers would, without a doubt, be very seductive.

2. All the same, the answer would be no. As before in the Batten and Seibert years, there were just too many aspects to such a move that were antithetical to the way JCPenney operated. Seibert had killed the move. Howell, as Seibert's man, would certainly do the same.

Texas!

The Americana Hotel was adjacent to the J. C. Penney tower on 6th Avenue. In its largest ballroom, fitted with theater-style seating, Bill Howell made an announcement in two successive jam-packed sessions (including all associates from other buildings as well). The news was stunning, and would shortly throw the city itself into a tizzy. The J. C. Penney Company was leaving its Big Apple roots for Dallas.

Some associates were ecstatic at the promise of a better lifestyle along with the trumpeted efficiency waiting in Big D. But they were the minority. Most, upon getting the news, were dazed, furious, or resigned.

"How can I *leave?* My parents and friends are here," said one person in tears.

"I'm a New Yorker, not a goddamn cowboy," said another who was steaming.

"So big deal," shrugged a third. "I've already moved seven times. What's another?"

And among Penney management there remained division, especially (but certainly not totally) between the buyers and store people.

A few months after the announcement, the annual Buyer Awards banquet was held in New York's splendid Pierre Hotel on 5th Avenue. Bill Howell had made the keynote address and said nothing at all about the upcoming move to Dallas. Dave Miller then kicked off the individual award presentations, also not mentioning a word about Dallas.

At a ballroom table near the dais, a buyer colleague leaned over to vice president Dave Fulcomer and said, "Okay, Dave, if you're so smart, answer me this. What is *the* subject on the mind of everyone here tonight?"

"The move to Dallas?" said Fulcomer.

"And what was noticeably absent from the remarks of our esteemed leaders?"

"The move to Dallas?" said Fulcomer.

"Then what the hell are they so worried about?"

"The move to Dallas?" Fulcomer said with a flat chuckle. "Pardon my jest."

"So weird," said the colleague, who then took a good draft of wine.

"It's the fart-in-the-elevator syndrome," Fulcomer said as he looked back toward the dais. "Everyone knows it's here, but nobody says anything about it." Dave Fulcomer himself—a merchandise executive known for his outspokenness as well as his quick humor—was scheduled to appear later as one of the award presenters. As he waited his turn, he kept thinking about *the* subject. This audience of *his* fellow merchandise associates deserved better. It was their night, after all, and the tension in the room was palpable, the sense of expectation enormous. "Well," he thought, "if the esteemed leadership won't address the subject, then I will have to do it myself."

When Jim Kennedy finished with his men's division awards, he introduced Fulcomer to cover the home division recipients. Trotting up to the podium, Fulcomer waved around the ballroom and then nearly shouted into the microphone, "Isn't this place great?!" Applause rose from the hundreds of buyers, family members, and guests—all in tuxedos and gowns. Then the applause rolled into a cheer. Fulcomer had astutely touched a nerve. While his reference was directly to the great hotel, symbolically it was also to New York City *and* J. C. Penney's presence there. He raised a fist and smiled—as he thought, "These people *really* need a release."

"This is New York at its best, folks," he continued. "And that's only fitting. You represent the best and brightest of the world's greatest buying corps!" That brought another cheer. "And before we continue with the awards, I have a sad-but-quick reflection followed by an upbeat, make-the-best-of-it announcement."

What came next was Fulcomer's stratagem to get everyone relaxed enough to buy into his main message: an appeal to retain as many of the veteran buyers as possible in the turbulent time to come. An appeal for them to come to Texas. First, he looked around and again indicated the ballroom. "Tonight," he said, "when we leave, every one of us should look around this elegant room for one last time . . . because it'll soon be good-bye New York City, good-bye Pierre Hotel, and hello Texas. And I'm sure you know that, because of the expenses involved in J. C. Penney's move to Dallas, certain economies will be necessary."

He took a folded paper from his tuxedo pocket. "And some of you may *also* know that the man who coordinates these company events, Bruce Ackerman,[2] has to work a year in advance." He held up the folded paper. "Well, *I* have been able to obtain a copy of Ackerman's work-up for the invitation to next year's Buyer Awards banquet in grrreater Dallas." And he pretended to read. "'The 1988 Buyer Awards *snack* [LAUGHTER] . . . will be held on Central Expressway at the *La Quinta* Motor Inn [BIG LAUGHTER] . . . Please come as you are . . . bring your own bottle [BIGGER LAUGHTER] . . . and dance the night away to the toe-tapping tunes of Lester Flatt, Earl Scruggs, and the Foggy Mountain Boys!'"

He had to wait, and then he continued. "Seriously, folks, and please hear me out on this. Without you, there *is* no JCPenney—which is something I hope the rest of them never have to find out! [CHEER!] So, wher*ever* this evening is held next year, *please* follow me and the others south. Dallas *has* advantages. And I hope that each and every one of you is in attendance next year. Because if J. C. Penney is nothing without us, *we* are nothing without you! So God bless you and let's get on with the awards!" [BIG CHEER!].

At the end of the evening, Howell returned to the podium for the wrap. He was scowling. Many additional awards had been given since Fulcomer had yielded to the next presenter, and Howell's initial remark surprised and then hushed the Pierre audience. "Before I congratulate you once again and conclude these proceedings," he said, "I have a question. Show of hands, please." He looked left and right, the master of all he surveyed. "Is there anyone else here besides Dave Fulcomer who went to Princeton?"

Howell waited for anyone to raise his or her hand. The few seconds felt like an hour—and everyone in the ballroom knew, if they hadn't known before, that there was a new sheriff in town. Not a hand appeared from the packed ballroom, and Howell finally said, "None? Well, I thought so."

In the eyes of Fulcomer and many of his friends, this event signaled the end of his highly promising career.[3]

Fail Safe!

In the book of Genesis, God directs Abraham and his family to Canaan (Palestine), a land of plenty that would bloom out of the

2. The same Bruce Ackerman who would promote the brilliant designer who figures prominently in Chapter 17.

3. Fulcomer retired in the late 1990s. His succinct recap of the Texas-move time: "Almost overnight, I went from an overachiever to a hanger-on."

desert. God promises that in return for absolute faith, the bountiful land will become the everlasting possession of Abraham's descendants. But a split in the family tree (Arabs this way, Jews that way), along with other casualties of time, have confused the covenant to this day. And if things can go amiss with the Almighty's plans, it has been known virtually from the time of Abraham that the schemes of mere mortals are extraordinarily vulnerable. Even a plan as dazzling and seemingly fail-safe as Bill Howell's move to Texas.

Basically, Howell directs his people to Dallas (a land of easy commutes, affordable swimming pools, and wonderful produce) and promises that in return for absolute fealty, everyone (and some more than others) will enjoy greater accommodations, escalating success, and everlasting security.

"You have to understand that there was a kind of technician's mentality or tunnel vision at work here," said Duncan Muir, Penney's senior PR executive. "And other than those who refused to move—and that's another story—I don't think my attitude at the time was much different from that of anyone else headed for Dallas. The workaday quality of life was going to improve significantly. And everyone felt it was justified. Howell's deal, after all, made it all a gift."

Muir was actually Howell's advance man. He introduced himself at the then two major Dallas dailies and the major TV outlets (where he was interviewed on camera), and he spoke to the Chamber of Commerce as well as virtually every other significant luncheon club and civic group. And he made a great impression, emphasizing JCPenney's values to the community (beyond the obvious financial impact):

> "And I believe," he would often end his speeches, "you'll find that the J. C. Penney Company is a truly outstanding corporate citizen. We will lead in the United Way and variety of other civic duties. We will pay our vendors and our taxes within two weeks of receiving invoices. And we will otherwise treat people exactly the way we would wish to be treated ourselves."

He would then pause, look around the room, and continue:

> "James Cash Penney's first store in 1902 was actually called The Golden Rule—truth. He ran the only cash-and-carry store

in the rough mining town of Kemmerer, Wyoming, and he could have introduced himself to customers with, 'Hi, I'm Jim Penney, and Cash is my middle name!' "

Another smile and a pause. Then:

"But he didn't. He just offered the best prices and service anyone had ever seen. And to this day we still do—and we still believe in the Golden Rule."

Muir would then tap his suit's lapel pin.

"And to this day every single one of our executives wears a lapel pin just like mine. It has four letters—HCSC—that, from our first convention in 1913 in Salt Lake City, have stood for the company's watchwords: Honor. Confidence. Service. Cooperation."

He would then pause and smile one last time, adding:

"A little corny, maybe. But that's the way we are. And we're something else, too. We're surprised and pleased by the Texas brand of friendliness we have found here. You have made us feel welcomed, and we are really thrilled to be coming to Dallas!"

In truth, of course, not everybody was.

chapter 15   Bill Howell

WHAT HAD HAPPENED? Why was the move ordained? Well, first of all, this was 1986, not the '60s or '70s. This was also Howell, not Seibert or Batten. Having transferred to New York from the Western Region only a few years before, Howell was a typical store nomad who was much more focused on operational efficiencies. Furthermore, he did not see the former negative arguments as applicable in this day and age. Fashion influences, for one, now originated in many places other than New York—and please name the vendor who wouldn't happily bring sample cases to such a big buyer.

The Big Move

Never even a fake New Yorker, Howell was also not bothered by the city's predictable fury over the company's exit. When the news hit the street, the *Daily News* was already being hawked with a front-page headline that read:

"J. C. PENNEY MOVING TO PLANO
(THAT'S 'PLANO' AS IN DRĀNO) TEXAS"

Speculation that moving would cause a mutiny of experienced talent cut no ice with Howell, either. Surveys were produced that assuaged various concerns, and plans went ahead for the move. Bill Howell, basically, just *wanted* this thing to happen.

In 1988, cattle still grazed on the land on which the new JCPenney headquarters would eventually rise—land that was a stunningly astute purchase. Located in what would become one of the nation's premiere corporate parks ("Legacy"), it had three times the acreage necessary for a sprawling headquarters complex. And this land was located at the corner of Highway 121 (a limited-access straight shot to Dallas/Fort Worth airport) and the Dallas North Tollway (straight shot downtown). By the year 2000, when Penney's stock had nosedived, the company's excess property would be worth many times the original purchase price.

Now the huge retailer moved,[1] and the temporary arrangements were elaborate. Among the march of ironies in this book, it is interesting to note that the company's office-proximity situation was worsened rather than improved by the move. In New York, Penney had occupied its 6th Avenue tower and floors of two other buildings within easy walking distance. But now the company was scattered in four north Dallas locations that were accessible only by freeway travel. The major address was Lincoln Center, where most of the Dallas newcomers and new hires took over three big buildings. (This was the complex visually known to millions as the home of amoral J. R. Ewing's oil empire on the television show *Dallas*.)

The most important address, however, was the just-completed Aberdeen Building two exits up on the Dallas North Tollway. There, leasing all seven floors, the company located its executive suite and several support departments.

For visitors from New York, the Aberdeen Building would hold a surprise. Oddly, in view of the comparatively simple accommodations left behind, here the top Penney executives had large suites, including individual conference rooms. The largest measured nearly a thousand square feet.

One of the smaller offices on the Aberdeen executive floor belonged to Gale Duff-Bloom. Newly established as director of investor relations, she was developing a rapport with Howell while working hard and effectively to present the JCPenney case to Wall Street. In a few chapters this narrative will follow Duff-Bloom's ascent from offbeat trainee to the executive suite. For now, she joined a few other observers in concluding that the fancy offices were the result of two factors:

1. Credit and systems, stand-alone Penney departments, had already moved to Dallas a few years before.

1. The more senior executives were suddenly quite prominent in Dallas and, as never before in New York, those who sought social and peer acceptance were able to easily find it in Big D.[2]

2. The premium building and new offices still represented a big savings per square foot compared to Rockefeller Center. So company officers must have thought "Why *not?!*"

"W. R."

It was also at the time of the Aberdeen occupation that Bill Howell changed his name. For a New York to Dallas transitional event, a senior producer had a brief meeting with the chairman himself in order to check any sensitive details. As the producer gathered his notes and rose, he remembered to ask, "Oh, and how do we address you in the scripted intro?"

"Call me 'Mr. Howell' or 'W. R.,'" came the reply.

For years in the field, Howell had contrived to be known as "W. R." It was different in New York, though. There his name was "Bill." Probably a "Mil" or a "Walt" or a "Don" had innocently started this, and Howell had never made an issue of it. But from this point forward he was never again "Bill" to anyone anywhere. Quickly, Lincoln Center watercooler wags picked up on the new name with comments like, "'W. R.?' Hmm. Rhymes with 'J. R.'" (Penney humor had an edge in those days because sales had taken a dive and associates worried about layoffs.)

Howell's name change was an interesting aspect of a complicated man. Raised and educated in Oklahoma, Howell always worked to enhance his image. When he became a candidate for the top job, he lost weight, quit smoking cigars, improved his tailoring, and (typical of many senior executives) took poise and elocution instruction. As the CEO, he always chose his publicized appearances with great care, favoring prestige events like serving on a White House blue ribbon panel (see photo section), Waldorf

---

2. Despite JCPenney's efforts in the later part of the twentieth century to move away from the company's commodity merchant identification, the retail and brand elite continued to see Penney as déclassé and its executives as comparative hicks (as always, there were exceptions; Mil Batten, who retired to run the NYSE, being the most obvious). In Texas these executives seemingly got their revenge.

speeches, and Penney's televised golf events. Yet the former head of Penney's meeting services, Jerry Convery, had a surprising story about the CEO's favorite music.

"I had a crew and equipment on one of the company jets to go to Kemmerer for an anniversary event. The planes were always scheduled tight, and, lo and behold, who else is riding with us but the chairman. For some reason W. R. had to get there the night before, too, so away we go to Rock Springs because that's the closest this plane can land to Kemmerer. I had a van waiting there and Howell had a Lincoln, which I picked up and volunteered to drive. He said fine and we headed out, my crew following behind. After about 10 minutes of small talk, the chairman starts fiddling with the radio and, lo and behold, he finds this country-western station and cranks the volume. Well, please understand that I have an unreasonable hatred of country-western in any form. Country-western makes me crazy. It makes me disregard social niceties like being pleasant to the powerful man sitting next to me as we drive across this desolate countryside with country-western hammering my head and blood pressure. I take all I can, which isn't much, and then I shout, 'I'm sorry, W. R., but if I'm doing the driving, there's no cowboy music allowed. It would not be safe for me to listen to that while I'm at the wheel.' Well, he gives me a scary look and then just snaps off the radio. Nothing more. He leans back, shuts his eyes, and dozes. Not another word all the way to Kemmerer, where he then gets into his leadership mode and of course performs very well. But I'll never forget two things. The look he gave me, and the fact that, lo and behold, W. R. Howell liked country-western."

The Man

In many ways, Howell is perhaps the most interesting (and surprising) player in this book. For example, unlike previous Penney leaders, when he became chairman and CEO, he was not known for any particular stellar accomplishment. In fact, his actual record was just average—except as a charismatic politician with an executive image. But if he had no signal achievement to hang his hat on, good-looking Bill Howell probably had the best outward leadership presence of anyone in the company's history.

To this day, Gale Duff-Bloom thinks that Jim Oesterreicher

(Howell's successor) was far more responsible than Howell for the company's fall. Duff-Bloom, however, never spent two days' time in concentrated abstract thought about the company, so entrenched was her career reflex to march on no matter what. Duff-Bloom also thought that Howell was the best teacher and boss she ever had, a more accurate appraisal. "I met a lot of great people in the Penney Company," she said. "But W. R. was open and supportive and inspirational and just the best."

Others, of course, would disagree.[3] A retired anchor store manager says of Howell: "A very slick customer. He listened but often didn't hear. He was an arrogant man in some ways. I never quite trusted him. He had his own agenda."

A retired Penney executive comments: "Bill Howell's rise to the top is understandable if regrettable. He was smooth, smart, controlled, experienced, with the presence of a potential CEO. Then there was the dark side: He was devious, egocentric, and a master at staying out of harm's way (not someone to share a foxhole with). It was said that the only thing Bill Howell really succeeded at was his own success."

As for myself (your author), in 16 years as a speechwriter for senior executives—mainly at big corporations—I never saw Howell's equal as a leader on his feet. Again and again he would improvise brilliantly. He was a special talent. And now the trick question: Was he the best CEO I ever saw? Not even close.

But someone in charge will always inspire a range of opinions. Penney CEOs Mil Batten and Al Hughes had their detractors. During his fall from grace, of course, James Cash Penney himself was disrespected by many in New York. And surely there had to be someone who didn't like Earl Sams, the man who ran the company for 40 years. Therefore, some hard scrutiny is necessary in appraising Howell's reign.

Howell's main weakness was a product of (or at least reinforced by) the times. He began early in the era of CEO stock promoters. Responding to stockholder and Wall Street clamoring for more market value growth, boards began selecting—and rewarding—executives whose primary focus and skill was in the present payout and resulting stock value. For the 80 years of company

3. The reader will learn that chairman Don Seibert, the man who picked Howell as his successor, would eventually have second thoughts.

history before Howell's ascendancy, however, the emphasis had been exactly the opposite: on the customer and on the future. If Wall Street didn't understand it or like it, tough.

Thus exacerbating other mistakes was a CEO who was literally not minding the store. Not a great idea, no matter *what* the era.

Empty Suits

And what about the executives Howell developed to fill the executive suite? Were they the best and the brightest, people of strong minds and razor-sharp abilities? Sure, in some cases (obvious in this book). But generally? No. One of the great business organizations of all time actually ended up with many mediocrities immediately below the main man.

How could this happen? Well, first of all, we have to drag out those perennial whipping boys, insularity and parochialism. Lash! Lash! And they deserve it. The Penney culture's almost jingoistic antagonism toward "outsider" points of view (and talent) was always a drawback. But there is more to the story, and like so much of the Penney downfall, it's loaded with more irony.

In addition to Howell's dominant personality, his insistence upon store-oriented *breadth* at the top led to weaknesses in the executive suite. How? Well, with the world's store of knowledge increasing exponentially these days, it is not the time for well-rounded generalists to run things. A really sharp management today needs a specialist at the top who somehow has a grasp of the overall picture and rides herd on a band of acute specialists. Andy Grove at Intel would have come quickly to mind a few years ago. But, toward the end of the last century, Penney management was the diametric opposite.

Breadth of (retail) experience, in fact, became so worshiped in executive offices that special "fast track" career paths were designated for those who seemed particularly promising for senior management. So after being dipped into store managing, the candidates were often whisked from one retail-related broadening experience to the next with such rapidity that one often heard exchanges like:

Associate A: "Is he really that good?"
Associate B: "Nobody knows. He's never been in one place long enough to find out."

What was lost in all this? As the frenetic well rounding of candidates continued, specialists—men and women with drop-dead knowledge and skills in some particular area of the business—became less and less important in the JCPenney executive suite (particularly expert buyers). Under Batten, when Penney got into new businesses like catalog, discounting, and fashion, he disregarded tradition and brought in top-level specialists from the outside. No more.

Even more damaging, specialists within the company became *disqualified* for senior management candidacy. Only the broadened store-oriented person need apply.

Thus, store-oriented shallowness finally reigned at the top, the executive suite largely populated by empty suits who were prey to the chairman's moods and whims. Just before Howell retired with a bigger package and bonus than any previous CEO, he unwittingly bragged about the shallowness of his senior managers in his 1995 annual letter to stockholders. Citing the "exceptional strength" of Penney's management team, it said:

> Thanks to the *retail experience*,[4] dedication, and skill of our company's managers and the professionalism of our *store* managers, JCPenney is well-positioned for this decade and poised for the coming century.

Oh? Five years later, with outsiders at the very top, most senior managers were given written tests (!) to assess their skills. Few graded well. With that message leaked into the grapevine, retirement packages were dangled. Soon, the officers from the 1990s were all gone as well, the old guard replaced by more outsiders with impressive and focused résumés.

But there was to be a surge of remarkable events before all the outsiders arrived.

---

4. Italics are mine.

chapter 16　The Taj MaHowell

"There is nothing worse in our type of company than executives being isolated, being insulated in their headquarters offices. Of course, there must be executive offices, which is why a general should always have his own tent. But otherwise senior managers should reside in an everyday environment with their troops. How could they lead otherwise? This is only common sense."

—MIL BATTEN

I N DALLAS, it was apparent that Penney's executive ranks had significantly changed from the traditional New York makeup. Like Gale Duff-Bloom, most of the new brass had migrated from the field under Howell. And all of these people, of course, praised the financial and operational soundness of the Dallas move. They also spread the idea that the move eliminated "deadwood," building a company more in synch with itself.

On the other hand, veteran buyers and merchandising executives moving on to other employment in New York City had a different take. As she moved into her new office at Macy's, former Penney senior buyer Lucille Klein said, "Oh, it'll be pretty funny, all right. Watch when the contracts start expiring, and see those so-called buyers start to panic."

The Overproduced Induction Ceremony

In 1989, all the new buyers and other green personnel added a more unsettled aspect to Penney headquarters—where people were still recovering from the rigors of the move south. And the time had rolled around for the quadrennial HCSC inductions.

Perhaps sensing a need to remind associates of the solid history of their company, or to distract them from the puzzling problems of diminishing sales, or both, W. R. Howell directed the communications department to make a show of the HCSC ceremonies.

The event was held at the largest Dallas/Fort Worth airport hotel and produced on a scale never seen before. Encompassing nine days, waves of associates came in for a day and a night. Two-thousand-plus inductees were greeted by a foyer and ballroom that had been transformed into a JCPenney time trip. After the lights dimmed, stirring visuals driven by swelling original music led to Howell's keynote module. Next, there was an enveloping mythic history leading to a "magnificent" modern company worthy of everyone's pride and commitment. The induction ceremony followed, capped by an effective production module that wrapped the show and spilled attendees into a sumptuous reception that had been laid out during the show. The evening's banquet and entertainment were equally first rate.

Nevertheless, many inductees and visiting associates felt compelled to contrast aspects of the show with realities of the current Penney Company:

➤ Howell's keynote described a bold organization where empowered associates could and routinely did take risks. Hello? The company's now-extreme addiction to process (including the locked-in consensus management mode) made W. R. Howell himself virtually the only one "empowered" to "take risks."

➤ The expensive affair seemed to be either a tasteless mistake or an obvious diversionary tactic. Participants had discussed the serious drop in store sales, and it was obvious to all that, without some miracle, the company was heading into a serious downturn.

There was no miracle. Weeks after the equipment was packed and the sets were struck at the airport hotel, a jarring sequence of budget cuts and layoffs began. Eventually, hundreds of new and old associates from Dallas, New York, and even the field were let go. The quality of life may have been better and less expensive in Dallas, but morale for the Penney multitudes had taken a plunge.

As Dickens wrote presciently without ever having the slightest notion of Big D, "It was the best of times, it was the worst of times . . ."

While ex-associates packed office belongings, bid colleagues good-bye, and walked out of Lincoln Center and Park Central, a special meeting was being held up the Tollway at the Aberdeen Building. Executive vice president and director of support services Terry Prindiville had day-to-day responsibility for planning and construction of the vast "Home Office" project. Now in his conference room were key members of Prindiville's team from the company and the architectural and general contracting firms that would build the headquarters. A model and plans, specifications, and deal documents were laid out on the expanse of mahogany. The working session had just concluded.

Prindiville rose and made some upbeat closing remarks, and then everyone else rose, shook hands, and left for a reception that had been prepared in the building's main floor restaurant. Prindiville lagged behind to dictate a simple message to his secretary for distribution around the executive suite. The big project, it said, had now officially begun.

What Is There Not to Like?

By late 1992, company communications producer Marti Gottl was finishing a video gloriously titled "Building for the Future." The pun was ironic in view of Penney's near collapse only eight short years into that future. But Gottl had nothing to do with the video's title or the retailer's future, and her powerful video would certainly mark the headquarters construction event.

The video's payoff would be a short sequence reprising the entire construction process from beginning to end from a single camera position. Gottl had found a good angle from the top floor of a nearby building erected on speculation and still empty. She rented a room and "locked down" a camera. Then, only having to keep the window clean and change magazines, over the major period of construction one of her camera people went to the room every day and exposed only a few frames of film. After 18 months, Gottl had a perfect 90-second "animation" of the real thing, the birth of a vast postmodern corporate edifice.

Edifices, actually. The complex comprised seven separate buildings all joined into one structure by eight atriums and three rotundas. Outside or inside, the expanse was immense. Each building was a uniform and extra-tall three stories above grade. There was also a lower level that, for the great cafeteria and private dining rooms, opened onto a sunken garden and fountain area. All together, there were nearly two million square feet of usable business and utility space.

After the breathtaking trick of showing the construction in 90 seconds, the video would build again to a grand climax. Gottl had an arsenal of shots from which to select. She had loving pans of the exterior elevations, the rich masonry aggregate, the fields of glass, the great copper hip roof. For interiors, she had tracking shots of sunlit floors opening directly onto atriums. She had shots that swept up to atrium skylights stretching on forever. Then, perhaps with music moving into a last crescendo, Gottl could select from angles spinning up into the twin rotundas at the north and south confluence of atriums. And to climax the whole show, she could intercut inside and outside the grand, airy central rotunda—the statue of Mr. Penney receding below in the middle of the rotunda's marble floor—and then finish with a view rising above the building's ceremonial entrance to the rotunda's peak, a helicopter panorama of the copper-roofed complex and all of the choice land beyond.

Marti Gottl dove into the final cuts for "Building for the Future." She worked in a Lincoln Center editing suite with much excitement. Gottl knew the video would deliver on its main job of glorifying a building. It would also, she knew, glorify the managers who knew how to run a huge enterprise that *deserved* such a building. And it finally presented their reward: the space, the elegance, the comfort of it all. And, after all, the whole thing would be free.[1] That, per se, wasn't in the video, but everybody knew it anyway. As Duncan Muir, a PR executive, would informally say during the building's official opening festivities, "What is there not to like?"

---

1. *Add:* The cash from 1301 6th Avenue's sale; the money not spent on necessary refurbishing; the cost-per-square-foot savings in Texas for maintenance and utilities; the conservative projected profit from sale of the excess land. *Subtract:* The cost of the move and construction; furnishings, fixtures, etc. *Result:* A wash—with much more space and a much better lifestyle thrown into the bargain.

Introduction to the "Home Office"

As Gottl continued her editing inside, Gordon Curry drove out of the big, open Lincoln Center parking lot. I was his passenger. We were headed up the Tollway to the far northern suburb of Plano for a meeting at Legacy—the first look at the new headquarters for both of us. Curry's title was manager of executive communications, and the business of this trip was a speech. I was in my first year of freelance speechwriting for Penney upper management. Our meeting was to be with Mike Restaino, communications director for Jim Kennedy, former head of the men's merchandising division and now head of the home division. The assignment was a Kennedy presentation to be guided and edited by both Restaino and Curry—before Kennedy then became involved with his own input.[2]

Because of staggered completion schedules for the different buildings in the complex, the home division and some support departments had been among the first to move from Lincoln Center to Legacy. They were not *the* first to occupy the new edifice, however. Penney's top dozen officers (making up the "management committee") had left the sixth floor of the Aberdeen Building and, along with vans of furniture, accessories, records, and office equipment, made the grand migration to what would become known to some outsiders as the "Golden Crescent."

Curry had a map that had been printed to assist in the transition from North Dallas to Plano. It showed the main routes to Legacy, the gigantic three-story parking garages, and the drive that circled the complex. Instead of driving directly to the garages upon arriving in the corporate park, Curry said, "Let's do a little rubbernecking." He then circled the property. Halfway around, he swung into the special driveway that cut across well-landscaped lawns and passed a large man-made pond with a fountain blowing higher than Old Faithful.

I indicated the building's approaching ceremonial entrance.

2. This typified Penney's evolved bureaucratic micromanaging process. Interestingly, I later reflected that if a speech assignment was for one of the very highest-ranking executives—Gale Duff-Bloom, for example, or the chairman himself—Curry was able to simply dispatch me to direct one-on-one meetings with the speaker. Guess which process usually resulted in the best speeches.

"Not many corporations have a main entrance fit for occasions of state," I said.

Curry smiled and checked his map. "That's the main rotunda, which has a statue of Mr. Penney. We can say hello to him after the meeting."

From there we circled back around to the garages and parked on the mid level of the south structure, close to the elevator and stairwell. We faced two ways to enter the building: down the stairs or elevator to a long gallery that led into the lower level, or straight ahead across an open walkway (over the gallery). Both ways had views of the terraced gardens that led down to a pool and another fountain blowing almost as high as the one in the fancy front of the complex. Beyond the fountain was a giant patio with tables and chairs fronting an expanse of glass. Again checking his map, Curry said, "Inside the glass is the cafeteria dining room, and there are supposed to be private dining rooms somewhere."

"It's huge," I said.

"Lot of people here, or will be," said Curry. "There will be two cafeteria lines, one at either end—not lines, but clusters, with different kinds of food, or so it says here. Only one open right now."

"This is some layout," I said, looking back at the garages with brick facades and sizable ornamental copper-roofed cupolas at the corners. Then I looked around again at the terraced gardens, the lower-level fountain, and glass-walled cafeteria. As we proceeded inside, neither Curry nor I had known to look *above* the cafeteria at the most interesting aspect of this elevation—something we would do with rapt attention within 15 minutes.

It Never Really Caught On

About halfway through the construction of the complex, two mid-level managers had sat down for a cup of coffee at Lincoln Center. One of them produced a wry smile and said, "Well, did you hear? It's almost certain. Howell has settled on a name for Plano."

"What? This isn't a joke, is it?"

"Depends on your point of view. He's going to call it—da-da-da-DAA: The 'Home Office.'"

"Well, that's certainly warm and fuzzy. Just like him."

The first manager held up his hand. "But. I *also* heard he's still considering another name."

"Another name?" said the second manager, an eager smile forming.

"Yes—da-da-da-DAA: The 'Taj MaHowell.'"

The listener did a take and burst out laughing. As others looked over, the most famous of the building's nicknames was born. Within hours it was being enjoyed at Lincoln Center watercoolers. Within days it was part of Penney folklore throughout the world. In time, the complex would acquire other monikers as well, names like "The Mall without Stores" (used among some vendors) and "Versailles" (used among the press). But locally it was usually known as "Legacy" (after the corporate park), while to out-of-towners it was "Plano" (the address). Almost never was it Howell's choice, "Home Office." Despite signs, printed matter, and executive speeches, "Home Office" never really caught on as intended.

Perhaps that was an outgrowth of superstition, a name too cute and cloying for a structure that bothered many. Some imaginative corporate historians have pointed out the dark fate that often follows pretentious relocations. The superstition says that if a company erects an edifice in honor of itself—and as a reflection of the prevailing management's heightened self-esteem—bad things are bound to follow. Surprisingly numerous examples are then given like the Bethlehem Steel headquarters and the Sears Tower.

This superstition is interesting in view of all the other relocations to the Dallas/Fort Worth area in the latter part of the twentieth century. These included American Airlines, Blockbuster, Burlington Northern, Exxon, GTE (Verizon), Lennox, and Nokia—*all* moving into comparatively modest accommodations. Only JC-Penney, the area's second-largest business (a distant second to Exxon), chose to build a monumental headquarters. And superstitions are always rooted in some moral point. In the case of self-aggrandizing new headquarters, say the historians, troubles follow because managements are so busy preening themselves that they slack off on day-to-day business.

Mixed Emotions

When Gordon Curry and I arrived at the south rotunda guest desk with two receptionists, I looked around in awe as Curry asked for directions. We knew this was one of two rotundas and that a third, the *grand* rotunda (which we had seen from the outside), anchored the symmetrical center of the great building. On our way up to our meeting on this wing's third floor, Curry chuckled and said, "Did you know that, as huge as this place is, there still isn't enough room? Everybody's staying put at Park Central, and I heard the credit division's moving into a building near the Aberdeen."

"Maybe they should've just built a cluster of high rises here instead of getting so fancy," I said.

"Maybe so," said Curry, with a shake of his head.

Mike Restaino was a pleasant young man, a dozen years an associate. He had just recently come to Plano after working in stores and district and regional offices (he was on the breadth-of-experience track). His background prompted an unpredictable turn in the small talk before we got into the assignment. Curry started it with an innocent question. "Well," he said, spreading his hands, "how do you like it?"

Restaino nodded at the question and thought for a moment. "Good and bad."

Curry and I exchanged glances, and then Curry said, "We were just talking. So what's *your* complaint, Mike?"

"Well, guys, I've just come from the stores. And I gotta tell you, when most store managers see this palace, they're not going to be too happy."

"Jealous?"

"More than that," said Restaino. "It's almost like the powers that be have no respect."

"How do you mean?" I asked.

"I'll give you an example I keep thinking about. A couple months ago I had a meeting in this store manager's office and a train goes by outside. We had to shout. Then, after the noise, he has to get up and straighten the pictures on his wall." Restaino waved at the complex. "But here *we* are in the lap of luxury. Have you seen the executive suite yet?"

"Not yet," said Curry.

Restaino stood up and nodded for us to follow him. He led us to an expanse of glass looking—to the right—down upon the cafeteria fountain and the gardens that rose beyond to the parking garages. He motioned the other way—to the left. We looked below at nicely placed potted plants arrayed across a wide expanse of special roofing aggregate. This had to be the roof of the cafeteria—

also serving as a visual deck for the occupants of the offices stretching around a wide crescent on the second floor below. Restaino motioned. "From right under us all the way around to the far corner on the other side is the executive suite."

"A lot of executives," I said.

"Just a dozen," said Restaino.

"And people thought Aberdeen was a little plush," Curry said.

"Kennedy and I were down there yesterday for a meeting. Everybody has a big reception room, a big conference room, and an office that's even bigger. There's also a kitchen, a couple of VIP living rooms, and you should see the boardroom, Gordon." Now he pointed across the broad executive crescent. "And see all the glass at the far corner over there? That's Howell. Someone said six rooms. And look." Restaino gestured at the beautified cafeteria roof, the fountain, and terraced gardens leading up to the brick and copper cupola background of the garages. "From down there you don't see people, just water and greenery." Turning to lead us back to his office, he shook his head with a sad smile. "I love this company, but I don't know." He looked at Curry. "What would Mr. Penney've thought about this?"

Not much. The last New York headquarters at 1301 6th Avenue was a tower reasonably acquired in the 1960s when the old man was still coming to the office regularly. It had certainly been practical and comparatively modest. Executive offices had been uniform, simple, and not large, and executives used the same elevators and plumbing as everyone else. But things were certainly different at the Taj MaHowell in Plano. Without a doubt, the old man would have been highly displeased.

We all sat down again, and Restaino outlined the assignment. Basically, it was to be a speech about JCPenney's constant reinvention of itself, its continuing change to meet new market conditions—as it related to changes in the home division.

On our way out of the building, I looked at Curry and said, "I'm a little confused on this reinvention angle."

"Yes, it's a problem," Curry said with a smile. "Since it basically doesn't exist."

"I wondered. But you didn't say anything."

Curry chuckled. "What was I going to say? 'Mike, that's really a stupid idea?' I don't know where Kennedy—or Mike—got such an idea."

"Maybe from Oesterreicher?"

"No, he's into fixing things, not ideas."

"So, where do I go on this?"

"Well, I can have Carol dig up some history, and then you can see if there's a through-line somewhere, something that relates to that stuff Mike gave you on how home is evolving. Make sense?"

"No." Both of us laughed.

"Well, who said it was easy? That's why we pay your rate."

Twin Failures

I studied the Penney history and, as an exercise to spark an idea, wrote a monograph about Penney's sustained success:

> Few companies last a century. How did Penney do it? Besides ethics, partnership, buying and service, there was another secret: a tradition of change. Because of the Founder himself, every so often when the company began to stagnate (as any company inevitably must), someone would issue a challenge for change. This thrust the organization into chaos—and rejuvenation.
>
> Wall Street, of course, always hated the announcement of a new cycle of change. It meant less money for dividends. Analysts would point out that the current model was still working beautifully. Penney's management responded with reiterations of the newest long-term plan, and then ploughed ahead anyway.
>
> In the Howell years, this changed. Wall Street *celebrated* the company's attitude. Now Penney was run by astute businessmen, epitomized by W. R. himself. And in the early '90s, the vision of the mid-'70s was still working and the payout looked especially promising for the immediate future.
>
> So the last decade of the twentieth century began with twin failures of values and vision. The ideas and ethics that built the company were now just quaint history, reinvention and rejuvenation discarded as inefficient. The company had lost its soul.

After admiring my analysis and brevity, I sighed and called Gordon Curry. "Gordon, I'm having an interesting time, but I still haven't found the handle."

"And the problem?"

"Well, just to reiterate. Kennedy wants to say JCPenney had reinvented itself as America's Department Store, right? And, within that, the home department, right?"

"Uh-huh."

"But the America's Department Store idea is 10 years old."

"Older."

"And you said there *is* nothing new in the works, right?"

"Uh-huh."

I laughed. "Gordon, you're not helping me at all."

"Okay, look. That's what Kennedy apparently thinks. But, he has to know what he's doing in the home division, so why not just take what they're doing that's new and cast it in the reinvention light. The company is 'always' reinventing itself, and the home division is a great example—exactly what Restaino said. It's a half-truth, but they might buy it if you keep it centered on home."

"You think?" I said, disconsolately.

"Worth a try."

I finally finished Kennedy's speech and never thought of the monograph exercise again until the company's bleak year 2000. Then I dug into the files one day and retrieved the Kennedy folder from eight years earlier (I never throw notes away). After looking over the monograph, I added the following postscript after the paragraph that began: "So the last decade of the twentieth century began with twin failures of values and vision . . ."

But who knew or cared? In 1994, after all, they had a record year of immense profit. The party was Texas-sized, with praise and rewards all around. It was a celebration of fools.

chapter 17   The Designer

AN EASEL IN HOWELL'S CONFERENCE ROOM displayed a big glamour shot of Lyn St. James standing in a logo-spotted jumpsuit beside her Indy racer. She looked like a movie star, but this was the real thing. Not only a female pioneer on the Indy car circuit, St. James had already established herself as a true competitor and was now looking for a big league sponsor to attack the Brickyard itself. St. James also had brains and brass. As a reflection of her self-promotion skills, there was a conspicuous bare spot in the heart area of her jumpsuit, a retouched "?" imposed upon it. Whose dominant logo would reside there?

It's About Who We Are

Jim Oesterreicher was Howell's number-two man and the workaday architect of Penney's emergence from the grief of '89–'91. Presently, he flipped his hand dismissively toward the photo. "W. R.," he said, "the ladies make it look nice, but I still don't get it. We don't sell tires or batteries anymore, so why are we even looking at this?"

Gale Duff-Bloom looked around at Kay Baker and subtly rolled her eyes. Baker, another PR executive under Duff-Bloom's wing, had been pushing the expensive sponsorship of St. James and had just made an adroit presentation.

Howell looked at Duff-Bloom and, in a very serious voice, said, "Gale, what do you think?"

"W. R.," she said, now seriously herself, "Jim has a point that's beside the point. We have launched the 'Spirit of the American Woman' campaign—which this company backed 100 percent because most of our customers are women. And, as Kay said and I reiterate, if we did that and if we can get St. James at Indianapolis with all that coverage plastered with 'Spirit of the American Woman' *and* the Penney logo for about the cost of some network spots, where's the argument?"

"You've just heard it," Oesterreicher said to Howell.

The chairman shut his eyes briefly and then looked only at Oesterreicher. "Jim, it's not a plug for tires and batteries. It's about who we are, what we believe in. This woman has overcome great odds, just like Mr. Penney did." He turned and winked at the women, adding, "And I like the numbers." He hesitated, teasing the moment, then beamed and said, "It's a go."

And, indeed, when St. James raced in the Indy 500 the following Memorial Day, her "JCPenney"/"Spirit of the American Woman" car and W. R. Howell himself seemed as prominent as the driver herself.

Why Would I Tell Him What to Wear?

The Lyn St. James promotion would seem to indicate that, for such a big, traditional company, JCPenney really had its progressive act together. But retailing is a yin-yang business if there ever was one. Just to survive, things naturally in tension must work in practical harmony. If events at a retail chain are not both earthbound and heaven-sent and if men are not in touch with their feminine sides (and vice versa), the business is in trouble. And in 1992, things were falling further out of balance at Penney—although almost nobody understood this at the time.

After all, the Penney Company now resided in a glorious and vast new headquarters and in two years they would set sales and profit records. But there is no better example of the real condition of the company than the roller-coaster ride of a young genius named Anthony Mark Hankins. Altogether, it seemed to at first confirm and then strongly refute the company's new marketing theme:

"JCPENNEY, WE LOVE YOUR STYLE!"

First of all, Hankins's résumé was controversial. He claimed five impressive stops in just a couple of years after high school, including Yves St. Laurent. While he probably did most of what he listed—he could accomplish a lot very quickly—he also probably pushed it a bit. He was only a kid, after all—an exuberant 23-year-old African-American at the time he gave his introductory fashion show for Penney brass.

One thing no one could fault, however, was the cleverness of his career plan. In the couture world, designers are often criticized for being impractical. But Hankins wished to embrace the whole business. So after his design training he wangled a job with JCPenney in the field, spending two years working as a factory inspector for the quality assurance department. He added a workmanlike knowledge of apparel manufacturing and quality control to his dream of designing for working women, women of modest means, the "urban contemporary woman" (but not just women of color).

Hankins worked in greater Los Angeles, where he was well received and well treated by utterly decent, hardworking Penney associates. He also got along quite well with the factory personnel and managers with whom he dealt every week (people problems would not appear until he got to the Plano headquarters). At night and on weekends when he wasn't in the factories, he developed a stunning portfolio. And he was learning how to deliver fashion and quality at a price, knowing that the customer he envisioned defined the majority of Penney shoppers.

Advised by his Penney field colleagues, he finally arranged to meet with Penney's vice president of product development, Don Scaccia, who was scheduled to be in L.A. on business. But Scaccia stood him up without a word, and Hankins also drew polite indifference from Jim Hailey, the head of Penney's women's division whom he managed to get on the phone. Were the Scaccia and Hailey responses connected? Hankins had no idea, but when other approaches fizzled as well, the designer's heart sunk. Then a quality assurance manager suggested one more phone call. Bruce Ackerman was now Penney's manager of minority supplier development in Dallas. He might be interested.

Hankins fired himself up and, on the phone and through the mail, gave the pitch of his young life. The manager bit. Ackerman was also part of a task force formed to explore ways of attracting urban, African-American women customers—an effort that higher-ranking Penney merchandising executives such as Hailey and Scaccia seemed unaware of. Hankins, although he wasn't technically a supplier, seemed a good fit. Ackerman set up meetings.

Tony Haake, vice president of QA, gave Hankins a paid leave and covered his travel expenses. Anthony was on. And he was a refreshing hit from the first meeting with ground-level buyers and staff. They lapped up his designs, ideas, personality, and energy. Yes, he was arrogant, but personably so. Everybody at that level also thought the overall concept—the marriage of Anthony's designs, specs, and know-how—was sound.

As the meetings moved up the merchandising organizational chart, however, problems developed. A merchandise manager seemed sincerely perplexed when she remarked, "Omigosh, what can I say? You've really got exciting work here, Anthony. But here you are, and way over there is JCPenney. And what I wonder is, how do we get from way over there to here?" Then a fashion coordinator drew Ackerman aside at the end of another meeting and in a low voice said, "No question, Anthony is a talent. But he isn't doing himself any good coming across like some freak show. Start teaching him the JCPenney way, Bruce."

Still, an Anthony groundswell was building, and Ackerman artfully banked it toward the one person who could make something happen for Hankins. He was able to arrange a meeting with the highest-ranking woman in the company, merchandising senior vice president Gale Duff-Bloom.

Hankins had been wearing a chartreuse jacket and an ascot to meetings, and one day Ackerman's boss crossly pulled Bruce aside to complain. "Why can't you tell Anthony to wear a suit to these meetings?" he wondered.

"He's a designer," Ackerman replied. "Why would I tell him what to wear?"

Another word about corporate attire at JCPenney (at that time). The suits wore suits. The mail droids wore suits. Among the parked sample cases in the reps' lounges, always suits. From research to human resources, from marketing to merchandising, from communications to information services: suits. From Armani to Brooks Brothers, everybody wore suits. It was a Penney tradition, a Penney law. Again and again it was heard that wearing a sports coat would corrupt one's thinking.

Despite Ackerman's protection, this suit prejudice eventually communicated itself to Hankins, and he was careful to wear a suit for the Duff-Bloom meeting—a brightly accessorized circa 1932 suit he had picked up at an L.A. retro fashion store.

"Nice suit!" beamed Duff-Bloom as they shook hands. Respecting the value of the executive's time, Anthony had streamlined his pitch, and in 15 minutes he made his sale. "Okay, make the arrangements. Do it all through this office, and try to keep the cost down. And good luck, Anthony," she finished, adding a warm handshake, a smile, and a sigh. "They won't be the easiest audience."

To present himself and his designs to the merchandising brass, Hankins needed to produce a fashion show with virtually no budget. The solution was found in equal parts of chutzpah, earnestness, and scintillating designs. Tony Haake provided some walking-around money, and Hankins and Ackerman put together a team of Penney volunteers. In Los Angeles, manufacturers familiar with Hankins were easily sold on providing 50 samples at no cost.

The Fashion Show

A telling moment came when Hankins began to accessorize his samples. First stop was the shoe buyer; Hankins was looking for just the right kind of shoes to complement his clothes (he had the sizzling sketches with him). It was a bad moment because of the bland styles the buyer displayed. Hankins desperately described what he was looking for, and suddenly something seemed to register with the buyer and she said, "Wait right here." She went back to her department storeroom and returned with boxes of fabulous shoes—sample shoes that had been rejected. This scene was repeated with other buyers as they dug around and found the right accessories for every piece—all among samples that had been rejected for the stores.

In late June 1992 the set was ready, a smart white-on-white tropical theme from one of the company's visual talents. Music was selected, and volunteer models were recruited, rehearsed, and dressed. Fancy invitations, courtesy of the Penney art department, drew the appointed big shots and the moment was at hand. Gale Duff-Bloom strolled in with a hand mike and said, "Good afternoon and welcome to the introduction of an outstanding talent we are privileged to consider recruiting into the Penney ranks. His goal is to create affordable and exciting fashions for women of limited means, and he has the factory background as well as the design credentials to back that up. So without further ado, ladies and gentlemen, let me now introduce . . . Mr. Anthony Mark Hankins!"

And what were the vibes in the whole room as a spirited Cuban salsa beat blasted from the speakers and Anthony Mark Hankins made his entrance? Keep in mind that Hankins was many things, among them about as good a couture talent as ever comes down the fashion pike. And, sure, he was young, he was passionate, he was temperamental and a little flaky at times. But he was also a clever self-promoter who appeared to have his head in the clouds but his feet firmly on the ground. He was also a one-of-a-kind personality, affectingly outgoing and energetically upbeat. And he looked great for this moment—assuming you don't want your potential designer to look boring. He was wearing crisp white tropicals with a dashing scarf, his hair cropped corporately short. He held a hand mike and wore a radiant smile as he sat on a stool beside the runway.

They hated him on sight.

"So!" he exulted. "Let's let the clothes speak for themselves! This fashion show is: Movin' *forward*, girlfriend!" That cued the first model, a tall African-American who entered and began sweeping down the incline in a knockout suit. The show was on—most of the men in the audience cringing. Anthony had been looking at *them*, not the model, when he said "girlfriend."

It was an extraordinary show, 50 exciting outfits from dressy to casual with four or five backstage changes for each model. Anthony didn't say much. For the most part he managed to control his excitement and just briefly drop impressively low projected wholesale costs. He also repeated an offer to go one-on-one with any buyer on how to cut costs without losing quality.

He slipped just once. After three especially saucy lookers whisked around on the runway, Anthony exclaimed, "These models look *hot* in my clothes and they know it! We're turnin' heads today," he said, looking right at his audience of mostly male suits. "*Aren't* we, girlfriend?!"

There may have been one or two grins out there, but to Gale Duff-Bloom it seemed as though all of the men sat in stony silence with mouths slightly agape. She herself was thrilled with the show, readily seeing the possible impact Anthony could have on the company's merchandising. She was angry that she seemed to be so isolated in this. She looked over at Hankins and thought, "What a trouper." He was keeping up appearances, still as upbeat and radiant as he was at the start, although the reaction of most of the men must have been hurtfully obvious.

The last model swept off the stage and the music buttoned. Hankins didn't leave a hole for applause that he knew would be embarrassingly weak or nonexistent. Immediately he spoke. "Well, now, Gale said that you would have questions, so please shoot."

At first nobody shot.

"Gale, do *you* have a question?" That actually got a little chuckle from the audience, and someone raised his hand and spoke up.

"Anthony, you seem to have a lot of confidence in a market out there for these clothes."

"Because it's so huge, that's why," he responded amiably. He then went on, making the man seem like an idiot. "Just because a working woman like my mother can't afford to shop on Fifth Avenue doesn't mean she doesn't appreciate style. She *loves* good clothes and she isn't alone. There are millions of women, and not just women of color, who would love to look good if they only could afford it. I can *give* them clothes they can afford." He waved at the empty runway. "JCPenney can. That's why I'm so confident."

A few more questions came now, and Anthony deftly answered them. Then Don Scaccia stood and said, "Anthony, some people have wondered about the veracity of your résumé—" He looked around at the other men with a big grin and added, "Not *me!*" This made everyone laugh. "Do you have any comment about getting all that accomplished at such a young age?"

"I do," said Hankins, prepared for the question. He later told Ackerman that he wondered if Scaccia had a son his age who was only getting out of college or beginning some entry-level job— wondered if other men in the room were bothered by where he was standing at his age. He smiled as he spoke, but there was an edge to his voice now. "First of all, Penney people have seen me at work." He nodded at the empty runway. "So there is no question that those designs are mine. And that's what today was supposed to be about. But let me take you again through my time after graduating from high school in Elizabeth, New Jersey, five-plus years ago." He proceeded to do so, as thoroughly and quickly as possible, sucking it up and disregarding the continuing insult.

You *Knew* the Rules, Anthony

Now there was a meeting in the conference room of Tom Hutchens, a merchandising executive vice president. Gale Duff-Bloom, Tony Haake, and other senior executives were there, as well as Bruce Ackerman. "Okay," said Hutchens, "I don't have a lot of time. So what are we going to do with Anthony?"

"Make him a designer," said Haake.

"It should be obvious," Duff-Bloom agreed.

"Well, it isn't, Gale," said someone else.

Another said, "For one thing, did you notice him mentioning his mother a lot? Could that mean he's got AIDS?"

"*What?*" said Duff-Bloom, tilting her head and looking at the man in disbelief.

Quickly from someone else, "But this guy *is* just a little weird, let's face it."

"What designer isn't?" asked Duff-Bloom. "Would you want your designer *not* to be?"

Then came, "I still don't buy that résumé, either."

"I can't believe this," Haake murmured.

"Forget the résumé!" said Duff-Bloom. "This is about the clothes. Did you happen to notice the clothes?"

On they went. Helping the situation for Hankins was that Hutchens, then one of the top five Penney executives, simply moderated and did not render an opinion. In the matter of corporate gravity, this somewhat befuddled the antagonists.

There was another worry. "There's no such animal here; we've never had a designer before."

"Yes, you have," said Ackerman, speaking for the first time. "He already works for the company and he's a designer."

"But there isn't any such job description in the whole company," somebody followed.

Ackerman was on that, turning to Duff-Bloom. "Gale, do you think we could write up a new job description for Anthony?"

It was common knowledge that Duff-Bloom was the hottest executive in the company, soon to be promoted into the elite of company management. Everyone assumed (correctly) that she would take over an important staff function, probably human resources.

"Well," she smiled, "I don't think that would be such a problem."

"Okay," said Hutchens, rising. He was a complex man, but now he was showing a side reflecting the company's historic receptiveness to new ideas. "So we have a designer. I gotta go, so, Bruce, you shepherd this. Make sure he's paid and accommodated right." Hutchens was moving toward the door as he said, "Meeting adjourned."

Young and Not Wise

Anthony Mark Hankins, all of 23, had his salary doubled and was given a good office, an assistant, a storeroom, and a modest budget. After celebrating with Ackerman and other new company friends, he began five months of 80-hour weeks. In November 1992 his line made its store debut and was featured on the cover and first eight pages of *Fashion Influences,* a specialty catalog for in-store and mail distribution to African-American customers. He was also invited to hit the road for trunk shows. The kid was living his dream.

But all was not wonderful, and Anthony's response was unfortunate.

Indy-car racer Lyn St. James had begun racing under the JCPenney ("Spirit of the American Woman") colors. St. James knew the corporate ropes and once in a speech outlined her approach to sponsors (especially) like Penney. "You must learn the rules," she said. "Then you play by the rules, win by the rules, and *only* then consider possibly changing the rules." Hankins should have been as wise.

He was told that he would be reporting directly to a vice president. This seemed like great news because it would scrape away a lot of bureaucratic sludge. Then the officer was revealed.

Don Scaccia.

Money in the Bank

Mainly to make a speech, Ralph LaRovere was happily back in New York. After a morning meeting, he headed for a midtown

JCPenney's headquarters (partial view, ca. 1992). Affording two million square feet of state-of-the-art space, it became a harbinger of bad times. PHOTO: JOHN RHODES, *THE DALLAS MORNING NEWS*.

Interior of headquarters complex. Eight buildings connected by airy atriums and elegant rotundas. PHOTO: JOHN RHODES, *THE DALLAS MORNING NEWS*.

View from the "Golden Crescent." This is what one sees from any of the large suites for top executives. A view uncluttered with people—except perhaps gardeners. Photo: John Rhodes, *The Dallas Morning News*.

Jim Penney's first venture failed because he wouldn't pay bribes. Penney is second from right; his beloved Berta is at far right (ca. 1900). Photo: AP/Wide World.

Penney at 93 (ca. 1969). Framed photo is of original "Golden Rule" partners. Back row: Penney, left; Guy Johnson, middle; Tom Callahan, right. PHOTO: AP/WIDE WORLD.

In a TV interview, Penney holds a drawing of his first store (ca. 1958). PHOTO: AP/WIDE WORLD.

At age 91 (ca. 1967), Penney shows his "off-the-rack" JCPenney Towncraft suit. Actually, his suits were custom made, but he never knew. PHOTO: AP/WIDE WORLD.

James Cash Penney, "The Man with a Thousand Partners" (ca. 1928). PHOTO: AP/WIDE WORLD.

Photo from a newspaper clipping about the great Jack Maynard, store manager in downtown Lansing, Michigan (ca. 1934). PHOTO: COURTESY *LANSING STATE JOURNAL.*

Earl Sams testifying (ca. 1946). He ran the Penney Company for 40 years! PHOTO: AP/WIDE WORLD.

Mil Batten, JCPenney's 4th chairman/CEO and a brilliant innovator (ca. 1970). PHOTO: AP/WIDE WORLD.

Soft-spoken Don Seibert, Penney's 5th chairman/CEO (ca. 1981). PHOTO: CLINT GRANT, THE DALLAS MORNING NEWS.

War hero and ultimate "Penney person," Walt Neppl as JCPenney president (ca. 1979). PHOTO: NEPPL COLLECTION.

W. R. Howell (ca. 1995), JCPenney chairman/CEO from 1983 to 1996. PHOTO: JOHN RHODES, *THE DALLAS MORNING NEWS*.

Unlucky Jim Oesterreicher, JCPenney's 7th chairman/CEO (ca. 1998). PHOTO: DAVID WOO, *THE DALLAS MORNING NEWS*.

Gale Duff-Bloom (ca. 1994) broke the glass ceiling—or so she thought. PHOTO: DUFF-BLOOM COLLECTION.

W. R. Howell (hand on chin) in his element at a White House briefing (ca. 1985). PHOTO: AP/WIDE WORLD.

Duncan Muir (ca. 2001), senior
PR executive and a fan of Gale
Duff-Bloom. PHOTO: MUIR
COLLECTION.

Talented Anthony Mark Hankins (ca. 2002),
whom the "suits" never understood. PHOTO:
CONRAD SCHMIDT, THE DALLAS MORNING NEWS.

Ralph LaRovere, vice president
and director of merchandising
(ca. 1996). Like Carol Edwards
and Gordon Curry, La Rovere is
another of the many "Penney
people" who figure in this book.
PHOTO: LaROVERE COLLECTION.

The author at Wyoming "mother store" (ca. 1999) (see photo of Penney on TV for drawing of actual store). PHOTO: ELAINE HARE.

The "lonely sentinel in a suit." James Cash Penney's statue in the headquarters' grand rotunda. PHOTO: JOHN RHODES, *THE DALLAS MORNING NEWS*.

The once-honored HCSC lapel pin. PHOTO: A. C. DENES.

Manhattan hotel. LaRovere was vice president and director of merchandising for Penney's home and leisure division at Legacy. An articulate man, he had gone to work for Penney in 1960 directly after college and service in the army. Today a pro who had risen through the old merchandise department in New York, he had always prized the results of the creative process. He and his wife, for example, had been avid theater-goers in New York, preferring off-Broadway shows. And today he was speaking to a business audience he knew well. His subject, and especially its manner of presentation, was calculated to stir them to action in a tricky area.

The J. C. Penney Company and its headquarters complex were so large that LaRovere would have no idea that his words that day would be tinged with a particular irony. He would be appealing to his audience for the very thing that, in another corner of the organization, would be meeting stupid and even cruel resistance. LaRovere was speaking to the New York Textile Council and his main message was:

Be more creative!

Find and cherish those who are talented, no matter how weird and different they might appear. Technology, the textiles hot button of the day, was great. But future survival, let alone prosperity, would hinge upon success with new looks and designs. This was a surprising message, meant to jolt his audience, and LaRovere would hopefully add a clincher. The J. C. Penney Company—a *huge* buyer of textile products—was depending upon the mills and manufacturers to come through.

LaRovere had been convinced that a really effective speech required taking risks. So would this approach work? Challenging an audience like this often succeeded. But often as not it failed—the audience feeling shoved around and tuning out. Which would it be? There was no way to tell before just doing it.

It was noon when LaRovere finally parked his briefcase with a checker and quickly worked the reception in the foyer of a large dining room. Then he retrieved his briefcase, joined the Textile Council officers who had invited him, faked his way through a convivial lunch, and then faced the whole room from the podium as the featured speaker for this quarterly meeting. He looked composed and confident. Inside, however, he was as nervous as he'd even been in his career.

He opened with a surprising warm and fuzzy about how good it was to be back "home" in New York. Then he said:

> ➤ Broad alliances—partnerships among everyone in the entire merchandise pipeline from fiber to retail—were the only way to succeed in the emerging global economy.

Then the main point:

> ➤ To *feed* those alliances, there was an urgent need to find, cultivate, and reward artistic talent. Good designers were money in the bank.

And he concluded with a pitch to:

"Farm the talent, nurture the talent, support the talent in our various institutes and colleges. And then in your companies. And, again, understand the talent." [HE PAUSED AND THEN INDICATED THE WHOLE ROOM]

"And to repeat, because it cannot be overemphasized, it will be the new designs and design concepts that will be increasingly important. And these will not come from your salesmen, your bean counters, your technical people. These will come from the people with God-given creative talent and good training who are to be absolutely cherished. So you must become flexible enough to properly utilize your talent once it's in place. Remember, the most important thing is not your process, not the way you used to do things. It's your product. It's the way you look and feel tomorrow that will capture business in the next big fashion trend that is identified or even created by your talent."

And now he dared to smile and say, "Thank you." After what seemed to him like an eternity of a pause, his audience burst into big applause—he even heard a couple of people shout "Bravo!" (this was New York, after all). He *had* entertained them with his message and they bought it with gratitude.

Meanwhile, Back at the Ranch

In an end run around Don Scaccia, Anthony Mark Hankins succeeded in winning approval for special oversized hangtags for his garments. He designed them himself, with his picture and signature prominent along with a short bio and statement about the line. Otherwise, though, the company would pay for no marketing at all. And no promotion either. So Hankins and his assistant put together 500 homemade press kits and, through a contact in the mail room, got them out. Then he made a poster prototype and sent it to top management in hopes of approval, which was not forthcoming. So every night before leaving he forced himself to produce four posters. When it was finally time to depart for the trunk shows, he had a portfolio case jammed with enough poster art to cover several stores.

With Ackerman's help, a last-minute coast-to-coast telephone blitz alerted fashion editors to look for the press kits. It worked, and a few editors actually flew into Atlanta to see his first show. There, the posters, hangtags, Hankins's personality, and especially his clothes worked magic. Good ink flowed from Atlanta, and other stories with his picture began popping up all around the country. Anthony was news and the line was launched.

Scaccia was furious. First, about going over his head on the hangtags and posters, then about Hankins's success with the press. The company policy was to sneak a new product into test stores under wraps, see how it sold, and only then consider marketing and promotion. Promotion and PR were verboten until then. Scaccia pulled Hankins off the road and confronted him.

"You *knew* the rules, Anthony."

"But they just don't compute in my case."

"And you think you're above the law around here, you can do any damn thing you want?"

"Don, be reasonable."

"Well, you can't."

"Look, it doesn't make sense not to promote a new line. How can you test it if nobody knows it's—?"

"You're not *listening*, you—" Scaccia gulped air and leaned forward on his desk. "Anthony. You're gonna do it the right way. Or you're not gonna do anything. At all. Got it?"

". . . Yes."

"From now on. Everything. Clear everything through me. In writing. And not a peep outta you from now on."

Hankins followed Ackerman's reluctant advice and began checking every little thing with Scaccia. He even tried to be lighthearted about it, entering the vice president's office the first time with a smile and the word "Peep!"

But his assistant was taken from him, and his small budget was cut back. Documents began disappearing from his office. Scaccia found fault with everything about Anthony: his vision, his office procedure, the dolls and toys that cluttered his bookshelves, the way he dressed (never in a suit), his mannerisms (which he began laying on for effect, girlfriend!), and even his race—very indirectly, but in ways that fed back to him. More than once after being called on the carpet, scolded, and ridiculed by Scaccia, he returned to his office and burst into tears. The little sleep he managed to get during the week became a fitful tossing and turning, and Hankins awoke in the early morning and dressed in a hungover stupor without having taken any drugs or alcohol.

He leaned on Ackerman, then steeled himself, praying and connecting with his mother for long nocturnal soul-searchings. He retaliated by dressing more and more outlandishly. He went from jeans, flannel shirts, and backward baseball caps to attire that brought a steady parade of rubberneckers by his office. One day he entered Scaccia's office wearing an Errol Flynn–inspired pirate's costume with his hair in a bandana. Once again the vice president gaped and leaned forward on his desk. "Where'd you get *that*? Some fag shop on Cedar Springs?"

And the Anthony Mark Hankins line was flying out of the test stores.

Then the Twist

So it appeared that a chance for JCPenney to light a fire under its women's apparel was being ignored. Hankins may well have been the most talented person under the Legacy roofs, but so far it only mattered to the few Penney store managers who had large numbers of African-American customers. And only the L.A. manufacturers who were plugged into that market were producing A.M.H. designs. Hankins always wanted to design for women—but *all* women of modest means, no matter. He felt he was now in the design ghetto.

Then a strange thing happened. Distribution gremlins caused the Hankins line to land at a Houston location dubbed "the country club store" where there were almost *no* nonwhite customers and the demographics skewed to upper-middle. Intrigued by the look of the clothes, the manager whimsically set them out instead of returning them.

They sold. Fast.

Hankins, of course, got word of this. *There*, he thought, is all the proof I need! He quickly jumped to the conclusion that he had earned a shot at designing for all of Penney's women customers. He thought he had also at last qualified for marketing and promotional support as well. After all, what more could he have done?

To No Avail (for All)

Corporations, of course, are slow and can be just as obtuse and confined as any person. Don Scaccia just laughed and, with the exception of Gale Duff-Bloom (whose interest and authority were now elsewhere), there would be no change in the Penney upper management's view of Hankins's value. So he felt battered and unappreciated and totally frustrated. So *close* to a wonderful, largely self-made opportunity, he presently felt bound and gagged and stomped upon. He didn't know what to do, which way to move, what to think. It never entered his mind that he had *already* made remarkable progress for such a young talent.

Hankins pondered his "stalled" career. He consulted with Bruce Ackerman, and both eventually concluded that designing was a fast track and there was now only one way to truly capitalize on his proven capabilities as a designer.

Leave JCPenney.

Incredibly, there was nothing in writing to keep him there. And, with Ackerman's advice and financing, he trademarked his name and signature. Then they were gone—Ackerman going along to run the business part. Quickly setting up a studio and office, they selected manufacturers to turn out the line and hit the ground running.

I was LaRovere's speechwriter and had known Ackerman from earlier assignments. So I told LaRovere the Hankins story soon after they had departed. Although he had not been aware of the designer, as a merchandise executive steeped in J. C. Penney's private-brands tradition, LaRovere immediately picked up on the company's loss. Likewise, he thought that Hankins would succeed.

"Style and quality for the moderate income shopper? How can they miss?"[1]

"I hear the label is already hot," I said.

LaRovere sighed. "And we let this kid get away?"

"Not only that," I added. "Guess who signed up first with Hankins?"

"JCPenney?—don't tell me. And now we lose half our margins because we didn't keep the kid happy." He looked stricken. "Unbelievable."

---

1. Hankins did go on to get extensive publicity; become a star on the Home Shopping Network; and expand his line into other major chains like Nordstrom, Dayton-Hudson, Target, Sears, Federated, and Army/Air Force exchanges worldwide.

chapter 18 Showtime

I F A YIN-YANG HARMONY had been absent around Anthony Mark Hankins at JCPenney, so too had it practically disappeared way up the ladder. Again, however, almost nobody knew this. But not long after I told LaRovere about Hankins, a sequence of events began on the Monterey Peninsula in the autumn of 1993 that would change Gale Duff-Bloom from the most ardent Penney booster to someone just going through the motions until she could retire. Alone among the company's top management, she would be shocked into realizing that something was very wrong at the core of the J. C. Penney Company.

God Forbid

Every now and then a Fortune 50 CEO makes a public speech that actually says something. Such an event usually happens because someone a step or two lower on the ladder had a passionate belief in the message. She (in this case) also had a vested interest in having the words come spilling out of the boss's mouth. And, as the reader will continue to see, she certainly had the political acumen to bring off this event. Gale Duff-Bloom, in fact, will become one of the principal figures in this book. She was a woman who seemed to break through the glass ceiling and for a while become one of the best modern Penney executives.

As usually happens between concept and delivery of such a speech, Duff-Bloom became somewhat distanced from the project after the completion of the writing process while a cadre of mostly anonymous staffers took over the coordination, PR, graphics development, and audiovisual aspects. These people would see little more than continued employment if the presentation worked. But some careers could be hurt if, God forbid, the CEO and his text should go down in flames. In November, three people from JCPenney—a sports marketing manager, a computer artist, and an audiovisual ace—converged at one of America's storied resorts. They had the final responsibility in staging the riskiest executive speech in their company's history.

The Secret Project

Carol Edwards carried her attaché case into the inn's main ballroom and pulled up short, her heart skipping a beat. The event being staged there was not hers. She turned and marched away to the hotel manager's office, where she registered a blistering but now pointless complaint and then, at the front desk, waited anxiously as a frontman turned from his computer screen with an accommodating smile. "Yes, Ms. Edwards," he said, "they're waiting for you at the fire pits."

"The pits . . ." Edwards mumbled. "Thank you."

For other guests, the tony inn's signature blend of rustic luxury was continually refreshing. Here, the lobby's towering cathedral ceiling framed a massive stone fireplace, in which a fire always blazed. For most, it was a warm, welcoming place, but Edwards now passed obliviously outside into the cool twilight.

She found Kim Lang, the inventive and resourceful computer artist, and Mark Shoener, the audiovisual ace, nursing sodas around one of the blazing pits. Dressed in suits, they looked out of place on the deck. But as Edwards strode up, she could see that otherwise the two Penney production people were behaving like everyone else—beaming at the ocean view, pleased with their surroundings, fully enjoying themselves.

"So," Edwards said, "I assume you've heard?" Her colleagues looked around with patient smiles.

"We've heard," said Shoener.

"Well, you don't seem very upset," Edwards said, dropping into a chair.

"Carol," Lang said, "this kind of thing happens all the time."

"So what do we do now?" A waiter was instantly upon Edwards and she waved him off with, "Nothing now." Her voice made it sound more like an assessment of the moment than a service issue.

Now Shoener hit Edwards with a big grin and wagged his fore-finger. "Carol," he said, "what you don't understand is, there's a patron saint of business conferences, and it's St. Murphy. And when St. Murphy finds out everything is going as planned, you know what St. Murphy does?"

"Please, Mark." Edwards had a sense of humor, but it was no-where to be found at the moment. She looked up into the evening sky as if for an answer. "Kerry Graham should have double-checked. Months ago. Or maybe I should have."

"Hey, not to worry," assured Lang.

"We'll just have a good dinner and set up when the ballroom clears," said Shoener. "Join us?"

"Thanks," said Edwards, rising. "But I'd better find Graham and make sure they know it'll be a late night."

Elsewhere in the inn, many of those who would form Edwards's audience were now enjoying a reception. They were LPGA touring pros and hierarchy, club pros, women's golf advocates, tournament staffs, marketers and vendors, many having arrived during the day to get in a round and enjoy a pleasant evening before attending the LPGA-hosted Women in Golf Summit.

As Edwards passed through the lobby, she felt a chill. Not only would the summit staging and production people now have to work far into the night, the tech part could actually be in trouble. If they did get everything finished tonight, the people at the controls would no doubt be operating on little or no sleep. And despite the ability and confidence of Shoener and Lang, tomorrow's general session and keynote speech could crash.

The Stakes

Realizing she was playing with a hot hand, Edwards had shrewdly cultivated *The Dallas Morning News,* which had sent a writer. She knew that "everybody" in JCPenney management would read a feature on the business page of *the* Dallas paper. Assuming that the report was favorable, this ink would nourish various agendas at the new Penney headquarters complex. Considerably down the food chain, this included those of Edwards and her colleagues in sports marketing.

Working through Penney's PR department on the sly, she also had several other media reps attending, including stringers for the national retail and sports trade press. So there was the press to worry about, plus the overall reaction to the material. When a corporate program strayed away from the expected, there was never any guarantee of success. And conferences with press coverage could be dangerous to careers.

Aside from the sporadic intense pressure, Carol Edwards had what appeared to be an enviable job at JCPenney. Because of the nature of sports marketing and Edwards' special competency, she had ready and frequent access to her company's executive suite. There, she had managed to catch the eye of new Executive Vice President Gale Duff-Bloom. Edwards's title was manager of sports programs, and she was, in effect, the producer of tomorrow's keynote and coproducer of the preceding two-hour Summit session.

JCPenney sponsored several women-oriented events, with an emphasis on golf. These included the LPGA "Skins Game" and the "JCPenney Classic" (a mixed team tournament), seen every year on ABC. Senior Penney executives were always visible at these events, especially chairman/CEO W. R. Howell. Now came a most unusual moment in the Penney sports scheme. The summit was a comparatively small corporate event with an offbeat team of only four from JCPenney—the three staffers and a Fortune 50 CEO. Yet this keynote event was so potentially important that it had started near the top (where conference matters almost never do) and, in the interest of secrecy and control, arrangements had completely bypassed Penney's company communications producers.

And I Run This Alone?

Seven months before, Edwards had received a surprise summons to Duff-Bloom's office, and after she had taken a seat in the capacious quarters, she was doubly surprised. "Got a special job for you, Carol. It's an LPGA event where W. R. speaks. Like a Catalyst conference for golf. Theme is access, inclusion, fair shot for women. The LPGA brings in advocates like the Women's Sports Foundation, plus a bunch of corporate women and apparel and equipment vendors. But no retailers." She smiled. "Except us." Edwards knew that Duff-Bloom loved getting the drop, loved exclusivity whenever she could get it for huge but homey JCPenney. "He'll be speaking to five-six hundred."

"So he's speaking on inclusion?"

"With a sports theme. And we want this real edgy. He says things you don't usually hear. So let's fly solo on this, pick and choose who we want, and not go through communications. We don't want a lot of people to know beforehand and worry and have meetings and fuss and send memos and hold things up for a century."

"Wow," Edwards said, loving this woman's insouciant clout.

Duff-Bloom smiled and said, "Yes, 'wow.' Doesn't it sound like *fun?*"

"Yes. And I run this alone?" Edwards asked.

"You're working for me on this, yes," Duff-Bloom said. "First off, I'll work with the writer, then you follow up getting it polished and then making the other arrangements. Here's the file, including some notes I just rattled off."

Edwards glanced at the pages and then ventured an idea. "Gale, the LPGA can't possibly have our resources, so maybe we should also volunteer to produce their screen support and help get their general session together. Make them look good leading into W. R."

"Done. Great idea. So you watch over that, too. Their producer's in the file. Okay?" Duff-Bloom rose.

"Okay," Edwards said, also rising. Then, "Uh, where is this?"

Duff-Bloom laughed infectiously. "Oh, good heavens, small detail! You get to go to Pebble *Beach,* which I hear is just fabulous." Duff-Bloom then reached to shake Edward's hand; said "Thanks, Carol"; and returned to her credenza, where she picked up the phone.

Edwards on the Line

Thanks to Duff-Bloom, women at JCPenney were now playing an increasingly important role. This was the chairman's basic theme for the Women in Golf Summit keynote, surprising as his approach would be. Inclusion, the overall theme of the conference, was very high on Duff-Bloom's agenda. Anyone who significantly abetted the inclusion program had a good future. Obviously, too, if the chairman ended up pleased with the event, Duff-Bloom's interests (and those of the favored women below her) would gain further force.

Inclusion was actually a hot topic nationwide. And the LPGA, as a progressive promoter, along with JCPenney, which had perhaps the nation's best corporate citizenship, was falling in to march beside organizations like Catalyst in the advocacy and advancement of women. Women in business. Women in sports. Women in government and the military. Anywhere there were leadership issues. Anywhere things were happening. Anywhere inclusion (and diversity) was overtly or covertly fought. And now, on the Monterey Peninsula, the battle for inclusion in America was Carol Edwards's responsibility tomorrow.

You're Going to *Say* That?

In the ballroom, the event that had pushed back Edwards's summit staging was finally over. By 11:10, the big room had begun a remarkable metamorphosis into a serious business conference theater. Mark Shoener, still in his suit, was all over the room supervising a large hotel crew. Lang, also still in corporate attire, sat at a table copying changes from Edwards's master script into several other script binders. Lang finished the binders around midnight and took four to another table at which Carol Edwards waited with Kerry Graham and her assistants. She laid a binder in front of each woman as Graham looked up worriedly.

"Are these all identical?" asked Graham.

"Of course," Lang replied, covering her annoyance with a pleasant smile.

"When do we go?" asked Edwards.

"Mark?!" shouted Lang.

Shoener turned on a riser near the projection screen being erected. As quickly, he anticipated the question and shouted back, "Half an hour!"

The keynote would be unusual in several ways. First, there was the speech itself. Then there was the screen support, designed more like a movie than a slide show—171 electronic images in 20 minutes. At the very end, the audience would see a lone woman golfer, then ugly jail bars animating down over the scene, "barring" the golfer. Howell, supposedly silent at that moment, would follow the visual zinger with a simple, "Thank you."

Dynamite, if all went according to plan.

At 12:45, Shoener was back in the draped control booth at the rear of the ballroom. He leaned into a mike and said, "All yours,

Kim." His now tinny voice was heard amplified over the ceiling PA speakers.

Lang rose and looked at Graham and the staffers. She gestured at the twin podiums now on either side of the screen. "Ladies? The podiums are hot, so we can go," she said. "Mark has me hooked up to that PA for tonight, so I'll be cueing you."

Graham and the others went to the half-completed stage. Lang went back to the booth after picking up her two tech binders. The LPGA staffers climbed onto the stage (no stairs in place yet), passed the drapers working on the back wall, crossed to the podiums, opened their respective binders, and waited for Lang's cue on the PA.

Lang sat in front of her monitor and keyboard. She tapped the cue key for the first slide and leaned into the mike. The ceiling PA spoke, "LPGA logo is up, dissolve to summit logo . . . and go."

At one of the podiums a staffer began reading, her monotone now heard richly on the full ballroom speakers. "Good morning and welcome. I'm Charlie Mechem, commissioner of the Ladies Professional Golf Association and your host for the 1993 Women in Golf Summit. . . ."

Alternating speakers podium to podium, they finished the run-through for the two-hour LPGA program—making the usual stops and starts with new script notations—in a shade over four hours. Graham would have taken longer but Edwards said, "Have a heart, Kerry! We need to start the keynote before the sun comes up!"

On the PA, Lang said, "Carol, you can just motor right through it and I'll hit the cues just to see if they're still in the black box." As Edwards got to a podium, Lang faded up the summit logo and said, "Okay . . . summit logo up, Kathleen Sullivan intro, Sullivan talks, and now JCPenney logo up, then W. R.'s title, and W. R. to the podium."

Edwards began reading as Howell's title slide dissolved to a sequence showing Howell, in candid shots, thoughtfully looking, frowning, and touching his brow (his red necktie the only color). Edwards, heard over the speakers, said: "Thank you, Kathleen. I'm going to tell a true business story that happens to have nothing directly to do with women's sports and golf. This is by way of pointing out something that does. And, I'm embarrassed to say, it involves the sad fact that my company—now with 1,100 department stores whose customers are 80 percent women—is represented by a ridiculous and regrettably small minority of women managers and executives. And this is not smart—"

"Hold it!" said Lang on the PA. "Minor problem."

Graham and the staffers had idled by the door to take in the beginning of the Howell presentation, of which they had no detailed knowledge. The producer was amazed. She called up to Edwards, "You're going to *say* that?"

"No," said Edwards's speaker-amplified voice, "W. R. is."

chapter 19   The "Golden Crescent"

A T 5:00 A.M., almost two hours before dawn broke over the Sierra Nevadas, the run-through continued in the ballroom of the Inn at Spanish Bay at Pebble Beach. But the sun was rising in Plano, Texas. Gale Duff-Bloom put her card in the slot and opened the heavy door to the southern end of the plush executive inner sanctum. It was seven o'clock there, the usual time for her office workday to start. She turned immediately into her suite, the first of a crescent-shaped string of 12 such suites for JCPenney's top management. In the middle of the crescent, dividing the office suites, were the great board room and related facilities. Adjacent were two "living rooms" for directors and VIPs as well as a large "Executive" reception room. This whole area was expensively furnished and detailed in subdued good taste.

Beginning of a Big Day

Duff-Bloom passed through her reception room with its uniform U-shaped mahogany workstation for executive assistants, where Cathy Rozelle would be on duty in an hour. To the right was a room for filing and storage, to the left her large conference room. Straight ahead was her even larger office, which she entered. As she set her attaché case down, the electric-eyed miniblinds on the expanse of window glass automatically adjusted to the sunrise. She glanced quickly at the day sheet Cathy had placed on her desk pad the evening before, when Duff-Bloom had been at a long off-campus dinner meeting.

She had a couple of quick calls to make before an unavoidable human resources matter had to be settled in her conference room at 7:30. Thirty minutes allotted. Then she would grab her case and drive south to Love Field, where Penney kept its planes. Her flight would be to Gainesville, Florida, where she would be met and driven to the University of Florida for a reception and lunch. The occasion was a national retailing conference sponsored by the University's Warrington College of Business. Gale Duff-Bloom was to make the keynote address at 1:30. Although not on the level of importance as Howell's remarks that same day, it was still the first major speech (with trade press ink) of Duff-Bloom's career. Altogether, then, a very big day.

Now she switched out her case, placing last night's reading on her credenza for Cathy to file or forward per Post-it notes. Then she picked up the fresh copy of her speech that Cathy had run and counted, placing the pages in her leatherette speech box that Cathy had placed nearby. Also close at hand were two groups of reading matter, one marked "U. FLA." by Cathy for absorption before arriving in Gainesville. The other, labeled "Home," identified pressing Penney matters for study on the return flight and later that evening. All went into her case.

After her speech, there would be an obligatory roundtable appearance followed by networking during a break—after which she would pay her respects and head for the airport. Hopefully, she would not have to eat on the plane and would be able to enjoy a relaxed meal with her best friend, partner, and second husband, Darryl. Then she would retire to finish her homework. Bedtime would be midnight, the alarm always set for 5:15. Happily, after all those years of lengthy commutes, getting to work now was a breeze. Her Jaguar practically drove itself the 15 minutes from their Plano home. And Gale Duff-Bloom, age 53, was always eager to get to work. She drew energy from her schedule.

Uncharacteristically, she did not sit down immediately to make her calls but walked instead to a window for a moment of reflection. She looked out through the half-closed blinds. The great deck dotted with planters spread out from her suite and the others. Below was the nicely set out fountain and the terraced gardens that rose up to the giant but well-scaled parking garages sheathed in brick with ornamental copper cupolas. The huge cafeteria was just below the deck, of course, but her view (like all those from the suites) hid virtually all other human beings except gardeners. It was an architectural triumph of sorts.

A special elevator, accessible only by the few with "Executive" access, connected this area with private dining rooms that were walled off from the cafeteria and had a different, more haute cuisine menu. And it was possible for a senior executive like Duff-Bloom to arrive and depart via either of two other small elevators and the underground galleries to the garages. This way one might avoid contact with virtually any of the nearly 3,000 nonexecutive associates who also dwelt in the Plano complex. Duff-Bloom had noted and strongly disapproved of several peers who did exactly that.

The area was officially known simply and haughtily as "Executive," another bit of post–New York posturing. An outsider, a vendor with access, had sardonically dubbed "Executive" as "The Golden Crescent." It was unlikely that any of Penney's senior management had ever heard the term, but its use spread among some outsiders and even a few associates with whom they had regular contact.

Duff-Bloom was not unaware of the changes within the J. C. Penney Company that were reflected by these executive accouterments. Yet, because she was a fairly recent arrival in the Crescent and her success had been by dint of extraordinary effort over the years, she tended to take it all as a matter of course and as her due—except for the dining rooms, which she rarely used and then only to observe someone's success.

Not Bad at All

Duff-Bloom allowed herself a brief reverie, her mind fanning a quarter century of career snapshots that ended here in this sumptuous suite, in this stately Executive cloister, in this grand Legacy complex. Click, another snap, this of her nearby new home in boring-but-pricey Plano.

A booming prairie suburb, Plano was bordered on the north by the prime corporate park where JCPenney, EDS, Frito-Lay, and other major companies were relocating. To the south were upscale merchants and restaurateurs whose establishments buffered Plano's core of expensive residential subdivisions—some of which were simply separated from shopping strips by tall, thick brick walls and elaborate landscaping. The houses, on surprisingly small lots, were mainly variations on the Texas Gothic McMansion theme, largely distinct from one another only in scale. These choice properties were filling up all of the remaining suitable land and were mostly celebrated by their new owners—"choice," of course, being a relative term. Compared to Connecticut or the Coast, the new Plano palaces could be had for a song. Therefore, after decades of painful commutes to and from mortgage manors, most high-ranking Penney people considered the move to Texas—engineered by W. R. Howell—an unexpectedly wonderful fillip to their careers.

Duff-Bloom certainly did. She owned a beautifully decorated 5,000-square-foot house with a patio, pool, pool house, and planting fit for a movie star. And there was, in the end, a lot more to being a very successful Penney person. In seven years she would enter into a retirement that would be the envy of older male counterparts all across executive America. Meanwhile she wanted for nothing, there was no help or favor she couldn't reasonably dispense, and no person in business or government she couldn't reach, including the White House.

Not bad, she thought, for a small-town Florida girl who had started adult life so humbly. She was now one of the most powerful women in the retail industry, and before retirement she would be profiled in a work entitled "The 50 Most Important Women in the U.S."

Duff-Bloom smiled to herself and looked across the deck to the far end of the Golden Crescent. There, with an expanse of glass double that of the other commodious executive suites, the chairman's windows were aglow in the sunrise. In a few hours, she thought, W. R. would deliver her baby at Pebble Beach. She felt proud and smart and accomplished because of this. (Privately, she considered herself one of the most effective executives in the company.) Some day her title might actually approach a reflection of her skills. Naturally, there would always be a man or two ahead of her. But a designation approaching her ability wasn't bad, not bad at all.

Are You Nervous?

At shortly after eight o'clock Duff-Bloom saw her human resources conferees to the anteroom door of her conference room, then crossed to give Cathy some be-on-alert-in-my-absence verbal

notes before returning to her office. She picked up her attaché case
and turned back for the door when her phone rang. She answered
the phone on her guest table, which was closest. It could only be
one person. Cathy was supposed to be holding calls.

"W. R.?"

"I'm headed down for breakfast with Charlie Mechem. Came
here direct from Chicago last night and have to go right back after
the speech. And I'd been hoping to play a few holes, remember?"
He had made it sound like her fault.

"Sorry. But are you nervous?" she teased.

"Yes," he said with a chuckle. "That's why I called."

"Oh?"

"Since this trip turns out to be all business, if I get shouted
down on this thing, you get fired." He chuckled again and added,
"Just wanted you to know. Gotta go now." And he hung up.

Aha, she thought to herself. It was a Howell trick, but didn't he
actually sound a touch nervous? Pretty funny, if so. Maybe he actually gets it now, she gleefully surmised.

Sure, sure, the whole thing could blow up in their faces. She
knew it long before anyone else. The speech could bring down
the wrath of the entire women's movement upon traditional J. C.
Penney. Rather than position Penney as heroes, what Howell was
about to make public could portray the company as the worst of
good old boy pigsties. But you had to take risks. You had to take
the chance that the audience and especially the media would get
it. That the company would be seen as gutsy and courageous and
visionary. That Penney, of all companies, had thrown off the
chains of the past and—good grief! She had been so much into
the event lately that she'd even begun to *think* like a speechwriter!

Now the executive vice president looked out and down at the
fountain's multiple plumes. That was her, wasn't it? Her spirit?
Energy in constant play, a presence and personality to be reckoned
with? A success! She shivered happily, giving in to a few rare
blinks of self-indulgence. How far she had come!

On her way across the grade-level walkway to the garage, Duff-
Bloom again looked at the fountain, her spirits soaring as if cued
by the dancing, foamy water. Then, backing up her Jaguar, she
once more caught sight of the fountain before wheeling away into
the biggest day of her career. She felt doubly good because what
she was doing was right out of the J. C. Penney tradition of altruism (increasingly unusual at the company, she worried). Today,

literally from coast to coast, by her own efforts as well as partially by her very own voice, the cause of women and minorities in corporate America could be significantly advanced. Might the day eventually even be marked as a milestone—? No, she admonished herself, that was getting a little carried away. What she had once heard phrased as the vagaries and vicissitudes of corporate life (she'd quickly looked up the words) meant that everything she'd been so energetic and clever about might amount to nothing.

But, she reassured herself, there *were* things she could count on. W. R. could lay a huge egg out in California, but his speech was a killer. And with his brains and self-confidence, could he really screw it up? She didn't think so, not at all.

And she had *no* doubt about herself. It might be her first "national" presentation, but she was ready. And, while her speech had to be less incendiary than W. R.'s, it was quite as timely and personable. It was also, she knew, tested and true and fail-safe and ready to go. Almost as important, she knew that *she*—Gale Duff-Bloom—was *equally* tested and true and fail-safe and ready to go.

Now, as she turned toward the airport and her Florida flight to a national business audience, she once again considered her roots. Wouldn't certain people be astonished, she thought, to know what had happened to the cute little cheerleader who dodged college for blue-collar oblivion?

I Think You're Playing God

Gale Duff was married to her first husband for nearly 21 years. Swept off her feet and in defiance of both parents and friends, she had married an excellent dancer who was headed for a noncom navy career. Despite her promising high school record, college was never an option as she gave birth to three boys and established as many new households in her first six years of navy life.

Then she was alone, her husband off on a noncombat tour of Vietnam. Shortly after his departure, her father passed away. As Gale was an only child, her mother offered to move in and help with the children. This allowed Gale to begin working. When her husband returned from Nam and they were transferred to Columbus, Ohio, on a recruiting assignment, she had made a fateful decision. She would always love and find time for her boys, but she now felt the need for some kind of career—something that would help her grow as a person. It was in this frame of mind that one day she looked around the J. C. Penney store where she was working on the sales floor and thought, "Am I already there?"

Because of the peripatetic military life, she knew she must join a national company. More important to her was the company's reputation. She had grown up equating the Penney name with quality goods, affordable prices, and thoughtful service. But it was after becoming a Penney employee and absorbing the company's values that she became truly captivated. A career with the J. C. Penney Company seemed like *the* answer.

Unlike many of her colleagues on the floor, she made a point of studying the organization. She was struck by the company's core values, its long and storied history of doing the right thing. Even to the extent that it may have been unpopular or uncomfortable or even costly, the company came through. Its *people* seemed to come through. There seemed to be fundamental unity at every level. And, abetted by a record of social responsibility, JCPenney had won a place in the lives of millions of Americans. To Gale, this seemed to resonate among the company's "associates"—and, in particular, the so-called Penney people, those talented individuals who had dedicated their entire careers to the company and its principles. A Penney person, she decided, was what she wanted to be.

The problem she faced was that the company accepted only college graduates into its management trainee program. After preliminary screenings, all applicants with potential were finally interviewed by managers of larger Penney stores—such as the man who ran the Columbus store where Gale presently worked. His name was Charlie Collins, and he would not soon forget Gale Duff's frontal assault.

"I'm only seeing you, Gale, because of your record in this store, which is outstanding."

"Thank you, Mr. Collins."

"But I'm afraid we have to turn down your application because you don't have the educational requirement."

"Why? Why do you?"

"It's the policy, Gale. I didn't make it, but I have to abide by it."

"Do you?"

"What do you mean?"

"I thought Penney managers had a lot of power."

"We do. To a point."

"What point is that, Mr. Collins? Is it the point where you have to turn somebody down that you *know* would succeed as a Penney person, turn her down just because of some stupid technicality?"

Collins drew a breath. "The point, Gale, is that we have reasons for rules. They don't just drop out of the sky."

"Well, I didn't just drop out of the sky, either. I walked into this store and performed as well or better than any management trainee you've ever had, because you can't *get* better reviews and appraisals than I get."

"That may be true, and I'm sorry, Gale. But my hands are tied."

She rose and insolently pointed at him. "I don't really think so, Mr. Collins. I think you're playing God and I don't think it's fair at all! And I had *thought* that this was a fair company!" Without another word, she turned and marched out of Collins's office and past his puzzled secretary.

A moment later the manager appeared in his doorway wearing an odd smile. "Well," he sighed, looking in the direction of Gale Duff's exit. "There goes someone I suppose we're going to have to bend some rules for."

Some weeks later Collins shook her hand and said, "Welcome to the program, Gale." He nodded and said, "So, we did reach out for you finally, didn't we? That's what Penney people do—as I trust you will yourself some day."

"I will, Mr. Collins. Thank you." The year was 1969 and she was 28 years old.

Gale was a star trainee from the beginning. And a lucky one as well. Because her faulty application had made waves through the district, regional, and even New York personnel offices, her name was known. As a result, her stellar appraisals won her better and more frequent reassignments.

Bill Howell (as he was then known) had risen up through the Western Region and in 1979, now in New York, was keeping an eye on Gale Duff as possibly the best emerging talent in the West. She was presently in charge of women's merchandising for the region's 300 stores. And, he knew, she also had a problem with her immediate superior in Buena Park, Bill Hovey. Duff had learned a lot from Hovey, who was a superb merchant. Their relationship otherwise had always been touchy. The boss was quite demanding, which was fine with Duff because she loved to respond to challenges. But Hovey was also frequently unreasonable in his demands, wanting everything to turn on his whim and by his clock. That was not so fine.

Every week, Gale had to spend Monday through Thursday on the road visiting stores in all of the region's districts. It was lonely, demanding work and difficult for her as a mother. Complicating this were office messages piling up in her absence, half of them marked "Important" or "Urgent." The first thing she tried to do on Friday mornings was return the calls, but complicating that was the presence of Hovey. The boss would often pointedly look in on her during these calls, catching her eye and gesturing obviously at his watch. Clearly, he felt that *he*, not her call list, should be Gale's immediate Friday morning priority.

But she was working for Hovey, advancing his agenda and policing his districts and, in her opinion, responding to a slew of important and urgent messages served him better and took precedence over the man's latest musings. One Friday morning it all came to a head. Hovey camped in her doorway and began tapping his watch and loudly clearing his throat. On the phone, Gale finally said, "Hey, I'm sorry, but something has just come up and I'll have to call you—*back!*" And she slammed the receiver down. Then she stood up and seethed, "What is it, Bill?"

He pointed at her stack of messages. "The message on top, Gale, said to please see me ASAP."

"And I was *going* to see you ASAP."

"But there you are gassing on the phone instead."

"'Gassing'?"

"What would you call it?"

"Doing my job, that's what I'd call it."

Hovey was getting hot under the collar himself. "Well, we would seem to have a little communication problem, wouldn't we?"

"Yes, we would," she burned.

"And I can't help but be struck by an irony, Gale." Hovey was a man who liked the sound of his own voice. He continued, indicating her telephone. "A telephone, of all things, seems to be the cause of this communication problem."

As if all at once possessed of a radiant truth, she regarded him with an almost grateful expression. "Oh. Well in that case, there really isn't any problem at all. I apologize. I was returning store calls, which was a mistake. So *here!*" She turned quickly, reaching down and yanking the phone cord out of the wall with both hands and yelling "*Sorry!*" Then she grabbed the phone, turned, and threw it at Hovey with all her might. He ducked aside as the instrument put a hole in the Sheetrock inches from the doorjamb.

Besides good reflexes, Bill Hovey had other redeeming qualities, including a nicely skewed sense of humor. He now straightened up and exaggerated shooting his cuffs. Then he said, "Well, and aren't *we* being a little edgy today." He then turned and paused by a wide-eyed secretary, saying, "She just threw the phone at me"—as though he had just realized it. Not knowing what else to do, the secretary began to laugh. Hovey returned to his office laughing. And Gale—now with the missile in her hands—appeared in her doorway laughing.

Not long after this (and possibly in self-defense), Hovey recommended Duff for promotion to the anchor store managing job that was such a necessary career stepping-stone.

The Big Break

Duff-Bloom had long since been initiated into the JCPenney fraternity of nomads. Like others who had been identified as candidates for upper management, she lived a life without roots. As her husband retired from the service (and then was finally retired from the marriage itself in 1981), her career developed in Columbus, San Bernardino, Austin, Houston, Buena Park (twice), Oakland, Walnut Creek, New York City, Phoenix, Dallas, and finally Plano.

Aside from her precious family unit, her life was the company. Her closest friends were Penney associates, the friendships flowering during one or another exhausting assignment at one or another new stop on the career path.

New assignments were almost never in familiar areas, the better (so it was felt) to eventually grasp the totality of what made JCPenney tick. Along the way, she was expected to behave ethically and expect the same from her peers and superiors. The conduct of business by all parties to it would be according to the Golden Rule, which, all associates knew, had actually been the name of James Cash Penney's first stores.

Yes, there was a double standard in this life. A glass ceiling was firmly in place. But there were several people, including some bright and brave women, determined to change that. Also, despite the best of intentions, the ills affecting corporate America in general were also visited upon the J. C. Penney Company, where, as at all other companies, human beings with weaknesses were running things. However, through cross-corporate meetings, conferences, and trade shows over the years, Duff-Bloom had become convinced that Penney was still the most upright and honest of all the major American businesses.

She believed that in 1979 after the telephone incident, she believed it in 1983 when Howell became Penney's CEO, and she believed it in 1988 when JCPenney moved from New York City to Dallas. With the move, Duff-Bloom had been promoted to vice president and director of investor relations—a position, of course, for which she had no experience.

It was her big break.

chapter 20 Onward and Upward

W. R. HOWELL was refocusing Penney's traditional view of the financial community. It used to be a nuisance matter, something barely tolerated. But Howell began paying a great deal of attention to Wall Street. This provided Duff-Bloom with access that, she knew, could become a real boon to upward movement as well as be nettlesome to the boys above her.

You Can Hold Me to That

Although she was a quick study, she had to put in even longer hours in order to (often barely) present Howell with accurate pictures of the company's stock performance as well as keep stockholders and the Street mollified. According to Duncan Muir, the veteran Penney PR pro, "Gale was really effective with analysts because of her personality and the fact that she spoke like a merchant, which was a refreshing change of pace. She had always done her homework and I don't remember her once making any kind of a slip. But the Wall Street types also knew they were hearing the real deal, not some management CFO-type mouthpiece."

Muir, who spent a lot of time guiding Howell's appearances and photo sessions, casually let the CEO know of Gale's success with financial audiences. Because of that and her direct reports to him, by the end of her first year she enjoyed an excellent rapport with the main man. And she was still secretly thrilled (as many others were then) to be in his presence. Then one day in his office Howell looked at Duff-Bloom as though considering her ability to absorb something particularly sizeable. He nodded dramatically, then spoke in a confidential tone that was new to her.

"There's a lot of stupid speculation about our move here, you know. But aside from scoring on the real estate, have you thought about one of the biggest side benefits? It's something we can't tell our shareholders, but it's true nevertheless." His eyes, which could argue so convincingly, now shone with cunning amusement.

"Side benefit?" she had to ask.

"All those people who refused to move down here? Lucky break, in my opinion. Gives us a chance to balance our workforce. Hmm?"

"I guess you're right."

"I *am* right, and we're putting people like you in those jobs— people who come from the field and know what's happening in the stores."

"People like me?" she said with a smile.

"Yes," he nodded. He gave her another instant sizing up and added, "Including women. More women. You can hold me to that."

She hesitated one second, then dared to say, "I will."

He regarded her, then smiled himself. "I know you will."

She had levitated down the hall after that meeting, euphoric with the new knowledge that unless she somehow screwed up, her career was going to continue at an increasingly upward angle. She had just been told so.

The hall she traversed was on the executive floor of the Aberdeen Building in North Dallas. In contrast to the modest executive offices they had left behind in New York, of course, the Aberdeen executive offices were quite spacious and plush. Executives showing off their new digs would explain the change with comments like, "Is it any wonder we moved here? This is what the company gets for *half* what New York cost."

As Duff-Bloom returned to her office, she reflected briefly on some of the top men who resided at the heavyweight end of the building. Besides Howell, she thought two other men were absolutely top-notch: Bob Gill (a merchandise pro) and Dave Miller (a stores expert), both of whom having been in the running for CEO. Others—capable enough execs without star quality—she didn't regard as highly. She wondered what it had been like in the executive suite during the Batten and Seibert years.

After another year of lustrous service, she was promoted to the number two spot in the Merchandising Division, which presented merchandise across the whole spectrum of the then 1,200 department stores. A year after that, she was made senior vice president and director of merchandising. Duff-Bloom had advanced to within one step from the executive suite of a $22 billion organization.

The Future Looked Great

At the Legacy complex in the spring of 1993, Gale left her merchandising office suite for the even bigger suites of the Golden Crescent. She had been summoned to see the main man, having been told only that it was "about a speech." Entering the chairman's anteroom, she was waved through by his suave executive secretary Trudy Morris. "He's with Chris, but he wanted you to wait inside."

Howell's suite was larger than any of the first Golden Rule stores. In addition to the main room where she was headed, the office included a midsize conference room; a full bathroom and dressing room; an office utility room; the anteroom reception area that included Trudy's mahogany workstation; and a really large conference room that bordered the rooms of "Director of the Office of the Chairman" Chris Sears, an executive vice president who was Howell's assistant.

Taking a seat at the table W. R. favored for one-on-one conversations, Duff-Bloom looked around at Howell's power walls. There were framed photos, honors and awards, plaques and mementos. There was a long built-in mahogany credenza laden with more mementos of crystal, silver, marble, brass, and gleaming wood. She turned toward an alcove and smiled at a symbol of Howell's position and personality: an expensive desk and accessories used for photo ops and nothing else.

Duff-Bloom smiled to herself and thought that of all the boys on this floor now, only W. R. really had the size to fill out his quarters—even if they were twice as big as the others!

"You want Chris's job?" came the jocular voice. "Right now I think he'd pay you to take it." Duff-Bloom turned and rose, returning Howell's grin.

"Trouble down the hall?" she asked.

"God," said Howell as he walked over to his desk and picked up a folder. He said nothing further about whatever the high-level skirmish may have been about. But his prolonged chuckle as he crossed to Duff-Bloom indicated how much he actually enjoyed the blood and guts of office politics at this level.

"For you," he said, dropping the folder on the table and sitting. Duff-Bloom also sat as he continued with, "I've hardly looked at this, but I got a call from Charlie Mechem, who said they wanted me to make the keynote at an LPGA convention." He tapped the folder. "It's all in here, from the LPGA producer."

"So I gather you've committed."

"We have the relationship."

"And you want me to handle this?"

He tapped the folder again. "You're the Penney point person on these issues."

"Well, at a guess, this ought to be a pretty good audience for publicity. Do you want to talk about inclusion?"

"Yes."

"How forceful do you want to be?"

"Forceful."

"When and where?"

"Pebble Beach, November 16, a Tuesday I think, in the morning." Howell's memory always impressed her. He had probably only glanced at the LPGA producer's letter. Now his eyes twinkled. "Hmm. Be almost sacrilegious not to play a couple holes as long as I'm there. Maybe Chris and Trudy can free up a few hours for me—not," he added with an eye on her only half-hidden disapproval, "that *golf* had anything to do with my accepting the invitation."

He was having fun with her. For years Duff-Bloom had been known for playing it very straight, and she still policed perquisites among her direct reports, sending a signal to the decks below. But here was the chairman theatrically flaunting executive privilege—but also, she knew, confiding in her. Which was a compliment. And compliments from the head of a $22 billion business were to be taken seriously—no matter how awkward.

She actually managed a smile with, "Oh, of *course* not. Who would ever think that?" He reacted with appreciation. Howell admired her spirit. She could tell by his eyes—eyes that on other occasions could freeze the strongest personalities in the company if he was displeased.

He tapped the folder once more. "By the way, since we're talking about inclusion, are we going to win the Catalyst Award?"

"1995," she replied with a confident smile. "Unless I'm totally wrong."

"Which these days would be very unlikely," he said with a smile, rising. Typically, he was sending her off walking on air.

Things were going so well for Duff-Bloom that on the way back to her office she made a confident prediction to herself. By the time Howell got to Pebble Beach, she herself would be residing in the Golden Crescent!

The Plan

Duff-Bloom would find a lot of satisfaction in the dozen diversity/ inclusion programs she backed over the years. As a woman who would successively head company administration, personnel (later HR), and communications, and who would become president of marketing—roles she ably assumed although far from her skills and experience in merchandising—she felt upon retirement that the major contribution in her career had been as an advocate and champion of the level playing field. And it had always been a struggle, despite the backing she received from W. R. Howell. In conversations and future speeches, Duff-Bloom would stress:

> "Of course we will *never* arrive at a point where everybody gets it, where everybody likes it, where everybody backs it. People are *always* going to erect barriers. But as long as we have a decent sample of people at all levels who *do* get it and who *do* support these programs, then our long-term success will be inevitable."

In practical terms, however, what would the programs really mean? A smokescreen obscuring the good old boys' club that still basically ruled the company? Yes, to some degree. A Howell tactic aligning Penney with politically correct numbers to make the company more attractive on Wall Street? Yes, that too. Nevertheless—and in view of zero previous personnel experience—did Duff-Bloom accomplish something remarkable by selling the equation of

SENSITIVITY + FAIRNESS = GOOD BUSINESS

Yes, absolutely. To an extreme, as it ironically turned out. Because, on a July day in 1999—to the shock and consternation of those same good old boys—a woman would be put in charge of the company with a mandate to change its culture.

But now, as she entered her office after the Howell Pebble Beach meeting in the spring of 1993, she thought again about his question regarding the Catalyst Award. As the lone woman on the management committee (Penney's most senior officers), Duff-Bloom was the chief promoter of good works within the company. And winning the Catalyst Award would signify distinction in the advancement of women in the business world and emphasize the overall importance of diversity to the fortunes of the company as no other recognition would.

No retailer had yet to be favored by Catalyst, the very adroit nonprofit research and advisory organization. So company prestige was a big factor. But more important to Duff-Bloom were the practical aspects—what it would do for her career, of course, but especially that positive everyday effect within the company itself. Winning the award would send energy-producing shivers of pride down the spine of every good woman in the organization. Yet, this would require an inspired and well-orchestrated campaign to achieve high evaluations against a range of demanding criteria. Among the considerations were measurable results, accountability, and senior-level leadership.

Howell, therefore, was priority number one. His backing of the Catalyst pursuit would prevent executive obfuscation of measurable results. Same for accountability. No matter who you were, you'd be in trouble if women were reeling from glass ceiling concussions in your area. Most important of all was the fact that W. R. alone was JCPenney's senior-level leadership. This totally negated the fact that most of the boys hated the very idea of the Catalyst campaign, let alone the possibility of actually winning the damned award. With Howell's approval, the others could jump up and down like Rumpelstiltskin until the floor buckled and it couldn't matter less.

And Duff-Bloom knew she could count on Howell for this. She had figured out some time ago that there was a genuine if limited streak of fairness and sensitivity in this feared and dictatorial CEO. And she had also seen, again and again, that he responded quickly and decisively to empirical evidence—such as JCPenney's increasingly diverse customer base and the fact that the company's fortunes were overwhelmingly tied to women shoppers. Therefore, more women and people of color in management had to simply be good business, and therefore, Duff-Bloom's team would receive all the resources and most of the cooperation necessary to achieve her goal.

The Duff-Bloom diversity/inclusion agenda had three other salient factors, all tied to the Catalyst Award. Internally, there was a range of programs with teeth, each aimed at raising the levels of opportunity for minorities and women, each aimed at raising confidence levels as well. Separately, there were both formal and informal efforts to source and develop promising women within the organization. The last thrust was a plan for external speech making.

The strategy behind the speaking was as ingenious as it was simple in concept. It was also unique in the company's history. First, of course, the topics were hot; and for any organization wishing to be seen as enlightened, it was certainly the good fight. So if a series of Penney speakers (working with compelling material) made favorable impressions at carefully selected conventions and meetings, the trade ink, house publicity, and word of mouth would not only reflect well upon JCPenney, they would actually force and reinforce progress within the company itself.

Howell's backing this campaign (and leading off with the Pebble Beach speech), then, was a lucky coup. But there was a vexing twist to his support, one that would frustrate Duff-Bloom to no end because she was helpless to do anything about it. Part of her plan was to also establish herself as a spokesperson for the diversity/inclusion issues—perhaps *the* spokesperson—and yet she would be denied the two most exciting and prestigious recurring forums on the JCPenney calendar.

Sports were a company priority regarding gender equity, and, of course, they sponsored the two entertaining charity golf events. Both broadcast on ABC, again they were the "JCPenney Classic," a mixed team tournament that attracted headliner pros of both sexes, and "The Skins Game," high-stakes match play featuring a foursome of the year's most popular players on the LPGA tour.

And the hitch? Not uncommon among CEO types, Howell loved the limelight and the company of celebrities. So there was no way the chairman would ever relinquish the job of hosting the two TV events since both were awash with celebrities, and both afforded national television exposure.

W. R. would relish each delicious sound bite leading to the feast of handing out Waterford trophies and big checks to the winners. And yet it was Duff-Bloom, not Howell, who should have fronted these events. She was, after all, not only the highest ranking woman in the company, but would eventually become perhaps the nation's number one businesswoman-champion of diversity and inclusion. Damn!

Aside from that one flaw, the plan was perfect. She knew that once her reputation as a speaker with something to say was established, in due course other presenters in the Golden Crescent and just below would follow her and W. R.'s lead. As to her potential effectiveness at the podium, she was encouraged and excited. In the few "talks" she had given around the company and in general sessions of small retail-related meetings, Duff-Bloom had discovered that she was pretty good on her feet. She also knew that she needed a top-notch speech (like Howell's), she needed practice before her premiere engagement, and she needed a perfect initial venue.

The Execution

The reader knows that I didn't think much of several of the senior executives I encountered in the Golden Crescent. Gale Duff-Bloom, however, was certainly an exception. Next to Howell, in fact, I thought she had the best business mind and the most talent. I met her when Debbie Litwak, Gordon Curry's boss, suggested I write a speech for Gale. The experience was good for all of us, and the relationships continued for several years.

Gale selected me to write her speech because she had bought into the approach I used to preach: *entertain* them with the message. I had written the Pebble Beach speech, which she thought was terrific. And, in a trade magazine, she had read good things about LaRovere's presentation to the Textile Council. She also knew that, as a writer and coach, I had made passable performers out of Penney executives previously known for curing insomniacs.

Duff-Bloom's material was easy; in one input session, I easily noted or recorded enough good stuff for a couple of speeches. It was exciting, too, that the presentation would have plenty of heart.

Duff-Bloom, for example, recalled Columbus manager Charlie Collins's welcome when she became an official management trainee, a story that touched me and I knew would move an audience.

"Gale," I said, "this is definitely the way to end your speech."

She smiled, liking the idea. "Can you make it pay the whole thing off?"

"That's the idea," I said, almost condescendingly. She later confessed that she was able to sit on her irritation with me, figuring she had a lot to learn and remembering experiences in other areas of retail where working with talent was often uncomfortable but important.

Practice in front of an audience had easy answers as well. Within the company she was a star. And there were so many JCPenney meetings going on every week in the Plano complex (her topic fitting almost any meeting) that she could practically take her choice. Likewise, she was easily connected to regional corporate conferences where there was interest in her speaking. The problem was her first "national" venue. It had to be just right. Not more important or more attractive than W. R.'s Pebble Beach audience, but a significant and pertinent gathering that would launch her nationwide.

Robin Caldwell was one of the impressive young women Duff-Bloom had "surfaced" who was presently running Penney's charitable donations department. This was no small responsibility, as the company had been giving away over $20 million a year to favored charities or appealing good works. Naturally, these donations all had an angle. There had to be some subtle benefit derived from every donated dollar. In the spirit of the company's record of outstanding corporate citizenship, however, the charity was basically sincere. No corporation in America, for example, put more effort into United Way drives than JCPenney. Education was another strong area of interest. An example was the "JCPenney Eminent Scholar" honoraria at universities like Florida and Texas A&M with strong marketing/retailing programs.

Gale called Caldwell one morning figuring that someone out there under the Penney umbrella might be interested in her diversity/inclusion message. She explained, "There's plenty of lead time, about six months. But don't you take more than a week or two. I need time to go out and practice this thing."

"So you obviously don't want to preempt W. R., so nothing before he talks at Pebble Beach—am I guessing right?"

"You are."

"I'll get back." She got back the next morning.

"Gale, you said not before W. R., right? And he speaks in the morning, right?"

"You've got something on the same *day?*"

"Gale, it's perfect. Afternoon at the University of Florida, national retail conference, accent on personnel, Warrington College of Business—I'll send up the details in a moment. Guy in charge, Bart Weitz, has real credentials, M.I.T., Stanford Ph.D. And all the media types you'd want. Everybody who isn't at Pebble Beach will be in Gainesville."

"Damn," said Duff-Bloom happily. "And how did you pull this off? I'm not exactly a celebrity."

"Yet. But you're not exactly unknown, Gale, number one. If there's any doubt, there won't be after Weitz introduces you. Number two is this interesting fact. Bart Weitz . . . is the 'JCPenney Eminent Scholar' there."

Duff-Bloom chuckled and said, "Nice work, Robin."

My first draft worked for her, and she didn't have many changes. Now she was ready to practice. She spoke twice to groups in the Home Office, having me make a few additional revisions after each. Then she presented the material up the road in Denton at the University of North Texas's "Executives in Residence" conference. She told me that the material was working like a charm. And she happily added that she herself was proving pretty darned good at delivering it.

Shameless

The day after Duff-Bloom's successful presentation in Denton, she was doing the mail with Cathy Rozelle, her ebullient assistant, when she stopped and pondered something. "Cathy, got an idea. Send the chairman my speech and highlight the part where I talk about the two best things he ever did. It's on the first page."

"A note?"

"Yes, say . . . I thought he'd get a kick out of the way I start off, but the whole script is included. Then say I'm doing it at the University of Florida next Tuesday afternoon, just a couple hours after he's finished at Pebble Beach. A coast-to-coast one-two punch."

Roselle's shorthand had it down almost as fast as Gale could say it. "I know you probably think I'm shameless," Gale said.

"Not really," said Rozelle.

"Well, I am. But it's for a good cause. I'm setting him up so I can go in someday and let him know there're some things bothering me."

"Yes?"

"Well, one thing I can tell you, we never talk about merchandise around here anymore. We talk about everything else, God knows, but not merchandise."

"Merchandise?"

"Yeah," Gale said with a grin. "You know, the stuff we buy and try reselling in stores?"

"Oh, sure, 'merchandise,' I *heard* about merchandise."

Doing mail three days later, Roselle handed over a large envelope from the chairman. Her speech and note had gone to him, the compliment highlighted on page one. He had shamelessly returned the speech with a note handwritten on her original note which was still clipped to the cover:

Gale—I completely agree!
W. R.

Duff-Bloom had one more rehearsal, giving her speech at a "Workforce Issues Network" conference in New Orleans. She returned to Plano as Carol Edwards, Kim Lang, Mark Shoener, and W. R. Howell were enplaning for the West Coast. Soon Duff-Bloom herself would again be airborne—in the opposite direction—to spread the same word. She was as ready as she would ever be for her national debut.

chapter **21**   The Speech

THE INN AT SPANISH BAY, Pebble Beach, 6 A.M.

After double-checking script changes, Carol Edwards managed to get back to her room, where she brushed her teeth, fixed her face, and changed. She then met Graham and the staffers for breakfast. Lang and Shoener had remained in the ball-room, where they loaded up with caffeine. Then, after reviewing the show with the stage manager backstage, they would take rest-room breaks and then kill time in the booth before pulling on their headsets. At show time, they would hear the first of the in-and-out verbal cues from the stage manager: "House down . . . walk-in music out . . . bring up summit logo . . . Mr. Mechem at the podium."

What If They Yell Back?

In the ballroom, a crew set the last of 650 chairs theater-style in front of the stage. From the dark velvet back wall of the stage now hung big banners reading "Women In Golf SUMMIT" and "1993" with the LPGA logo. The room lighting was set at half, the spots playing on both podiums also at half. The big screen between the podiums had been framed and totally encased in the velvet wall.

Lang and Shoener were relaxing in the booth with gossip about Penney people. Suddenly Lang looked away thoughtfully. "Mark . . . ?" she said, now very abstracted. "Remember the re-hearsal with W. R.?"

"Yeah?" The rehearsal had been especially memorable because it was so unusual for the chairman to rehearse anything at all.

"Remember how he was? Ad-libbing until Gale and Carol said

that he couldn't because of all the cues? Then he reads through the rest fast and flat?"

"Yeah?"

"I mean, like he still didn't get it?"

"You have a point?"

Lang waved at the empty ballroom. "These are mostly women. Sisters. It will be a rally for sisters."

"And?"

"And what if they really respond to him, to what he's saying? What if they yell back? What if they really get into it?"

"W. R. will be in heaven."

"No, the first time could scare the crap out of him. He could crater. Think of the stuff he usually says. Bor–ing. He's never done a show like this."

"So what?"

"I think we should alert him."

"Isn't that Carol's job?"

"What if she doesn't? She's pretty uptight. Excuse me." Lang moved her coffee and reached for one of the booth binders. She checked her watch, then skipped the LPGA presentation and opened the binder at Howell's speech, scanning the text for particularly hot or surprising lines. The text itself had speaker cues in CAPS—[PAUSE] for example, at the very end before the zinger. But now she added a few red-felt-pen notes in the margins throughout the script of 18-point type. At the bottom of the first page she wrote "AUD. *SHOCKED* AT HONESTY!" At about the five-minute point of the speech, she thought for a while and then printed "*WAIT!!* THEY MAY ANSWER!" after a certain sentence. She continued to the last page, then closed the script and opened the other booth binder.

The Show

At 7:44 Shoener faded up the music cassette, and he and Lang pulled on headsets. Shoener said, "Lang and Shoener here, all present and accounted for. Walk-in music up." The backstage stage manager replied with ready cues.

At 7:45 the ballroom doors were opened and the summit audience began filling the room as upbeat music played from the big speakers. Edwards and Graham took seats on the edge in the back row—leaving the first seat empty. Edwards held Howell's light leatherette speech box and Graham uselessly opened her show binder. At 8:07 the houselights and music faded—and W. R. Howell slid into the empty seat. The LPGA logo came up on the screen and then dissolved to the summit logo as light rose on Charlie Mechem at one of the podiums. The audience heard his rich, full voice over the big speakers.

> "Good morning and welcome. I'm Charlie Mechem, commissioner of the Ladies Professional Golf Association and your host for the 1993 Women In Golf Summit . . ."

He sounded so much better than the staffer had seven hours earlier that the two women almost managed to relax a bit.

The LPGA show went well, principally because Mechem was such a good speaker and master of ceremonies. There was only one anxious moment for Lang and Shoener. One of the other speakers, presenting details of the 1994 LPGA Tour, inadvertently turned two script pages at once, swallowing several of Lang's slide cues. In a twinkling, Shoener managed to kill the screen as Lang frantically located where the speaker now was in the script. She advanced the electronic slides, and the screen faded back up as the presenter, after a panicked glance back at the screen, said with relief, "So much for July," and continued on.

Mechem wrapped with his overall theme. "The LPGA doesn't seek to be noisy, only to be heard. We don't expect center stage, only to share the same stage . . ." He said the Women's Professional Golf Association ship of state was under full sail on good seas—as Shoener sneaked the house and music up to signal a break.

The two hours had gone quickly enough, the overall show impressive enough, so that when Mechem added, "And now let's take a 20-minute break," Graham could stand with great relief. Howell just looked at Edwards (who still held his speech box) and said, "I need some coffee." As Graham headed backstage, Edwards followed the chairman to the ballroom lobby. Back in the booth Lang and Shoener rose and stretched without comment. Then both again headed for the rest rooms.

Banzai!

At 15 minutes into the break, ballroom music was heard through the open lobby doors, but only a few of the hundreds enjoying coffee, pastry, fruit, and chat began moving back to their seats. The chairman at the moment was laughing within an encirclement of LPGA stars and was displeased with Edwards's attempt to extricate him in order to head backstage.

"W. R., we're supposed to check in backstage now," she politely admonished.

"They're going to start without me?" he replied in a flat voice.

But in a minute she had Howell moving in the right direction. "You're just about on, W. R. And you could tell by the buzz out there, this morning is *happening*." She emphasized the moment by handing Howell's speech box to him. Then she continued with comments about how exciting he was going to be. When they arrived backstage, the chairman was almost oblivious to Edwards and the activity around him—until Kim Lang came forward.

"Mr. Howell, I'm Kim, I worked on the slides." The chairman was not pleased. So? What the hell was this? "Mr. Howell," Lang continued, brazenly holding out her hand, "I need to borrow your speech to mark a few places where you need to wait a sec for the audience to respond. We think they will, and you don't want to be talking over them. I'll be back in a few minutes."

After a cross glance at Edwards, Howell unhappily handed the speech box to Lang as though he could not think of a reason to refuse. But unscheduled intervals like this were strictly taboo with the chairman. That the cause was someone from the ranks did not make the moment any better. As Edwards looked a little sick, all Howell could manage was, "Well, don't get the pages out of order."

"Of course not," replied Lang, covering her annoyance with a pleasant smile.

"And please don't be late," Edwards said in a strained voice.

"Of course not," repeated Lang with another smile—now adding just the slightest shade of condescension. "Plus, nothing can start until we say it can."

Edwards next spent an uncomfortable minute explaining to Howell that Lang was just reemphasizing the material's kick. That, again, they all thought when he took the stage it would be the beginning of something special. And then she did the reminders.

"Now we should remember what's happening here. There're about 600 women in the audience who are going to be surprised and thrilled with what you're saying. And please remember what Gale said. No ad-libs because of all the screen support, all those pictures playing on the screen reinforcing your words. A hundred and seventy-one slides, one after the other, so it's like a movie backing you. It happens like magic. You never look at the screen or even acknowledge it, everything cued very tightly to every word you say. Which is why we don't want to ad-lib. So Kathleen Sullivan gives your intro—there's a canned intro for her. We wrote her words, so that'll work, and then you walk up, open your speech box, say 'Thank you, Kathleen.' Then you deliberately slide the title page over and down to the left side, look back at the first page, and then look up and out over the audience like you know they're going to be surprised with what's on that first page. And they are, of course. And this is important, to just look at them before you start. It says this is going to be important, that something's on your mind."

Howell liked Edwards's act. She had an expected function and one had to accept her ingenuous passion. To a point. He grinned and said, "Carol, you do earn your pay, don't you."

Kim Lang returned in less than 10 minutes, having duplicated her new margin notes (like ". . . *SHOCKED* . . .") in Howell's script. "Here you go," she said quickly. "Just a couple margin notes, in case they react. And pages are in order. Good luck, sir." She handed over the speech box and departed.

Edwards did not return to the back row with Graham. Instead she paced in back of the ballroom seating. The lights and walk-in music faded and up came the summit logo. Kathleen Sullivan walked into podium lighting after the canned announcer intoned, "And now! Ladies and gentlemen, please welcome television sports personality Kath-leeeen Sullivan!"

"Oh, get *on* with it," Edwards thought irritably as the introduction began. But actually, Sullivan's words were fairly adroit, dealing out the obligatory praise without being especially cloying and lending a soft air of mystery regarding the content of the keynote coming up.

And then here came W. R. Howell himself. He said, "Thank you, Kathleen," placed his speech box carefully on the podium, opened it—and seemed to flinch slightly. Probably nobody noticed except Edwards (Lang's and Shoener's eyes were on the script), but she saw enough to make her heart skip.

To remind Howell about upcoming margin notes, Lang had printed two words on the title page in large red-felt-pen letters. The page read:

Good Luck!

WOMEN IN GOLF SUMMIT
KEYNOTE SPEECH BY

W. R. HOWELL
CHAIRMAN AND C.E.O., JCPENNEY COMPANY
PEBBLE BEACH—TUESDAY, NOVEMBER 16, 1993.

This simple gesture unhinged Howell. He moved the title page to the left lower half of the speech box and, instead of pausing and looking dramatically at the audience, he began speaking right away.

It didn't matter.

There was no warm-up. The speech got right into it, and Howell's words shocked the audience. In four sentences he had cut to the quick of the conference's central issue. He had confessed embarrassment and regret. He had admitted that the position of a Fortune 50 colossus with regard to the inclusion issue simply wasn't smart. He had said things out loud, then and there, that CEOs just didn't say in public. Something now happened that was foreign to the experience of Charlie Mechem, Kerry Graham, the LPGA staffers, Carol Edwards, Kim Lang, and Mark Shoener (who were now looking). An almost palpable hush fell over the audience. An eerie silence, as if everyone was holding their breath.

Howell was not the speaker Mechem was, but as a larger-than-life personality, he was still a force at any podium. But now he staggered, thoroughly rattled, as if the sudden stillness in the room were an invisible cloud moving in to suffocate him. His voice became thin, reedy, rising in pitch. A cold sweat rose on his brow. He soldiered on in agony.

The funny thing (later) was that the audience didn't realize any of this, seeing and hearing only what they wanted. This was because they were enraptured, captivated, carried along by the most exciting speech they had ever heard. So you had a speaker who thought he was dying a slow, torturous death. And you had an audience that thought they were having the experience of a lifetime. This dichotomy was building to an explosive moment just a few pages away.

Howell had glanced at the margin notes with further irritation, not really wanting to take them in. His galloping discomfort made the first words of the speech itself seem abstract and meaningless as they sputtered out of his mouth and were boomed from the great speakers. But the chairman had a keen mind and, as an executive expedient years ago, had taught himself to speed-read with excellent retention. Hence, he was not able to totally ignore the notes, and the sight of them, the insolence of them made his blood boil—or would have, had time allowed. Instead, a half-second sting of fury interrupted his main suffering, and he continued to read.

> "And, yes, we say that JCPenney is committed to breaking the glass ceiling. But it will be obvious to you, as it is to me, that we still have work to do."

Now he was desperately afraid that they *might* shout him down! He was *encouraging* it! If he had been the superb extemporaneous speaker that Mechem was, he would have abandoned his text right then and there, backpedaling to back and fill and rebuild the company's power and integrity. But despite his IQ, this was something he could not do. He was inextricably tied to his text.

> "Not too long ago at the Penney Home Office, we had a meeting of our 100 top executives—only nine of whom at the moment are women. This featured a report on the 'Expo' women's conferences that we pioneered as an exclusive joint sponsor. You may have attended one of these trade fairs that draw well over a million women across the country."

Only Howell's innate courage and years of summoning whatever it took for appearance's sake kept him from collapsing on the spot. And his trouble was now beginning to make him sound angry. This, of course, made the *audience* even happier with what they were experiencing. And the stillness began to dissolve into a low, appreciative murmur—sounding now to the speaker like the precursor to a building tenor of insurrection! Soon the commune to the barricades!

> "Now it happened that the Dallas Expo had been held the previous weekend. And so when I went to the podium to wrap up the meeting, I said, 'By the way, how many of you attended the women's Expo at the Info Mart last weekend.' I raised my own hand and added, 'Hands?'"

An insolent, goddamn red margin note was coming up!

> "Remember how many of our top 100 executives at that meeting were women? The number is nine—which, incidentally, is nine more than it *used* to be not too long ago, and we have a number of very talented women who will be added to our top management in the near future." [PAUSE]

He took a breath, glaring at them.
"Anyway, can you guess how many hands went up?"
He looked at the margin note, seeing it clearly now. *"WAIT!! THEY MAY ANSWER!"*
And it happened! A massive shout came from the audience! It sounded like a World War II Japanese death charge! **Banzai!** He could see the women in the first rows clearly as they shouted. They were beaming, eyes shining, faces spread with wide smiles!
Then *what* they were shouting became clear. *"Nine!"*
Oh.
He had elicited a thunderously positive response from his audience. *Oh! Sonofabitch! This wasn't just good, this was wonderful!*
Something else now happened that was foreign to the experience of Charlie Mechem, Kerry Graham, the LPGA staffers, Carol Edwards, Kim Lang, and Mark Shoener. Before their very eyes, Howell turned into a speaker as good as Ronald Reagan. He read his next lines exactly right, holding up a forefinger and unforgettably extracting drama from the story.

> "Counting mine, actually 11 hands went up. Besides me, only one other man had bothered to go. One. I looked at them and said, 'Only two men? Just *two* of us? [SHORT PAUSE] Fellas, have we forgotten who our customer is?'"

Howell ad-libbed. He leaned into the mike and repeated in a low voice, "Forgotten who our customer is?" It was a dicey moment for Lang and Shoener, with a slide cue coming up a few words later. They didn't breathe until he was back solidly on text and the cue came and went. It was, they would later admit, an inspired transgression.

> "Then I said, 'And *who* is the only other one besides me? Why, he happens to be head of women's merchandise! He *had* to be there!' [PAUSE] Then I surprised them, saying, 'But now I have a confession to make. I was there to receive an award. If that hadn't been the case, I probably would have been out playing golf myself!' [SHORT PAUSE] 'Fellas,' I concluded, 'this is a lesson we don't want to learn *twice*.'"

It is no exaggeration to say that not since Vince Lombardi gave his landmark motivational speech at the Waldorf had a business audience been more moved. Howell had them totally. He soared when speaking of sponsoring women's sports events. He agonized about the restrictions to women's play still in force on too many golf courses. He thrilled at the progress made since Billie Jean King beat Bobby Riggs in the Astrodome and Title IX was enacted in Washington. And again and again his audience responded out loud in all the right places.

Howell built to his climax by shaking his fist and ad-libbing once more (Lang and Shoener now relaxed completely):

> He added, "And by *God*," continuing with, "one day soon, I know that women will be teeing off at *any* course that is compatible with their game and income. And they will be teeing off at *any* time on *any* day of their choosing that is compatible with *their* schedule."

A lump was actually in his throat as he concluded:

> "And, ironically, when they do, these women golfers will be *doing* so with the very sensitivity, caring, and tolerance that was *so* unjustly denied them for so many years."

Lang tapped the last cue and the jail bars animated down over the lone woman golfer with the red sweater.

Howell hesitated, then again leaned into the mike and spoke in a voice approaching a whisper:

"Thank you."

One-two-three . . . The Penney people held their breath. And then the ballroom erupted, the audience rising en masse with cheers and applause.

Edwards stood by as the radiant chairman accepted joyous handshakes and high fives from Mechem, Graham, and other well-wishers. The press was also hovering nearby, the *Morning News* writer catching Edwards's eye and giving her a two-handed OK sign.

At length, Howell turned for her. But he simply handed over his speech box, pointed to the rear of the ballroom, and said, "Something to do." Edwards tagged along as Howell marched back to the booth and surprised Lang, shaking her hand and uttering the most sincere "Thank you" either woman had ever heard.

The moment the ballroom had emptied, Lang and Shoener began busily packing up their equipment. They left Pebble Beach without fanfare, typical of the staffers who, far below the executive suite, keep corporate America going. Managing to check their cases at San Francisco International in time for the four o'clock flight to Dallas/Fort Worth, they arrived at their respective homes just before midnight. Both would spend short, restless nights before awakening in time to report for work at 8 A.M.

chapter 22   Where Have All the Values Gone?

LET US NOW SEE the continent from the height of a satellite, looking almost coast to coast, from Pebble Beach to Gainesville—where another audience is gathering to hear about diversity, inclusion, and enlightenment at JCPenney. And at about the halfway point in-between, we can also see—as we drop down—Plano, Texas. And there is the grand Legacy complex of the Penney Company. Inside, from atrium to atrium, building to building, rotunda to rotunda, nearly 3,000 associates are at work as though Anthony Mark Hankins had never existed. Everything appears normal, functional. But is it really? Is everything really in synch with the messages of Howell and Duff-Bloom? The Hankins departure (no matter who knows or cares) would suggest otherwise. But, on balance, that story was just a tick in the giant company's clockworks. So—overall—*is* JCPenney really as solid as its speech-making officers and Wall Street think? Or are serious cracks beginning to form in the vast foundation?

Mr. Penney Is Unhappy

Now let us move outside, to the western elevation of the complex awash in sunlight. There is the glassy ceremonial entrance that virtually nobody ever uses except the few borne by limousines or company cars. The doors, of course, open into the symmetrical center of the complex, the tall, airy grand rotunda. The only adornment across the main expanse of the rotunda's glistening marble and terrazzo is a bronze statue of James Cash Penney at the age of 65. There, the frugal Main Street Merchant stands watch, a lonely sentinel in a suit. He seems a little uneasy, as though unsure of his luxurious surroundings. Mr. Penney is extending a hand, perhaps reaching to touch a memory in the distance of time. Perhaps he is thinking back to the Golden Rule store and the rush of all that has happened since. But look carefully now, for this pose is important.

Fittingly, Mr. Penney faces the outside, the Texas horizon stretching away to the west under the big sky. His back is to a winding staircase leading up to the Penney "Executive." And now one can understand his gesture and the sad, hooded eyes. It is as though he has just turned back from looking around toward the Golden Crescent. As though he *is* now reaching back to the past, reaching away from the plush suites to a time when a man virtually lived in his store in order to serve his customers.

Great Inconsistencies

Despite constant posturing to the contrary, W. R. Howell and his administration were morally very inconsistent. While he could say, with all his heart, that he believed in James Cash Penney and everything the founder had stood for, he did not, and his administration did not *act* in accordance with the ancient precepts. Lip service was constantly paid while company communications produced endless and artful documentation of the rich Penney legacy. But in terms of contemporary relevance, most of this was pure puffery.

Below in boldface are three of the key "Penney Idea" precepts that formed the foundation upon which the great organization was built. The incidents related after each precept occurred during or just prior to Penney's 1994 banner year.

To do all in our power to pack the customer's dollar full of value, quality, and satisfaction. The year was shaping up to be one of the company's best ever. Looking to such results, Howell had given a speech at the Waldorf-Astoria in which he predicted a bright future for his company. After the speech, the CEO and his entourage took a limousine to Teeterboro airport, where a company jet was waiting. En route, Howell pontificated about the success he saw on the horizon. Then he chuckled and added, "You know, guys, there's really no mystery to making it happen. All you have to do is keep your costs under control." Possible cost-cutting measures then dominated the conversation for the rest of the trip back to Dallas. Not once was the Penney customer mentioned.

To serve the public, as nearly as we can, to its complete satisfaction. "4 Billion or More in '94" was the name given to an internal promotion begun in the first quarter of 1994. The goal was a fiscal year increase in revenues by that amount (or more). Profits, it was assumed, would rise similarly. Posters went up in every Penney office around the world. An expensive video was produced. Rallies were held. The whole system was revved up to sell more merchandise or to support anything that would do so. More, more, more in '94! Inventories were expanded—and hidden in some cases, to be marked down and written off the following year. Where was the customer in all this?

To expect for the service we render a fair remuneration and not all the profit the traffic will bear. Joan Gosnell was manager of the extensive JCPenney archives. ("If it's old or dead, it's mine.") One day she finished compiling memorabilia and notes for an executive's speech, including a favorite anecdote:

> Earl Sams, in charge of the company for four decades, had always worshiped the founder's customer-first precepts. Once Sams wrote store manager Al Hughes (later a Penney president) to gently scold him because his store had shown too much profit!

Gosnell returned to her office—where a small package awaited her. She opened it and found an L-shaped Plexiglas desk plaque that read:

> "IF IT DOESN'T HAVE TO DO WITH PROFIT,
> I DON'T HAVE TIME FOR IT."

Since this plaque landed on hundreds of managers' desks throughout the company, she wondered if anyone was supposed to have time for the customer anymore. Apparently the administration thought not.

The National Speech

Gale Duff-Bloom landed at the Gainesville airport at the time Charlie Mechem was calling for a break at Pebble Beach. She was met by an assistant to the Warrington College dean because Professor Bart Weitz was wheelchair bound. In the car, as they began passing through the main University of Florida campus, Gale felt a pang. She had immediately liked the size and appearance of the school and suddenly suffered the recurring regret that she had never experienced a true on-campus student's life. She knew that all the business books, meetings, and seminars would never add up to the same thing.

The reception at Warrington was disappointingly flat. She hoped this wasn't a bad omen. Then her spirits were elevated at the late lunch. Her host, Professor Weitz, was an amiable and interesting companion in addition to being an impressive business scholar. They sat at a ballroom front table, the lone podium on a low riser close by—already adjusted, she could see, for her 5'3" height.

The briefing material Gale had read on the plane gave her a good idea of her audience: about 400 corporate personnel-related executives along with several business school names from around the country, all with impressive credentials (panel and break-out speakers). Weitz immediately pointed out the table occupied by the local media types and some national trade press reps. She would also be taped, and two cameras were already set up and manned. She was getting psyched.

Halfway through dessert Weitz was given a hand mike and his voice was suddenly heard from the room's speakers. He reintroduced himself and went over some conference housekeeping and then segued right into their keynote speaker without notes. Gale smiled to herself. The man's memory was as good as W. R.'s. And then she was on. The applause lifted her to the riser and the podium. On her way up to face the audience, she wondered about W. R. He would have finished his speech—*the* speech—by now. She felt a rush as she wondered what the hell had happened. Good? Bad? Triumph? *Disaster?*

Then she laid her speech box on the podium, opened it, slid the top page across and down to the lower left half, looked at all the people, smiled, and surprisingly exclaimed:

"Go Gators!" This was a national conference, yet she got a good laugh and applause. She was off on the greatest moment of her career.

"Professor Weitz, distinguished faculty from Warrington College and the other great institutions represented here today, corporate friends, including several of you who actually *are* my friends . . . and Steve Spurrier, if he happens to be in the room."

More laughter and applause. They loved this woman and she hadn't said a thing yet!

[LOOK THEM OVER SERIOUSLY] "And—why in the world did the Penney Company develop initiatives for the advancement of women and minorities and invite all the stress and strain that inevitably accompany such moves? Well, to begin with, it had as much to do with making a buck as doing the right thing. [HOLD A BEAT] Diversity and inclusion are just good business! [THEY WILL LIKE THAT!] But before I get to the whys and wherefores, I want to say something nice about my boss. [SAY IT RIGHT AND THEY WILL CHUCKLE] The two greatest things our CEO, W. R. Howell, ever did—in my humble opinion—was, first, to reposition our company from a mass merchandiser to a national department store in the value fashion business. And, the second thing was: he wholeheartedly backed *all* the JCPenney diversity and inclusion programs!" [IF THERE IS JUSTICE IN THE WORLD AND A GOD IN HEAVEN, THEY WILL APPLAUD!]

I used to lace my work with notes like that—what I called "afterburner cues." Immediately or eventually speakers (including Duff-Bloom) would have their secretaries excise them, hopefully after some of the direction had sunk in. But for this speech and the next one Gale told me that she left the remarks intact as good luck talismans. Early on, she wanted the extra support.

After citing various milestones of progress (her title and those of another woman and an African-American officer, etc.), the speech got to work with a flair. The bulk of the material presented the JCPenney diversity/inclusion story (the basic menu for winning the Catalyst Award). She proudly enumerated all the programs and built up to gender equity in sports. She stressed the total commitment from the top, and followed with the good-for-business numbers.

Then the surefire close.

[HOLD UP FOREFINGER] "One last thing. I am proud to be part of a proud company's proud tradition—which once affected me in a very personal way. [LOOK AT THEM] I began as a Penney management trainee in 1969 at a big Columbus, Ohio, store run by a typically outstanding Penney manager named Charlie Collins—rest in peace. But they didn't want me at first. I was just a floor sales associate and I didn't fit the model for a Penney management recruit. I was too old, I had three children, and I had no college degree. But I was persistent, and Mr. Collins finally petitioned the regional and New York offices to make an exception in my case. And, on his word, they did. We had a little ceremony where Mr. Collins said—and I'll never forget it—'So you see how we reach out at the Penney Company, Gale. And, someday it will be your own turn to reach out as well.' [LOOK AT THEM] And so today it *is* my own turn— and my privilege—to reach out with our diversity and inclusion initiatives. As it is also my privilege today to do so for such a special audience. Thank you so very much for the opportunity."

The applause was totally heartening. And now the well-wishers began to gather around the professor's table. Several of these people gave Gale their cards. One got her particular attention.

A middle-aged African-American in a well-cut suit reached to shake hands. "Ms. Duff-Bloom, I'm Coleman Peterson. I'd like to talk sometime if we may. I really loved your speech and wondered if you'd consider giving it at Wal-Mart's Saturday Morning Meeting—which is a big deal for us."

Gale had taken in the essentials on the card:

COLEMAN PETERSON,
EXECUTIVE VICE PRESIDENT
THE PEOPLE DIVISION
WAL-MART

She pocketed the card with a smile and said, "Certainly, Mr. Peterson. I've heard of the meeting and I'd be honored. Call me anytime."

At that moment someone handed the professor a plain #10

envelope with "Ms. Duff-Bloom" hand-written on the front. He handed it up to Gale, with, "Message for you, Gale."

"There's no escaping, is there?" she said with an amused roll of her eyes. "Excuse me a moment." She ripped open the envelope and unfolded Weitz' stationery with the following typed after the date:

MESSAGE FOR MS. DUFF-BLOOM
TELEPHONED AT 2:40 PM:
W. R. WAS SENSATIONAL. DETAILS TOMORROW.
CAROL EDWARDS

I Felt Absolutely Humiliated

Not long after Pebble Beach, Penney's second in command, Barger Tygart, called together his top direct reports and announced a pleasant assignment. All were to clear their calendars and together attend a San Francisco retail conference in early 1994. The purpose (beyond the scheduled symposia) was to share learning experiences as a *group*, to interact with others in the retail industry as a *group*, and to bond as a *group*. Here was an opportunity to get to know one another in ways that the normal pressures of working together precluded. They would return a stronger team. In addition to Tygart, Jim Oesterreicher, Tom Hutchens, John Cody (another executive vice president), and Gale Duff-Bloom formed the team—aside from Howell, the company's top talent.

After the first full day in San Francisco, all agreed that both the conference and the bonding were going well. That night as guests of Levi Strauss,[1] they dined in a private room at the landmark Ernie's Restaurant. Here, in Duff-Bloom's words, is what happened that evening and the next morning:

> "Toward the end of dinner, I saw something like the old game where someone whispers in your ear and you whisper in the next person's ear and so on around the table. I saw this topic being passed from ear to ear, but nobody whispered in my ear. When we were leaving the restaurant, though, Barger told me what was up. The men were going to skip part of the confer-

---

1. LS&Co., headquartered in San Francisco, sold far more Dockers and Levi's apparel through JCPenney than through any other retailer.

ence the next day and *really* bond at some famous golf course, guests of Levi's, of course.

"Well, I'm not a golfer and I said that certainly wasn't a problem with me. In fact, I had been looking forward to all of the next day's presentations at the conference and would be happy not to miss any. But some of the other men were standing close by, and I believe it was Tom Hutchens who said, 'Oh, no, no, Gale, this is bonding and you've got to come with us. Even if you don't play, you can ride along and enjoy the view. It's a beautiful course.'

"And so I reluctantly agreed to go. To 'bond.' But when the Levi's people picked us up late the next morning, they were surprised to see me. And, with the men's golf bags, now the van wasn't big enough, and it was an uncomfortable squeeze out to the club. Then at a very nice lunch somebody went over and whispered to Jim Oesterreicher and it started again, whispers around the table but not to me. Finally, Jim came up after lunch and gave me the bad news. This was a day when no women were allowed on the course. Didn't matter if they weren't playing, no women, period.

"*Why* didn't the Levi's men, who were members, say something back at the hotel when they stopped to get us? This date had to be prearranged, so why wait until we got all the way out there? Did they want to torture me? I couldn't believe this was happening. And then one of the Levi's men came up and said, 'Gale, it's going to be okay. I have a car coming that will take you anywhere you want to shop.' *What?* I just looked at him, and then I told Jim to tell his friend, 'No, *thank* you.' Then I called a taxi.

"Then I went out front to wait, and I started to get a little emotional. The theme of W. R.'s Pebble Beach speech kept coming back to me, and there I was living it! An outcast, a second-class citizen! How terribly unfair. I felt absolutely humiliated. And then Jim Oesterreicher came out—and I wondered when things were going to get better instead of worse.

"Jim says, 'Gale, what should we do? Do you want us to leave?' And I turned and faced him and said, 'If you have to ask, Jim, you couldn't possibly understand my answer.' He just stood there a moment, then he says, 'Well, I'm sorry about all this.' *As*, of course, he goes back inside to get ready to play."

When the taxi arrived, Duff-Bloom got in thinking about the fact that Howell's top four lieutenants had just made a mockery of his Pebble Beach speech.[2] The men had behaved selfishly and unethically. To her, they had violated the Golden Rule and everything it meant to be a ranking Penney person. As the driver pulled away, Duff-Bloom announced the hotel destination and then leaned back, shut her eyes, and tried to concentrate on breathing.

As a woman, she had needed rules for survival and progress in the corporate world. One—to never hold a grudge—would now be severely tested as never before (the group was scheduled for dinner at the hotel that evening, for example). But she would come through, as she always did. In the future, with dignity, she would manage to work with these men again and again—Barger Tygart eventually extending the presidency of marketing to her in appreciation.

As the course disappeared behind her, though, she would never again have the same feelings for her formerly beloved J. C. Penney Company.

2. It is interesting to note that W. R. Howell was and is a member of the Augusta National Golf Club.

chapter 23   What If I Talk to W. R.?

J. C. PENNEY DID WIN the Catalyst Award in 1995, one of only three companies to be singled out by the women-in-business advocacy organization. Duff-Bloom and the other women who sought and facilitated the appraisal process were ecstatic. Working with company PR and communications personnel, they began two campaigns to publicize the success, one internal and one for the business world at large. Arrangements were also made with the Catalyst staff for ceremonial appearances in New York. Howell would accept the award at an evening banquet at the Waldorf, with Duff-Bloom to be featured in a widely covered panel discussion that afternoon.

Gale, I *Like* the Man

On the big night, W. R. Howell flew in late and arrived at the Waldorf just in time to change in his suite and descend to the reception for banquet dignitaries. Later in the Grand Ballroom he accepted the Catalyst Award "with pride and humility." It was a time to savor, and Duff-Bloom celebrated with Penney friends—some of whom were not sharing her philosophical dismissal of the chairman's "absentmindedness." "The man has a lot on his mind," she had said, waving the question away. Really? Most thought otherwise—that it had been wrong for Howell to accept the award without ever mentioning Duff-Bloom's name.

Duncan Muir, the PR executive who often guided Howell's appearances, was one. "What could W. R. have been thinking?" he wondered aloud.

"About running a $22 billion company?" said Duff-Bloom. "I keep saying."

"Well, at least you were sensational this afternoon."

"You were *there?*" asked Duff-Bloom, surprised.

"Of course," Muir smiled. "W. R. was going to be late, and I wanted to see you in action again anyway. Very impressive, Gale, and I mean it."

She knew he did. She had always liked the PR executive, as both a person and a professional. Their relationship was solid and forthcoming, and Muir was relaxed and direct with her despite Duff-Bloom's quite senior rank.

"There *is* one thing," Duff-Bloom said thoughtfully.

"What?"

"Well, I have this network of friends—all Penney people, all women, all scattered everywhere now. But the thing is, we *talk* to each other. And, aside from personal issues, they're my ears to the ground. You know?"

Muir nodded, knowing he was about to hear something interesting.

"Well, for a while now I've been hearing that we've become much too bureaucratic."

"Your friends have a point."

"Then how about this? W. R. is also too much of a dictator?"

Muir looked conflicted. "Gale, I *like* the man. Warts and all."

"I don't?"

Muir waited, then said, "Okay, forgetting the dictator bit, I agree. And I have a good story about knee-jerk bureaucracy. About Bob White."[1]

"Oh, I'm *sorry*. I never apologized to you!"

"You didn't have to."

"The goofy *policy*—I was *told* to give that job to Bob."

"I figured." Then he smiled wryly. "But bureaucracy? Did you know Bob was badly infected?"

"No. But I'm not shocked to hear it."

"Okay, remember when W. R. lets it be known that we shouldn't change our minds?"

"But I always thought he really just meant for people to think things through."

1. Muir's former boss and presently store manager.

"I agree. But not everybody saw it that way."

"Don't tell me."

Muir nodded with, "Bob White took it literally."

Muir had known that White was cycled to Plano from the field and was scheduled to return as the manager of a big store in a year. He also had reasoned that the "broadening" policy was behind White's being put in charge of company public relations despite having no previous experience in the field.

Muir now related this story. One day when he stopped by his boss's office to announce a change of mind due to some new information, White became upset.

"You can't do that."

"What?" said Muir.

"You can't change your mind like that."

"I can't? *We* can't?"

"No."

"Why not, Bob?"

"It's a sign of weakness."

"But this is PR and we have new information."

"I'm sorry."

"Things have changed, Bob."

"You still can't."

"Bob, we *have* to."

"I won't allow it."

"You what?"

"It's not our culture."

"*Huh?*"

Muir leaned back shaking his head and chuckling. "Do I have to tell you the trouble I went through end running that?"

"No," Duff-Bloom said, shaking her own head. Then her eyes sparked. "Duncan? What if I talk to W. R.?"

Muir regarded her admiringly. "He'd certainly listen to you."

Amazing Grace

Duff-Bloom sat at the chairman's guest table as Howell finished up some work at his desk and then came over. "What's on your mind?" he asked pleasantly.

"W. R., I've been worried about a couple of things."

"Shoot," he said.

"Well, I want you to know I've been waiting on this for over a year now, so it's not like I'm jumping to any conclusions here."

"Fine. And?"

"And have you noticed that we don't talk about merchandise around here anymore?" With the words "around here" she had nodded back in the direction of the Golden Crescent hallway. "We talk about everything else, but never merchandise. And this is still a merchandising company, isn't it?"

He issued a dry chuckle, his eyes probing. "You have a point. Why don't you talk to Jim about it?"

"Because I don't think Jim is actually comfortable talking merchandise." She shrugged lightly. "Or so it seems."

"Ah, we're being confrontational today."

"I think it's important, W. R."

"Okay, I'll *tell* Jim to talk to you about it."

"No, please. He'll just end up mad at me." With resignation, she said, "I'll talk to him."

"The other thing, then?"

"Well, you know my ear's always to the ground. And I do have sources. I hear things nobody but me would tell you in a million years."

He smiled. "Should I brace myself?"

"In a manner of speaking, yes."

Howell often was in a quicksilver mood, something that his petitioners feared greatly—all but Duff-Bloom. Now she leveled an even smile at him, and said, "Well, I hear this company has gotten way too bureaucratic. Makes us too predictable."

This drew a noncommittal nod from the chairman. She continued.

"Plus some think you're too much of a dictator." Beat. "I don't think so, for heaven's sake. I think you're a terrific boss, W. R., the best I ever had. And I think you've done an outstanding job with this company, a fabulous job of leadership. I only wish the next guy had half your ability."

"We *are* being confrontational," he said, his smile returning.

"Jim aside, W. R., but there *is* something wrong with this company now, and you're so close to retirement, I doubt that you would even notice."

"Oh?" he replied. The gamble had worked. She had his complete attention.

242 • Bill Hare

"Well, did you ever know that last year I went up to Wal-Mart and gave my inclusion/diversity speech at their Saturday Morning Meeting? Coleman Peterson heard me at the University of Florida and invited me. He runs their personnel."

"I know who Coleman Peterson is. And, yes, I heard. And one or two of the boys down the hall didn't think you should've been up there." He delivered a half-grin.

"I'm sure," she said. "But I'm glad I went because I learned something. And I'm sure the boys will at least agree that we 'might' just be able to learn something from the world's biggest retailer?"

"What was it?"

"Well, overall, W. R., I'm afraid to say that Mr. Penney, I think, would've liked some things better in Bentonville than here."

"Oh?" said Howell, in the flattest of tones.

Duff-Bloom continued as if he hadn't said or indicated a thing. "One thing, though, that Mr. Penney *wouldn't've* liked and I *do*: everything is casual there. Casual dress, no scripts in the meeting, the management people talking without notes and everybody really into the business and free to respond. They're free to speak their minds, the people in the audience. And there's this tremendous enthusiasm. It got me thinking."

"Oh?" Howell repeated, now with a new shade of wariness.

"We ought to make some changes around here. First of all, just consider that we *sell* more casual apparel than anyone else on earth. And yet, here we all are, still wearing suits. So I think, to begin with, we should change to casual dress."

"No way," Howell said.

"Oh, come on, W. R. It's time we considered changing that old tradition. It's time we loosened up some. I think some people here *are* afraid to speak up. Obviously *I'm* not," she laughed. "But I think speaking your mind should be encouraged. What's it going to hurt? And I think that when we make speeches and presentations internally, we shouldn't be scripted—it should be from the heart and people should be free to respond. I think we should look around for any other ways to liven things up around here. Take management council,[2] for example. It is *so* formal and so stiff and usually so boring. You should see that Saturday Morning Meeting

---

2. The name at that time of the monthly meetings of Penney's top 100 executives.

in contrast. Really, about the only leadership and excitement in management council is when you get up there and pull something to get their attention or to make a point. I could get together with some people and prepare a presentation on all this, by the way." She smiled. "We'd memorize it."

He was relaxed now. "God, I'm going to miss you when I walk out of here." He looked outside at the fountain as he continued. "Look, I'm not going to say what they do at Wal-Mart is in the least way wrong. They're a great organization and really moving." He looked back at her. "But I'm also not about to strike down any of our traditions at the J. C. Penney Company either."

"You don't think my points are valid?"

He smiled. "Your points are *always* valid. But I'm tempted to just remind you that you already have a lot on your plate. But I'm not going to do that because I like you too much. Instead?" He gestured sideways like a quarterback. "I'm going to lateral the ball. Go see Jim about this, too. Please allow me a graceful exit. Let me work with the board and do the ceremonial things and have a little fun. I'll let Jim know we've talked about your main ideas here, and I'll say they're something for him to listen to. And when you see him, you're clever enough to also work in your merchandise complaint. Fair enough?"

They chatted a few minutes longer, accomplishing nothing further, and Duff-Bloom rose to leave. Howell said, "Oh, wait a moment," as though he had almost forgotten something (which he *never* did). He went to his desk and picked up an audiocassette in a container with a printed label. "This is a preacher I heard recently. Just amazing." He smiled and handed her the cassette. "Amazing grace, I guess I should say."

The Successor

On her way back down the long, plush, quiet hallway of the Golden Crescent, Duff-Bloom took another fond look at the cassette. The label had a photo of a woman in ecclesiastical robes, along with her formal name and the titles of two sermons. The pastor's church was prominent, and Howell's message to Duff-Bloom was obvious: In conservative and traditional Dallas, look what a talented woman can accomplish! This tape is just like W. R., she thought with gratitude—and sadness.

Although she couldn't wait to play the tape in her car on the way home that evening, the gift actually made her heart heavy. It reminded her of W. R.'s appointed heir, someone from whom she would never dream of receiving such a thoughtful gift.

Duff-Bloom was not a big fan of Jim Oesterreicher. He was just on a far different wavelength than she was. While she would never have explained it as such, Duff-Bloom was used to thinking in abstract terms. Oesterreicher, she knew from experience, just didn't get abstract thoughts. Things had to be set in concrete terms for him to respond. And retailing, in her view, was a creative business where imagination was the principal currency.

Also, while it was popular to extol his considerable staff accomplishments, she feared that Oesterreicher would not remotely approach Howell in the leadership role. Beyond his problems with abstract concepts was his difficulty in making decisions. For example, when she did follow through on Howell's suggestion and see Oesterreicher about morale and merchandise, she figured he would hem and haw and just leave her thoughts on the table. She was sure of it, and she was right.

So Duff-Bloom anticipated Oesterreicher facing tricky industry issues in the future and delaying his response as long as possible. If the matter was truly pressing, she knew he would fall back on the need for consensus, throwing it to a top committee that was compelled to act. To Duff-Bloom, this meant that under Jim Oesterreicher the company was going to be run by consensus-bound committees. That, in turn, indicated that the possibilities for decisive innovation in the future were nil.

part **IV**

The End

chapter **24**   Jimmy-O the Farmer

J IM OESTERREICHER CAME from one of Michigan's many German-American farm communities. He was the first on his family tree to attend a university, graduating in 1964 (Michigan State, B.S. in marketing and retail). He trained at the J. C. Penney downtown Lansing store built by the legendary Jack Maynard. Like many successful Penney people, he had never known another employer. When he settled into the enormous chairman's suite in 1996, Wall Street was still singing his predecessor's praises after three consecutive record-breaking years. But now Howell was history, and the title and company were Oesterreicher's. All he had to do was keep the money ball rolling.

Jim

Winding up his first day in the chairman's suite, Jim Oesterreicher could have looked out and gazed at the fountain and terraced gardens in the twilight before heading home for a late dinner with his wife, Pat. He could have allowed himself a moment of reverie. A succession of images might have played across his mind's eye. The Michigan farm, MSU, the Lansing store, all the other stores, offices, and distribution centers he had come to know. He could have reflected on the 11 times he had uprooted his family in his 32 years with JCPenney. Or he might have studied the fine appointments of his sumptuous suite and savored a sense of accomplishment.

But he did none of that. Instead, he dictated memos and then checked his mail, a chore he never delegated. Once his desk was clear, he packed his briefcase and headed straight home—as he did every evening when he wasn't traveling or obligated to appear at some function.

On that particular night, Jim and Pat Oesterreicher may have allowed themselves a congratulatory glass of wine with their food. But after dinner, they probably worked together on the contents of his briefcase for another hour or so before going to bed— usually by 11, because he was always at his desk by 6:00 A.M.

The Farmer

Oesterreicher had not always been seen as the most promising of comers. As he rose through the ranks, nobody ever said that Jim Oesterreicher wasn't a decent guy. Nobody ever said he wasn't tough, either, whenever his responsibilities required it. And *nobody* ever worked any harder. Many, however, thought he lacked the leadership qualities necessary to become a top Penney executive. Still, at the end of the day, "the Farmer" had always gotten the job done.

Some called him that behind his back, less out of disrespect than as a warning. It was as if to say, "Be careful and don't pull anything fancy on this guy. He's basic. Go highbrow and he won't understand it and you're in trouble." And Jim Oesterreicher's interests did seem limited to the basics in his life: the business of retailing (not fabric, not style, not trends, but the *business* of retailing), plus family, church, and community service. Allen Questrom, the man who eventually replaced Oesterreicher at the top, once ran the Neiman-Marcus chain. Jim Oesterreicher would never have gotten to first base at Neiman's—assuming the unlikely possibility of his even applying for management training there.[1]

As often happens, Oesterreicher changed when he became CEO, and shortcomings surfaced that seemed odd for a top man.[2] If the essential difference between a senior executive and the CEO is the difference between follow-through and decision making,

1. Oesterreicher once said, "When I graduated I was married and had to get to work. The business school bulletin board had only two notices that made sense for me: selling vacuums and J. C. Penney. Vacuums paid better, but I thought that a big company like Penney was better for the long haul. And I had majored in retail, so that was that."
2. Was this an illustration of Penney's insularity weakness? Would another CEO with such drawbacks be found among the Fortune 50? Probably not.

Oesterreicher's inability to make important decisions until the last minute was a big problem. He also found it difficult to communicate exactly what he wanted. Sometimes it seemed as if he was giving clear instructions, but when the meetings were over, subordinates were often left grabbing at air. He did command immediate attention because he was quite self-assured and had *always* done his homework. But did he really have the vision or the soul of a leader? People wondered. He was quick with business platitudes and epigrams, but how about an *idea*?

Once, a rising upper-middle manager with access to the Golden Crescent sent Oesterreicher a memo politely requesting his thoughts on the most important aspects of an executive hire. She was making a presentation to an important outside body (a career boost) and wished to feature his quotes (clearly to be the meat of her piece). Later that week she met with a Golden Crescent executive on another matter. As she sat down, he regarded her with an unhappy chuckle and said, "So you're the one causing all this trouble."

"Huh?" was all she could reply.

He held up a copy of a memo. Hers. "This trouble," he said, sliding it to her. She saw that Oesterreicher had scrawled a note on it:

COPY THIS TO MANAGEMENT COMMITTEE—
WHAT DO YOU THINK? PLS GIVE ME YOUR THOUGHTS.
—JIM

She produced a sheepish smile and mumbled, "Oh, m'god. I only wanted a couple of his own thoughts, whatever came to mind." She picked up the memo copy and indicated a sentence. "I made that clear."

"Ah, yes," said the executive. "And now I've got to put some people on this, have some meetings, watch over my own damn memo—I mean report."

"I never dreamed."

"Well, now you know," he said. "It's always wise to think twice when you deal with Jimmy-O."

The End of Camelot

Complicating his often vague instructions, Oesterreicher also liked to surprise people, keeping things a little off balance. He achieved this often by accident as well. Occasionally, his grammar would lapse, or he would startle people with some curious misunderstanding or lack of knowledge.

For example, the chairman was going to speak at the Greater Lansing Chamber of Commerce and wanted to engage his audience with some reminiscences about Michigan State and the downtown Lansing Penney store. I was doing the speech and during the input session, he mentioned "Not believing my ears" when, driving across campus, his car radio program was interrupted with the news of President Kennedy's assassination. "That's it," I said.

"What?" asked the chairman.

"The way to build to the theme. After Kennedy, things were not as pleasant anymore. Things happened faster, were more cynical."

"Okay."

We agreed (I thought) to base the speech on the age of accelerating change that began after the national tragedy. I then completed a draft,[3] tentatively titling the speech "The End of Camelot." But when Oesterreicher saw the work, he X'd out the title and the reference to "Camelot" in the text, which had been the heart of the build. Later, I reacted with dismay in a meeting with Kris Carlson, the chairman's able adjutant. Here was the passage:

> It was suddenly, unthinkably, a nation in transition. As the President's body lay in state in the Capitol rotunda . . . everyone on the State campus was reeling from a sense of great loss. It was the end of an age of innocence, the end of a time of grace. It was the end of Camelot.

Oesterreicher had slashed the last two sentences.

"Kris, that's good stuff," I pleaded.

"I know it, I agree."

"Then why the hell did he kill it?"

Carlson was loyal and conscientious but was burdened by the missing pages in her boss's onboard encyclopedia. She replied uneasily, "Because he didn't know what Camelot meant."

---

3. The first of many to come. Oesterreicher always kept changing or adding things with every draft, making coherent and structured presentations impossible.

"He what . . . ?"

"I know. But he didn't. I explained, but he was still uncomfortable with it."

"*Camelot?*" I blurted. But it was true. The chairman had never heard of the myth, or the musical, or the name for the Kennedy years. And that was the end of Camelot.

He Never Gives Up

W. R. Howell probably never gave Oesterreicher's lack of depth a thought. It was Oesterreicher's ability to come through and provide support that was held in high regard, and from the moment he left the West Coast regional office in 1988 for a brief stint in New York before the Dallas move, he was increasingly seen as the heir apparent. And if there remained any doubters, they were silenced in the early 1990s.

The year 1991 had been a disaster. Sales had sagged or dropped in the previous two years, but now they plunged, and profits plummeted. Some in Penney senior management hastily worked at repairing bridges to the investment community. Others led highly visible cost-cutting efforts. But Howell put the spotlight on Jim Oesterreicher as the one to repair the basic machinery of the corporation (as he saw it). Howell then watched "the Farmer" work quietly, with military precision, setting the stage for the turn-around that began in 1992.

In the next three years, Howell led Penney to the greatest sales and profits in the company's long history, including a record $1 billion to the good in 1994. And he made no secret of his appreciation of Oesterreicher's efforts. Still, many wondered why Howell had tapped Jimmy-O the Farmer instead of the more obvious original candidates like handsome and adroit John Cody or smooth and skillful Tom Hutchens. But when Oesterreicher took over stores in 1991, he had emerged as the front-runner, the position having become *the* stepping-stone to the top job.

By 1993 Oesterreicher had a lock on the job. A popular cocktail party explanation was that Howell, like most strong leaders, did not want any kind of big personality at his side or a hot leader to follow in his footsteps.

Of course, any CEO candidate at a major corporation will have strong personal attributes, and Oesterreicher was no exception.

➤ He was unusually steadfast. It was felt far and wide that you could take his word to the bank.

➤ He really tried to practice the Golden Rule (as opposed, for example, to Howell's lip service).

➤ While ignorant of the fine points of buying, he knew the business of running a store inside and out.

➤ And at times he had a completely unexpected capability for showmanship.

Oesterreicher's good points, however, were not enough to arrest the company's decline. And after his honeymoon in 1996 when sales sagged after the record years, he was increasingly seen as culpable. Media attacks rose during the five-year span of Oesterreicher's administration, the stories and commentary hammering on JCPenney's tailspin and calling for the chief's head. A lesser man would have been totally subdued or even killed by the pressure. But Oesterreicher kept slogging on—even, in his way, trying to fight back.

The Surprising Script Doctor

Penney's business was bad (and going to get worse), but it wasn't catastrophic. It just appeared that way in contrast to the tech and dot-com stocks that were at their crazy heights. In another speech that would be heard by the financial community (twice), Oesterreicher wanted to retaliate. He wanted to say, in essence, "Hey, give us a break. Our Eckerd drugstores alone are worth more than you're valuing our stock."

It wasn't an easy sell, and I suggested first disarming the audience with humor. I had extensive experience in scripting and production, was familiar with the Dallas talent pool, and guaranteed a presentation that would work. I promised that when the actors finished each of the (three) sketches, the audience would be nicely delivered for the chairman's knockout blow. Remarkably, Oesterreicher agreed.[4] Even more remarkably, everything worked like a charm. And, even *more* remarkably, Oesterreicher turned out to be a good script doctor.

4. How many CEOs would agree to share a stage with professional actors?

The sketches I wrote centered around an arrogant dot-comer, "Wanda Wonder," who was hustling an underwriter. During an interview at a conservative firm, she replied to a question about her background by saying, "I was a math and computer science genius at MIT. I also pitched softball in the Olympics and graduated first in my class at the Cordon Bleu Culinary Institute. (TO AUDIENCE) All at the same time. Then I started Wonder Woman dot-com which, of course, is the talk of Wall Street." You get the idea.

Oesterreicher liked the writing and loved the actors, Kathy Morath and Mark Fickert. But he pulled me aside after we played the sketches for him. "Bill," he said, "I've *met* people like Wanda. I don't think you've made her arrogant *enough*. And I also don't think Mark should use that character voice. I think he should play it straight. Make more of a contrast. If you don't mind my suggestions."

Oesterreicher would, again and again, whimsically change anything in a speech, but he would not change a comma in the sketch scripts without my agreement. Moreover, those were good (if amazing) notes. So I had Mark play it straight and changed a few lines and gave Kathy some over-the-top business that (yes!) really worked. This got big laughs, all the better setting up the chairman to make his points. The presentation got very favorable press and seemed to diminish the attacks on Penney and Oesterreicher for a while.

Still, the company's sales and profits continued to fall.

chapter **25**   There's Nothing There

OW HAD JIM OESTERREICHER gotten to such a God-awful point? How could he make such arrogant, ego-driven mistakes (as the reader will see)? It is a sad, unfair story, where Oesterreicher really was a sort of patsy—on the one hand. On the other, nobody ever put a gun to his head and forced him into the chairman's suite. And once there, at the very top of a big public company, he was vulnerable to the kind of scrutiny—then and now—that the power, money, and responsibility of the office must always attract.

In the final crunch, Oesterreicher suffered the worst of leadership mistakes—executive hubris.

At issue is the big leap that Mil Batten addressed at the top of this book. No one knows how a CEO-in-waiting will change once the mantle of leadership is on his shoulders. And Oesterreicher certainly changed—but in unforeseen and unfortunate ways. His consensus-driven administration was weak in leadership and barren of viable new concepts. It was wholly incapable of the kind of introspection that might have detected and averted the ruinous drift of the company. And there was also a regrettable moral slippage when the surprising arrogance surfaced.

Sideline

The reader will recall Walt Neppl's contemplating a lesson learned about expertise. "After spending our lives selling sheets and shoes," he told Don Seibert, "why did we ever think we could sell brown goods?" Indeed, the impetus behind Penney's returning to a soft goods emphasis was reflected in that statement. The company *knew* "sheets and shoes" and had from the very beginning. It did *not* know "brown goods" (hard goods, appliances) and was wise to abandon such trade to the Circuit Cities of the world.

But the "all everything" store had been a product of the 1960s, brown goods a necessary burden. In contrast, relearning the expertise lesson with the Eckerd Drug deal was just an embarrassment.

Despite its ownership of a few hundred Thrift Drugstores, drugstore retailing at Penney was a sideline, not a specialty.[1] In no way was drugstore retailing a reasonable target for a costly major acquisition. This was because of very different retailing natures. At JCPenney, basically, apparel and soft home items were sold. At a big drugstore chain, it was a matter of managing a zillion disparate SKUs (stockkeeping units) in the front—cosmetics to lightbulbs to crackers to antacids—and a managed-care-dependent prescription counter in the back. Apples, oranges, and bananas.

Yet JCPenney bought—and bought poorly—the Eckerd Corporation and its 2,800 stores. This hapless event was Jim Oesterreicher's doing and it eventually amounted to a financial millstone. Worse, from a remarkably lax and superficial due diligence to cosmetic bookkeeping that softened the downside of the acquisition, it was an odoriferous deal[2] that would cause many to ask, "This is *JCPenney?*"

Once, Jim Oesterreicher was about the last person on earth you would have associated with such a thing. So what had happened? Well, here was an utterly decent man with modest talents who had worked very hard all his adult life, played it straight, and achieved success—only to have the rotten luck of landing in the chairman's suite without a compass. And, naturally, searching for a direction in that plush land of Oz was not the best way to maintain one's grip on nitty-gritty reality.

---

1. Of Penney's other sidelines over the years, only direct marketing insurance (sold in 2001) enjoyed any real success; and Penney developed it from an inexpensive start-up.

2. As this book's manuscript was approaching completion, the financial media reported another negative impact on Penney stock because of bad Eckerd news. The gap between same-store sales in Penney's drug unit and other drug retailers was widening in favor of the competition. Observers wondered if Eckerd would *ever* stabilize long enough for Penney chairman Allen Questrom to sell off the star-crossed division without taking too much of a hit.

He *Had* to Have It

Hence, the Oesterreicher announcement that the J. C. Penney Company was negotiating to buy the Eckerd Corporation. In asides to his upper-level compatriots, the chairman said the acquisition was going to be "my legacy," alluding to a dazzling show of business imagination and acumen. The deal would reveal a practical pot of gold just waiting to be exploited. It would be, in fact, the essence and glory of synergism!

In time, an agreement in principle was reached with Eckerd, and the due diligence process began—at length, moving too slowly for the chairman. He was apparently afraid that his deal was losing momentum. Earlier, in a highly unorthodox move, he had anxiously called Frank Newman, head of Eckerd, late one evening. Oesterreicher urged him to do whatever was necessary to make the deal go through at his end. "We've *got* to get this done," he told Newman. Now, in his second unorthodox move, Oesterreicher greased the skids under Penney's due diligence. Originally and appropriately headed by Bill Alcorn, a CPA and company officer fresh from ably running Penney's credit operation, Oesterreicher eventually switched due diligence leadership to his longtime colleague, stores man Tom Hutchens.

One day Hutchens slumped into Gale Duff-Bloom's office and sat heavily on her couch. "How's Operation Synergy?" she asked cheerfully. She was not close to Hutchens but admired the executive for his talent and intelligence (if not for his golf passion). She also felt sorry for him. After a highly successful career, he had had a run of bad luck lately, culminating with an embarrassingly public sexual harassment trial caused by clumsiness with a former woman executive. Hutchens no longer had much to do in the Golden Crescent; Oesterreicher had given him a fancy title with limited responsibilities to ease him through to retirement. He would certainly have time to do whatever the boss wanted.

"Synergy?" Hutchens answered in a tired voice. "There *is* no 'synergy.'"

"*What?*" Gale exclaimed. This was a bit of a shock.

"None. There's nothing there."

"Good grief, Tom. That was the whole point."

"I know," he said sadly.

She hesitated, thinking, then just asked, "What are you going to do?"

He shrugged. "Give the man what he wants."

So Duff-Bloom was one of the first to know that Jim Oesterreicher's pet project wasn't nearly what it was cracked up to be—that the company might be paying heavily for a pig in a poke.

Synergism!

Jim Oesterreicher's favorite word was the Eckerd deal driver. Why, just look: Penney knew the catalog business, and there was a huge amount of new business just lying there in every one of Eckerd's 2,800 drugstores! Just put a catalog desk in all those stores and double profitable inventory overnight! Add health-related items too big to stock in a drugstore, like walkers and hospital beds! And, while we're at it, how about some high-turn apparel and soft home items! At the same time, expand Penney's own catalog to include drugstore items! Add the fact that most Eckerd stores are in the Sunbelt, where everybody retires to play shuffleboard, live longer, and buy more prescription pills, and this deal cannot miss!

It was obviously a seductive rationale. And was Oesterreicher alone in his specious thinking? Hardly. The assumption-of-efficiencies lesson is evidently one that must be learned again and again. In late 2002, a notable example surfaced right in JCPenney's own backyard. Tom Hicks of Dallas, acknowledged as a brilliant financier, had successively bought the National Hockey League Dallas Stars and the Major League Baseball Texas Rangers. Immediately, the operations of both clubs were combined except for player matters. Synergy—like combining broadcasting rights to leverage lucrative deals—was expected to reap wonders.

For the most part, it didn't work. As Stars president Jim Lites said in March 2002, "The process is completely logical. It looks like you can throw things together and get these efficiencies. [But] there just weren't efficiencies in many of the areas we tried."[3]

The Eckerd deal eventually went through. Penney paid a pretty price, and the Hutchens due diligence effort never uncovered what

3. Reprinted with permission of *The Dallas Morning News.*

St. Petersburg Times investigative reporter Mark Albright later referred to as the deal's "dirty little secrets."[4] Here were two big ones:

1. Eckerd's "shrinkage" (shoplifting, employee theft, etc.) had been significantly underreported. "Once Penney began accounting for losses at the rate Eckerd actually had been experiencing for years," Albright wrote, "it added a $74-million ball and chain to Eckerd's annual expenses in 1999."

2. Ten percent of Eckerd's stores were unprofitable and had to be closed. Eckerd officials said the stores were marked for closing before the company was acquired by Penney. But the deal, Albright reported, "went through so quickly that nobody had time to sort out the losers. Now it's become painfully obvious that JCPenney really was not buying profitable stores, just real estate." Asset write-down: $110 million.

As Albright wrote, "Such things happen when companies stray too far from what they know best."

More Dirty Little Secrets

After the Albright articles got around, more bad news bubbled up from other sources:

➤ No provision was made in the deal for the fact that data software at Eckerd was totally incompatible with Penney's.

➤ Not only that, the basic systems infrastructures could not interact. Penney ran a 56K frame relay system, Eckerd a satellite system designed by Accenture, the IBM arm, that was contracted for several more years.

➤ Reportedly, no one from JCPenney's information services spoke to their counterparts at Eckerd before the deal was signed.

4. This was of interest in the Tampa Bay area because of Eckerd's headquarters in Largo, a St. Petersburg suburb. This quote, along with the Albright quotes that follow, are reprinted by permission. Copyright © *St. Petersburg Times*, 1999, 2000, 2001.

➤ Eckerd was being sued by federal and state governments for fraud in filling managed-care prescriptions.

➤ There were also several public perception problems that were bound to hurt Eckerd earnings. Examples were Eckerd's low ranking for value and service and practical mistakes like forgetting to apply for pharmacy licenses in the confusion of all the store conversions.

➤ Eckerd had "gone private" earlier and carried the usual heavy debt associated with LBOs (leveraged buyouts). While deal accountants had to acknowledge this in so many words and numbers, its importance was obfuscated by burial in annual report "notes" (that few stockholders bother to read).

So how did synergistic catalog desks in 2,500 (net) Eckerd stores play out? Only 330 were installed before the program was tabled. In January 2001, Albright reported that the desks were being dismantled, beginning with immediate removal of two-thirds of them. Drugstore desks were "just a test," said Penney's new PR head, Rita Flynn. And all that easy prescription money from seniors in the South? The business was there, but as hospitals and physician groups have learned, contracting with managed-care providers requires the smarts and finesse of a derivatives dealer. A tricky task for a sideline.

Farewell

The Eckerd arc, from Oesterreicher's acquisition announcement in 1996 to Albright's reports, also follows and accents the overall decline of JCPenney's performance and market value along with a steady rise of confusion and panic in the ranks. Only the appearance of the *real* Wanda Wonder in mid-1999 and then shimmering Allen Questrom's arrival in late 2000 kept the situation from deteriorating into utter hopelessness.

Another thing the Eckerd arc described was the practical end of the traditional J. C. Penney operation. And one of the casualties was the lamentable disappearance of The Penney Idea as a companywide doctrine and discipline—especially the last and most quoted precept:

To test our every policy, method, and act in this wise: "Does it square with what is right and just?"

Gale Duff-Bloom, who had fought so hard to square company employment policy with what *was* right and just, would particularly feel the sting of this loss.

Madam Marketing

Some time after Oesterreicher had taken complete charge of the company, Barger Tygart, still the number-two man, called in Duff-Bloom and said, "I just sold Jim on the need to fix our marketing. He said, 'Do whatever you think.' And what I think is, you've got the best marketing instincts on this floor. You also know how to make things work. So you are now, or soon will be, Penney's new president of marketing."

Duff-Bloom was thrilled. This was a choice assignment, her first "line" responsibility and a chance to directly affect the company's bottom line. "Barger," she beamed, "I think I can fix things there. Thanks."

"I know you can if anyone can. But I also know you've now got too much to do. So Jim's bringing in Gary Davis, and he'll take administration and HR off your hands. You keep communications since it's a fit."

Duff-Bloom got results almost immediately. Meetings with the agency in the past had been tortuous, senior executives with no advertising background pontificating on things like art direction and music. Duff-Bloom stopped that. She brought in a top-notch executive art director, John Thomas, to fix the frumpy look of Penney's print. And, responding to a common complaint, she initiated an ambitious process to finally get merchandising, supply, advertising, and promotion all on the same page.

She fixed the talent problems (by going outside) but was less successful with a coordinated, well-focused marketing program. Her enemies here were three: turf troubles, the chairman's consensus management, and the deteriorating value of JCPenney merchandise. Still, the efficacy of Penney's marketing had clearly improved. So she was hardly prepared for what happened 18 months before her retirement.

You Mis*spoke?*

On a late January morning in 1999, Duff-Bloom entered the board-room for a management committee meeting. As she sat down and opened her folder, a team from administration was changing en-cased bulletin boards throughout the complex. The main printed poster announced several personnel changes and events. One of the names featured in boldface type was that of Gale Duff-Bloom. In the boardroom, until the meeting's end Duff-Bloom had no idea that she was in the company news that morning.

"Anything more?" asked the chairman.

"Just this." Gary Davis stood with some handouts, now ad-dressing the other committee members. "This is a press release from our New York PR firm. Went out first thing this morning—personnel changes."

"You know," Duff-Bloom cut in, speaking not to Davis but to Oesterreicher, "we ought to be careful about using those New York people too much. And remember, this is an area I know some-thing about from my days running investor relations." She ordi-narily disapproved of this kind of interruption. But she was certain that whatever Davis was passing out was of less immediate impor-tance than what was on her mind. And Howell had taught and encouraged her to always speak out in this meeting. "I know for a fact that Duncan Muir has to fix half the stuff they do, because they just don't know us well enough. In fact, why do we even use them? Duncan and his people can do anything the New Yorkers can do, and not screw it up in the process."

This statement was a direct affront to committee member Don McKay, Penney's CFO, who (exercising a senior officer perk) had retained the outside firm. The rationalization was that PR special-ists from the financial district could handle the likes of *The Wall Street Journal* more effectively. But Duff-Bloom was right: Muir could and did ably handle anything in the financial sphere.

McKay made his displeasure apparent, and Duff-Bloom re-turned a flat smile. As this happened, Davis flicked a look at Char-lie Lotter, corporate counsel. Lotter glanced at Oesterreicher, who rose and said, "Taken under advisement, Gale. And, okay." The meeting was ended.

"Wait for your copies," said Davis, as he began handing out the releases, beginning with Oesterreicher and working his way around the table—starting on the side *across* from where Duff-Bloom sat.

With committee members already filing out of either board-room door, she was one of the last to see that:

> "Scaling back her responsibilities in anticipation of full retire-ment in the near future, Gale Duff-Bloom is giving up presidency of JCPenney marketing. She retains company communications and corporate image. Her replacement will be sought through a marketing-oriented search firm. James E. Oesterreicher, Pen-ney's chairman/CEO, praised Ms. Duff-Bloom for her strong contributions to the company's marketing effort."

"*What?*" she blurted, eyes still on the sheet. She turned and rose, seeing Oesterreicher already at an open door. "Jim! We have to talk!"

But the chairman disappeared wordlessly and, as Duff-Bloom moved toward the door, Lotter and Davis stopped in the doorway to "chat"—literally running interference for the chairman.

"Well, 'gentlemen,'" Duff-Bloom seethed, "I guess *we* have to talk, as a poor substitute." And Gale Duff-Bloom, who had pre-viously outranked Lotter and Davis in every measurable way, moved with the men to the foyer of Davis's nearby suite.

In the minutes that followed, nothing was accomplished. Lot-ter, with the quickest mind on the Crescent, had finally gestured hopelessly and said, "Gale, it was just one of those things that slipped through the cracks." At that very moment, along came James E. Oesterreicher, bound for another appointment. "And *here* comes the biggest crack of all," she said, then shouting, "Jim!"

The chairman, looking surprised and distressed, pointed ahead and said, "Gale, I'm sorry, but I'm late."

"Too bad," she said, as Lotter and Davis backed off. She nodded into Davis's office and said, "We have to talk. *Now.*" Inside the office, Duff-Bloom shut the door on Davis and Lotter and faced the chairman. "Did we have a conversation about this? Ever? I don't recall one."

"Gale, I'm sorry. I guess I misspoke."

"You mis*spoke?*"

"Yes. I'm sorry. I'll do whatever I can. Should we send out an-other release?"

"Saying what? You've obviously made a decision. You just forgot to tell me about it."

"I'm sorry."

"That doesn't do much good, Jim. Not at this point." She turned and marched back to her own office, passing Cathy Rozelle wordlessly. She shut her office door, crossed to the couch, sat heavily, and began to cry silently.

It wasn't over. Days later John Thomas hosted a private dining room luncheon in her honor. Attending were all of Gale's direct reports and, incredibly, the chairman. After orders were taken, Oesterreicher tapped a glass and rose to speak. "It is an honor and a privilege," he said, "to thank Gale for the fine work she did on our marketing. I just wish I hadn't misspoken."

Thomas—who would angrily leave the company within the year after a few months under Gale's replacement—was not about to let the chairman off easily. "Do you realize, Mister Oesterreicher, what damage was done when you 'misspoke' to the *Dallas Morning News,* the *New York Times,* and *The Wall Street Journal?*"

Still later Duff-Bloom received a disturbing phone call from a New York friend she had met during her investor relations days. Previously, they had spoken immediately after the friend read about Gale in the New York papers.

"Gale," the friend had said, "I was shocked."

"*You* were shocked?" Gale had laughed.

Presently there was some gossip. "Gale, I thought you'd better hear this. Did you know that your chairman made a presentation to First Boston this morning?"

"Vaguely."

"Well, I covered it, and in the Q and A he said that Penney had retained an executive search firm—quote—'several months ago,' and he was expecting to announce a new marketing president soon."

"'Several months ago'?"

"Several."

"See?" Duff-Bloom said wistfully. "He can't even keep his own lies straight anymore."

Duncan Muir:

"Gale? I had been on vacation and heard about it upon my return. I was shocked. What they did was unconscionable and something you would *never* have associated with the old J. C. Penney. I went to Gale's office and told her how badly I felt—for her and for what this company had become. I said that, as of then, I was going to reconsider the VERP [voluntary early retirement plan] that I had turned down earlier. Clearly, the Penney Company was no longer the organization that I had eagerly joined years before."

(Muir retired soon after Duff-Bloom.)

Wonder Woman

In June 1999, Oesterreicher appointed Steve Farley, formerly with Payless Shoes, to head up marketing. Farley, who would last only 18 months with the company, immediately fired the ad agency of record (Temerlin McClain) and began searching for a replacement. He asked the candidates, as part of their pitch, to define a marketable image for JCPenney.

A month later the new COO, Vanessa Castagna, blew in like a hurricane. She had achieved breakthrough results at Wal-Mart in apparel merchandising. She was a smart, strong, and talented leader who was also imaginatively decisive. A tall, athletic-looking woman who wore high heels, she was an imposing presence who, with her take-charge manner, caused great consternation among the boys on the Crescent and below.

Castagna's arrival scored two Penney firsts. Never before had an outsider come in at such a high level, and never before had a woman been put in charge of running things day to day. As Gale Duff-Bloom observed with wry amusement, "This sent a signal that *nobody* could disregard. Things were going to change, big time."

Immediately Castagna began an exhaustive search to determine the true state of the company. After a few weeks of getting the headquarters drift, she hit the road to visit stores, distribution centers, and regional offices. Many in Plano were relieved to see her leave for a while, which was a mistake.

While Castagna was searching for the company's identity, and Farley was outsourcing the creation of one, Jim Oesterreicher seemed to lose further faith in the organization in which he had spent his entire career. Because of his consensus methods, he had always been partial to outside consultants (who relieved him and others of decision making). Now more and more consultants arrived at Legacy. By March 2000, Arthur Andersen (not yet notorious) had 26 separate projects working at JCPenney. It was the largest consulting effort ever launched in retail by Andersen, and the biggest consultancy contract in Penney history. And that was just Andersen. Other work was being done by PriceWaterhouse-Coopers, McKinsey, and KPMG.

Upon her return to Plano, Castagna began a remarkable reorganization effort. It was kept under wraps until mid-January 2000 when she held the biggest meeting since a companywide convention in 1925. The giant main ballroom of the Adam's Mark Hotel in downtown Dallas was the site. In attendance would be every one of JCPenney's 1,100 store managers plus several hundred district, regional, and Plano executives. Shock waves would emanate from this event, and they began the night before at a small gathering in the hotel when Castagna stood up and said:

> "When I joined JCPenney, I assumed that its store managers would be generally competent and up to speed. This did not turn out to be the case. When I joined the company, I also assumed that the correct systems and procedures would be in place. This did not turn out to be the case. Finally, when I joined the company, I assumed that senior management would at least be on top of things. This did not turn out to be the case, either. So I knew that I had really gotten myself into a challenging situation. But I thrive on challenges and I *never* back down on anything."

In the ballroom the next morning, there was the predictable motivational video with a sports metaphor. There was the predictable motivational speaker with lots of heart. And there was the predictable name speaker to give the event sizzle (a vague Colin Powell in his big-fee speaker days). Nothing very exciting so far, and when Jim Oesterreicher made his "welcome" speech, the audience began to wonder why Penney had bothered to bring everybody into the Adams Mark during such a time of pain and strain.

The first pages of Oesterreicher's speech typically beat around the bush before he moved into general statements about the pressing issues before them. Not very scintillating, and this was an audience that increasingly *needed* scintillation.

But then they got it, right between the eyes.

Castagna's speech was the most amazing thing they had ever heard. First of all, it was immediately clear that this woman was loaded with energy and charisma—as opposed to their beleaguered chairman, who an observer once said "had all the charisma of your local pharmacist."[5] Then, as Oesterreicher looked on from the wings with a pale, bland expression, the whole ballroom seemed to tilt on edge as Vanessa Castagna unloaded. Performing with an amiable and bright enthusiasm, what she *said* was absolutely stunning.

The store and catalog operations were, as of that day, entering a period of *total* reorganization (including retraining or replacing *anyone* who couldn't cut the mustard). And—yes, the impossible—the Penney methods were going to change, as everything from this day forward would be keyed to centralized merchandising! The historic J. C. Penney store autonomy would soon be a thing of the past! Moreover, Penney would change from a "pull" company to a "push" company!

Everyone was breathless. And well-designed, surprisingly detailed handouts would anchor her words in forward-march reality. How had she and her team accomplished all this in only a few months' time? For the changes coming were as comprehensive as they were revolutionary.

Then when Castagna finished speaking, an astonishing thing happened. This was an audience made up of many who would not survive the coming transition. It was an audience at least partially *responsible* for the company's crisis. And what was she doing now but basically taking them to task? Yet this audience was so starved for answers and leadership that they rose en masse and gave her a roaring, standing ovation!

5. From the November 25, 1999, *Dallas Observer* article "Penney Pinched," by Miriam Rozen; reprinted with permission.

chapter 26   Standing in His Underwear

IN THE NEXT FEW MONTHS, first impressions were confirmed: Castagna *was* a very forceful leader (too forceful for some, who began referring to her at watercoolers as "Can'tstandya"). By her forthright announcements and actions, it also became apparent to all that Oesterreicher's administration had been flatly inept. It was fascinating and embarrassing because there was no attempt to cover this up. On the contrary, she spoke to the point publicly. Again and again in simultaneous comments to the press and Penney associates, she referred to the company's "outmoded management" and the pressing need to "change our culture." (*What?!*)

Castagna began communicating to the ranks as no one in modern times had ever done before. With banners, posters, company-wide newsletters, and "Straight Talk" broadcasts, she laid out her plans and appealed for extra effort. It was time to "ACT!" ("Accelerating Change Together"). And it was hokey, yes. But it all seemed fresh and vital because it was so new to the modern JCPenney. In another first, she backed up her appeals with a personal pledge to work harder than anyone, to get results, and to never be less than 100 percent up front.

Yes, the hiring of Vanessa Castagna meant that the board of directors had *finally* done something right.

What Was Wrong with the Penney Board?

The reader may have wondered about Penney's board during the Howell and Oesterreicher years. Why were they seemingly so quiescent? Supposedly representing the best interests of stockholders, why were they apparently blinded to the lack of a solid plan for

the future—à la the company's historic reinvention cycle—
including a war chest? Why did they praise and reward the Howell
administration for record sales and profits in 1994 when the numbers were often "bought" with heavy promotion at the expense of
future inventory disarray and costly markdowns? And why did
they reward Howell so well when he retired? And, in so doing,
why did they set up the biggest payout so that Howell received it
after his bitter (and unsavory) divorce was finalized?

Dave Binzen[1] was a bright light in the New York merchandise
department for some 30 years. He retired in 1981 to pursue several
interests from a Vermont farm, having been known as a literate
and highly skillful executive with an upbeat demeanor. But in 1998
Binzen wrote an uncharacteristically angry letter to Jim Oesterreicher.

Binzen cited egregious mistakes by the Penney brass and very
poor oversight by the Penney board. It opened by calling the
board "incompetent" and its actions "outrageous." And what fu-
eled Binzen's complaint? Simply that he had known a time when
the Penney Company put ethics before business and thereby *built*
a great business. He had also personally known two of the three
great leaders in Penney history—Mr. Penney himself and Mil Batten. And he found the cast of characters in the '80s and '90s badly
wanting in comparison.

The Howell boards okayed the move to Dallas. For 86 years
before this move, J. C. Penney had thrived. In another 12 it was
nearly in the tank. Mil Batten had warned about disregarding the
intangible benefits of headquartering in New York City. But that is
a subtle and abstract concept and perhaps beyond a workaday
board's grasp (as it was certainly beyond Howell's). On the other
hand, wasn't it easily foreseen that the move to Texas might virtually destroy the company's wholesale buying expertise? Howell
may have been oblivious to the importance of the buying function, but a board is supposed to add perspective and balance to a
company's business. So where were they on this one?

What About Bentonville?

Perhaps the board was beguiled (as was Howell) by Wal-Mart's
ability to buy well in Bentonville, Arkansas, its home town and

---

1. Son of Bill Binzen, the early Penney vice president.

still where it is headquartered. Or, likewise, Target's success in Minneapolis. To this day, there are people at or recently retired from JCPenney who would swear that the company can buy as well in Dallas as in New York. So it's time to check a premise or two.

First of all, we are discussing JCPenney, not Wal-Mart or Target. We're talking about Penney's roots being in New York, as the other two chains have never left their own roots. And we're talking about the kind of defining soft-tone business Penney does, which is *done* in New York City more than anywhere else on earth by far. Why did most of Penney's professional buyers quit and *stay* there? Because that's where this particular action is.

Some, then, would quickly ask, "But what about L.A.? What about Hong Kong?"

They are satellites, important but no more than satellites. The situation could change, of course, and someday *New York* could become a satellite. Possible, although it really doesn't seem likely.

Most important, whereas Penney was torn from its roots, Wal-Mart and Target still *have* their roots. They never moved anywhere. They didn't lose their talent. They don't have amateurs posing as buyers. Penney still does. The others are booming. Penney is not. (Maybe it will with the new management, but it will have struggled for a time before it really does—*if* it does.) Companies are like people, as this book has endeavored to demonstrate. Uproot people, and bad things can often occur.

It is interesting to speculate how people like Bill Clinton's favorite fixer and longtime Penney board member, Vernon Jordan, did not get a handle on the acquired weaknesses in the company as a result of the move. And how about the board taking so long waking up to Jim Oesterreicher, a man clearly in over his head as CEO? The company's historic parochialism may be as close to an answer as we will ever have in this regard—and one that is hardly satisfying. Out of all my attempts to contact and interview the outside directors in the Howell and Oesterreicher years, only one director—George Nigh—bothered to reply. And Governor Nigh simply and politely declined. Not a word from the other 20.

There is, of course, a remarkable postscript to the mysterious ineptitude and inaction of the Penney board. After waiting far too long, and with equal mysteriousness, the board suddenly sprang into action. They hired Vanessa Castagna, arguably the best person in the world to take over the company on a day-to-day basis. The board gave her a mandate to institute the sweeping changes and, after a year, acted again with utterly surprising effectiveness. They brought in Allen Questrom, arguably the best person in the world to conceptually frame a possible recovery and provide incisive, classy leadership.[2]

The Trouble, in Brief

In May 2000, a month after Gale Duff-Bloom retired, perhaps the sorriest moment in the history of the J. C. Penney Company occurred in Lenexa, Kansas, a suburb of Kansas City. In order to fully appreciate this rank (and finally dramatic) episode, a brief philosophical review would be helpful.

The decline and fall of the Penney Company is a classic example of the curse of corporate arrogance. One imagines that around the country today there are bright and capable young men and women who, remaining ignorant of the lessons of business history, are condemned to repeat them on some future stage. They, it seems, will be the last to understand that if a company's leaders come to view their own presence and process as the heart of the business, a heart attack is bound to follow.

Over much of the twentieth century J. C. Penney was among the world's best-managed business organizations. It had been founded with a strong sense of identity that became even greater as it developed into a power. It had known what it was and where it stood, and so had its customers. A Main Street Penney store had been essentially about trustworthiness, service, and value.

In the march of years, however, the emphasis widened to include a variety of other businesses as the stores swelled with an ever-increasing range of merchandise including an emphasis on value fashions. With those changes, the difference between JCPenney and its competitors narrowed. What had been unique retailing became increasingly similar to everyone else's. Penney had shifted from being a company of merchants to an organization of managers, with its focus changing from serving customers and communities to maximizing sales and profits. Finally, the actions of its

2. Since his arrival, Questrom has apparently so dazzled the board with his erudition and leadership skills that the directors may at last be performing with some consistency of competence.

leadership became both soulless and silly. This was embarrassingly evident when a shareholders meeting was convened in the Kansas City suburb.

Giving Them an Earful

Lenexa? Why there? Well, it's where Jim Oesterreicher, the Penney board, and senior management traveled in an attempt to dodge the press and hold a potentially volatile shareholders meeting with little notice or damage. This plan did not work, of course, and the company's management was again exposed as the foolishly incompetent husks they had largely become.

Shareholders saw the ruse for what it was, and enough showed up in Lenexa to cause trouble. When Duff-Bloom read newspaper accounts of the shareholders meeting, she could only shake her head in tired dismay. Here is the sort of thing that she read, representative of the handful of reporters who attended:

JCPENNEY CATCHES HEAT FROM INVESTORS
THE RETAILER MOVED ITS ANNUAL MEETING TO KANSAS, BUT IT COULDN'T HIDE FROM ANGRY SHAREHOLDERS
St. Petersburg Times

PENNEY'S TOP RANKS CRITICIZED
SHAREHOLDERS BLAME CEO AND DIRECTORS
Dallas Morning News

J. C. PENNEY SHAREHOLDERS HAMMER CEO
Reuters

Officially, the shareholders meeting was moved to Lenexa in order to emphasize the company's excellent capability in catalog fulfillment. Lenexa was the location of a typically big Penney distribution center (like Don Seibert's original giant in Atlanta). Highly automated, the warehouses supplied stores and processed a stream of catalog orders—*and* JCPenney Internet sales. Filling orders was a big hang-up for most of the new Internet retailers, and Penney, because of its multibillion-dollar catalog business, found itself fortunately positioned to move as fast as JCPenney dot-com could go. In COO Vanessa Castagna's reorganization, Internet sales were to be a priority effort.

Nevertheless, because the real reason for Lenexa was obvious to everyone, no attendee was in a mood to cut management any slack.

Past meetings had been embellished with fashion shows, videos, and other production values. Not this one. Held in a plain, open room at the warehouse, the meeting was as minimalist as possible. Folding chairs with a center aisle faced a small stage made of hotel-type risers with a curtain backing. On the stage were other chairs and a miked podium. The PA system and mikes on stands for the audience completed the staging.

In attendance were the board and senior management, with chairman Jim Oesterreicher conducting the meeting. Beforehand, reporters familiar with the Penney beat had agreed that with Oesterreicher's announcement of his pending retirement, it was time for him to finally communicate with some candor and clarity. All the same, just as in his opening remarks at the Adam's Mark meeting, he piled bromide upon cliché and then made fanciful projections as—never losing his dogged faith in "synergism"—he argued for the stockholders' confidence. But with his company in disorder, its stock down the tubes and little synergism actually in sight, the effect was the opposite. Only the stockholders' anger kept them from dozing off.

Finally, Oesterreicher went through the meeting formalities. In a sort of class action, a key piece of legislation was up for a vote. Proposed by Calpers, the giant pension fund, this would considerably increase director accountability. The proxy count was read, and the proposition was defeated, but only by a whisker—to the vocal disappointment of the audience and the visible relief of the directors and officers. Little else raised similar interest until it was time for commentary from the floor.

Now angry shareholders came to the audience mikes. Ten people managed to speak. The criticism ranged from management failures to excessive compensation. Nobody was remotely complimentary, everyone highly exercised. But one speaker's moment was so dramatic and struck such a nerve that his remarks were summarized in virtually every newspaper account from Dallas to St. Petersburg to London.

The Loss-Prevention Manager

Gary and Dee Nystrom hefted his scooter into the station wagon and drove from their Vacaville home to the Sacramento airport.

Since Gary's accident and disability, travel had been particularly difficult. Today it became worse because of severe weather in the Midwest. Instead of flying direct from California to Kansas City, they would have to route through Seattle and land in Omaha, driving the last leg. They managed to check the scooter on Northwest, and the airline found Gary a wheelchair for the trip to the gate.

After 21 years in the U.S. Air Force, Nystrom had retired at the rank of master sergeant in 1987. He became a loss-prevention manager at two JCPenney stores between the Bay Area and Sacramento, also becoming devoted to the company's traditions. Then, at the time of Penney's accelerating decline in 1998, Nystrom was hit by a car and sustained serious neck and back injuries. The surgery was botched and he went on total disability.[3] (He can stand for short periods and walk short distances, but he has to be careful. He spends a lot of time in pain on his back or in a hot bathtub.)

As a positive distraction, Nystrom has become a sort of "father communicator" to an e-mail group of Penney retirees and long-time employees. He also regularly writes Penney management (with input from his group). While impressed with Castagna and aware of the handicaps of Penney insularity, he is one of those who has never been convinced that the traditional Penney company had to be totally abandoned.

In March 2000, Nystrom decided to attend the upcoming shareholders meeting and make a statement from the floor. He e-mailed requests for ideas and language, then began writing and handing material to Dee for editing. When he learned about the shift in the meeting's location, rewriting began on his already unsparing remarks. He would issue a blanket condemnation of the board, of Oesterreicher, and of company officers.

The Nystroms arrived in Lenexa late in the evening but did not check into the motel immediately. Instead, they drove the route to Penney's distribution center in order to eliminate surprises and be certain of the timing. The meeting would start early the next morning, and Gary had to be ready.

As they drove, the Nystroms passed a Dairy Queen. Had they arrived several hours earlier, they would have seen an odd sight in a drive-through that usually saw more humble traffic. To scout

---

3. Collecting benefits has been a constant hassle, with his major medical fortunately covered through his wife's government job.

meeting site preparations before retiring to their hotel, Oester-reicher and a company party had driven to Lenexa in limousines. The chairman felt hungry and told the driver to pull into the DQ. As the trailing limo followed suit, both highway passers-by and DQ employees were treated to the sight of two dark limousines in line for burgers and shakes. What well-to-do people would be so eccentric? Was it a rock band or a Mafia party? No, it was JCPenney management!

A Rightfully Angry Man

That night, after practicing and practicing his presentation, Gary had trouble sleeping. Blessedly, his neck and back were just stiff. His problem was excitement and apprehension. His nerves did not abate in the morning after he mumbled the presentation over coffee and then put away a hearty breakfast. It wasn't fear of making a public address—he was steeled to the idea and the importance of the event. The nervousness came from a growing concern about messing up his opportunity. As they drove their pretested route in plenty of time, his apprehension grew.

Nystrom steered his scooter into the distribution center meeting room and parked it by one of the audience mikes. Seated two rows back were Walt Neppl and his colleague from times past, Bob Gill. Neppl and Gill, retired 18 and 9 years respectively, had been unhappily comparing notes on the company's dismal performance. Walt then looked around at the bare-bones setting, at the podium and mike, and shut his eyes with a sigh. He was instantly back making a speech himself just before retiring:

> "I'm proud of our management team and because I know these people and how we've all grown, I have no qualms about leaving the company. I think we've created a highly effective team environment and a powerful management. The future looks super. One thing, though. I said 'no qualms.' I didn't say no regrets. You can't work with the Penney people I have and not be terrifically impressed. I'm going to miss these guys."

"Hey, Walt," Said Gill with a smile, nudging Neppl's shoulder. "You're daydreaming."

Neppl opened his eyes and nodded. "And you know what,

Bob? I was wrong about some people back when I retired. Not you, of course. But some."

Nystrom pulled the presentation from his coat pocket and began rereading the words. He had done so on the plane, had practiced the speech in the car from Omaha and several times at the motel, and this morning he'd mumbled it at breakfast. Still, his hands trembled and the paper stuck to his fingers.

Oesterreicher began the meeting . . . and, it seemed, in no time Nystrom was raising his hand, was acknowledged by the chairman, and was beginning to read:

> "Mr. Chairman and members of the board of directors. First, I want to thank all of the stockholders who were able to make this meeting, as well as those attending in spirit only. Many stockholders feel that you moved this meeting for the sole purpose of limiting who could or would attend. Well, I am going to speak for those absent individuals today."

It was not going well. His voice was breathy and cracked with emotion, his eyes glued to the words and his wet hands gripping the paper so hard that he feared ripping it.

> "Mr. Chairman, I personally want to tell you, the directors, and other senior managers how very disappointed I am in each of your performances with regard to the leadership and operation of this fine company. Each of you should be ashamed of yourself."

His heart was racing and he was having difficulty getting his breath.

> "All of you have failed in your fiduciary responsibilities to JCPenney shareholders. You have (1) failed to maintain our confidence, (2) failed to maintain shareholder value, (3) failed to communicate to us, (4) failed to properly adjust compensation for poor performance, (5) failed to remove people who have not performed at acceptable levels, and (6) failed to maintain the morale of the associates. But instead, at a time when the market value of our stock has plummeted, and the company has performed so poorly as to become a takeover candi-

date, the board increased management salaries and gave a new severance package to senior managers and possibly them-selves."

He had to choke back tears at this point. Every eye in the audience was on him, every eye on the stage cast downward.

"This board has gone against the wishes of Mr. Penney, who believed that management should be paid a salary and their bonus should reflect their performance. According to a recent Bloomberg article, the chairman's performance has gone from bad to worse to terrible in the biggest bull market ever. And you? You have almost doubled his salary!"

Now Nystrom did start crying. So he shouted his next words in order to be understood.

"Well, do you know what the chairman should be doing today by Mr. Penney's standards? He should be standing here in his underwear!"

There was a sound from the audience, a quick exhalation of pleasant surprise accompanied by some random claps. All of the reporters were taking notes. Now gaining control of his voice, Nystrom went on to detail several of the transgressions and call for the CFO's resignation. He also called for a new accounting firm along with an emergency audit and report, with emphasis on the Eckerd acquisition. He concluded by calling for Oesterreicher's im-mediate resignation.

The chairman said, "Thank you, Gary," and went on to con-clude the meeting. After a brief and tightly controlled press confer-ence with the board and officers, the reporters all headed quickly outside—along with the PR head, Rita Flynn, who said she was going for a smoke.

On the curb, Nystrom waited in his scooter for Dee to drive up. He was downcast and exhausted, convinced that the whole trip had been an exercise in futility. Then the surprises began. By the time Dee drove up, Mark Albright of the *St. Petersburg Times*, Maria Halkias of the *Dallas Morning News*, Carey Gillam of Reuters, and the rest of the press contingent were crowded around in an appreciative interviewing session. Rita Flynn hovered nearby, an ear bent to the questions and answers. After Nystrom answered the last question, there was a tap on his shoulder. Walt Neppl stepped into view and reached to shake hands. "Gary? I'm Walt Neppl. I used to work for Penney's."

"Oh, my gosh, Mr. Neppl, I know my Penney history. It's an honor, sir."

"Well, I just wanted you to know that Bob Gill over there and I listened closely to what you had to say, and we thought you made some interesting points."

"Thank you, sir. Thank you very much."

It was a wonderful trip back to Vacaville. Worrisome thoughts about the lost traditional company were suppressed until the Nystroms got home.

chapter **27**   The Funeral and HCSC

GALE DUFF-BLOOM WAS INTERVIEWED for the last time in the summer of 2002. She is a strong personality, and her retired contentment is no act. She is relaxed and happy, and she talks about grandchildren, travel, some speaking engagements, and reunions with Penney people from the past. But she still hurts. As the interview concluded, she asked to make a statement, a summary of her life at Penney's. Here it is:

> "I was aware of problems and I worried about them, but I must say that altogether I was very happy with my career at JCPenney. I made many wonderful friends. I feel like I had six careers in one company. I had the opportunities and took advantage of them and worked hard and loved it, loved what I did and loved the people. Of course in 31 years you're going to have some good times and some hard times, and I experienced both. But when I think back on the Penney Company, back on my career, there was just a whole lot that I brought home from what I learned at JCPenney and a whole lot about who I was at home that I took back to JCPenney. I think I contributed to a lot of people's lives—they tell me that. Every function that I attend today where I run into Penney people, I am told that I'm missed, and I think it's sincere. And there's great love from me to many, many Penney associates."

At this point she hesitated—one had to know her well to even notice it. But she hesitated, and then as she finished her statement there was the slightest catch in her throat, her face showing the slightest change in coloring, as though a cloud were passing overhead:

"So, after 29 years, with the turf wars and the lack of trust, the lack of common decency, the last two years were not good. We had forgotten The Penney Idea, which, with all the rest, was a shame. Still, again, looking back, for the most part it was a great ride in a wonderful company, and they can never take that away."

Jimmy-O Comes Through

When Vanessa Castagna took over day-to-day operations with vision, skill, guts, and panache, a greater contrast to Jim Oesterreicher could not be imagined—until Allen Questrom arrived. And, even among the best, the most resolute of men, the cascade of woe that Oesterreicher went through before his forced retirement would have been totally subduing. The flogged CEO would have shuffled through the final wreckage of his career bent in abject humiliation. But not Jimmy-O, the Farmer.

Oesterreicher went through his last months at JCPenney with his back straight and his chin up. Having made many mistakes—including moral slippage regarding Duff-Bloom and the self-centered recklessness of the Eckerd deal—he concluded his career once again trying to do the right thing. It was a mystifying performance that had to be admired.

His last official act came when radiant Allen Questrom was the new Penney presence. The venue was an HCSC Club annual convention in Orlando, a convening of retirees who wore the pin. There could not have been a less receptive audience for Oesterreicher—the man they blamed for their loss of net worth. At the big banquet, he was introduced in a perfunctory and brief manner that was almost rude.

And what did he do? He walked to the podium and produced the trademark out-of-synch Oesterreicher smile, then began his speech stupidly with a couple of bad jokes about the weather. Next, after a sorry segue that compared changeable climates to the stock market, he told them how good it was for everyone there to be together. You could have heard a pin drop. And, at a front table, no doubt Allen Questrom and his wife, Kelli, wished they were anywhere else *but* there as Oesterreicher acknowledged them and asked them to stand. Next, he also acknowledged and thanked his wife, Pat, who stood with a proud smile (as possibly the only happy person at a ballroom table).

Then—talk about guts—a totally surprising thing happened. He addressed the reality of the moment in a strong, clear voice. And then he apologized! Finally he called Questrom to the podium, shook his hand, and said, "Allen, I'm sure that now this company is going to be just fine."

Robust applause rose from the audience, the ex-chairman now descending to the front table. There he kissed his wife, both Oesterreichers smiling at each other and no doubt unmindful that the level of applause was for the savior who was heard to gracefully repeat "Thank you, Jim" three times and then begin a new era.

Good-bye, My Friend

"One of the toughest duties I ever had was Don's funeral," said Walt Neppl, who was the same age, 78, when his friend passed away. "We were so close. Each of us had strengths the other didn't, and together we were a great team. At my age, we're supposed to accept these things. But I don't know. It was hard to say good-bye to Don."

Don Seibert's funeral was held on the last day of August 2000. With his family and friends, Seibert's second family of Penney people moved slowly into the church. As both close friend and Penney person, Walt Neppl was the surviving leader of that special senior congregation. They were people who had been part of one another's lives as their respective careers had crisscrossed the country over the years. Theirs was a bond beyond the norm in the corporate world, all sharing fond memories and belief in the founder's watchwords of honor, confidence, service, and cooperation. All of the men wore the HCSC lapel pin that day.

They had attended the kids' weddings, the conferences, the reunions. And the funerals. This year had already claimed legendary Penney leader Mil Batten.[1] Now another was gone, and during a time of bewilderment and despair about their company.

Neppl had been well known within JCPenney as someone to-

---

1. Longevity seemed to often go with the top jobs at Penney. The founder, of course, was 95 when he died; Batten was 89; and Ray Jordan (who died in 2003) was 98.

tally without cant. What you saw was what you got, and today you saw real grief. He did his best with nodding acknowledgments and muted greetings, but he was relieved to finally be able to sit with his wife, Marian, and shut his eyes.

When he opened them, he saw a younger Penney person who was not part of this sad ritual of reunion. Jim Oesterreicher had arrived with his wife, Pat. They sat at the side, apart from Neppl and the other old warhorses—who looked in Oesterreicher's direction with no love in their eyes. They had all lost paper fortunes[2] and, almost worse, had seen the diminution of their company's great stature. The once-grand chain bore little resemblance to the organization that had shaped the lives of so many in today's gathering. It had passed from being their company to something pretentious and then vastly troubled.

Yet one had to respect the quiet decency of Oesterreicher on this day. He had made the effort to attend the service despite the painful disarray of his last days in office.

Other great changes had occurred since Seibert's last days in charge.

Neppl recalled the idea that Seibert and he had worked on prior to retirement: the way to develop a smaller, younger company's energy and speed of response—the way to drive individual responsibility into the gut of the organization. What the idea needed—but never got—was a commitment from Seibert's handpicked successor, dynamic Bill Howell. Instead, Howell of course went his own way to "America's department store," to Dallas, and to the three most profitable years in company history. Then he retired just before the problems surfaced.

Neppl was aware of something else about Howell that Seibert had mentioned to only a very few during his final illness. After taking over, Howell became the first Penney leader who never sought counsel or comment from his predecessor. In fact, he avoided all but the obligatory contacts like board meetings. Unlike any other Penney chief in the company's history, Howell kept his own counsel. Seibert had finally recognized his complete misjudgment of the man. So to Neppl and the other few in the congregation who knew this, it was appropriate that Howell was the one person conspicuous in his absence today.

2. JCPenney stock had dropped from $78 to $8!

Those who did pack the church were soon moved by words and music that spoke to them of life, mortality, and remembrance. After the final notes from the brass choir faded, there was a reception set amid photographs and mementos of the former chairman.

Penney people gathered in small clusters, sharing news of events since their last meeting. And then without exception they quietly began asking each other about the J. C. Penney Company. Walt Neppl told friends that he felt doubly betrayed—by Seibert's death and by the performance of their once-cherished company.

"Who would ever have thought," he wondered out loud, then taking a breath, "that this could happen to J. C. Penney?"

What If?

As of this writing, Vanessa Castagna *has* changed the Penney culture. And there is certainly no hard argument against the course Questrom and Castagna took. The old company was just too far gone. Too many incompetents were on the bridge. Drastic measures had to be taken. And, recalling the mutinous stockholders who tried to unseat the great Mil Batten, there is no room for sentiment in business.

Despite all the key people Castagna and Questrom have brought in from the outside, however, and despite all the new systems and procedures, the JCPenney makeover remains an extraordinary demanding endeavor. And to what final avail?

Whatever happens, one can't help wondering what the effect would have been if the same mandate, the same brains, the same energy and talent had been applied to the traditional company in order to get *it* turned around.

Remember that for most of the twentieth century the J. C. Penney Company was a big winner. So could it somehow have survived in its original form? Could the traditional operation somehow have succeeded in the early twenty-first century? Probably not. But are we absolutely sure? No. There are two reasons. First, the real J. C. Penney leadership was quite troubling after W. R. Howell (né Bill) took over. From then on, those in the executive suite increasingly postured as Penney people, paying lip service to HCSC and The Penney Idea while other things dominated their agendas. This culminated in the move to Texas.

Running a company built upon the concept of thrift and hard

work first, rewards second, the Howell administration tore JCPenney from its roots because they wanted to live in affordable Mc-Mansions on golf courses in gated communities. They wanted easy commutes and commodious office suites with custom-made views. They wanted geographic centrality with a good, accessible airport. While the old generations ate, slept, and drank merchandise and stores and put up with any abuse and inconvenience in communion, the Howell crew was dedicated to getting the numbers and driving the stock.

The second reason is that however informed and sound it may be, the Castagna/Questrom makeover has a weakness. The stores are going to have a chic, updated, uncluttered look with a strategically narrow and deep inventory. The centrally bought merchandise itself will have a chic, updated, uncluttered presence with strategically coordinated advertising and sales floors—with promotional items in stock. (It used to be that the chances of finding a preprint-advertised item at the store was no better than 50/50.)

There is only one problem.

JCPenney will seem like everyone else. Or, at least like those who operate pretty much the same way, and there are several. Whereas the traditional J. C. Penney Company always stood out, always offered unique combinations of value and service and had the local heartbeat of a *person.*

Ah, but the reader has just thought, "The traditional company didn't have centralized buying. How could those cluttered and dowdy stores compete today?" Well, the esteemed Walt Neppl, weeks shy of his 80th birthday roast, had an answer to the first complaint:

"Whoever said centralized buying was bad? I certainly didn't. The problem, as always, is execution. Execution is where the company broke down, in my opinion, not whether or not to buy centrally."

And how to fix unexciting, confused stores? Check the premise at work in Plano when the Questrom team assumed full command. Big Brother and Big Sister *had* to start calling the shots. To restate the case, any director would have heartily approved *any* radical move Questrom wished to make (having already approved what Castagna had been doing for a year).

But the *only* way? James Cash Penney built a retail empire by tirelessly searching out the very best raw managerial candidates, relentlessly training them, providing them with the opportunity of a lifetime, swearing them to the cause, and then trusting them as responsible *individuals* to succeed. Result? An army of fiercely competitive individuals who were bonded into a cooperative fraternity of honorable achievers. Of course, there was a wide range of competence among them, from relative dolts to the really extraordinary people like Jack Maynard. *Overall*, however, they were a force of remarkable power—only fading in stature when values and standards diminished, management lost its merchant/merchandise balance, and the cancers of bureaucracy and nepotism spread.

So what if an idealized version of Mil Batten had taken over Penney early enough to stomp those out—along with the creeping status-seeking arrogance? Could the traditional company have *then* prospered into the twentieth-first century?

Yes, it seems, if Honor still had currency with employees, suppliers, and customers.

Yes, if the Confidence of an executive's convictions stood stronger than consensus and committees.

Yes, if Service to the customer and the community—however defined in contemporary America—was still rewarded by the customer's patronage.

And yes, if Cooperation still made an organization hum and business relationships soar.

It's hard to deny the ghosts and echoes of the past.

acknowledgments

Again and again I have read and heard about the Golden Age of Publishing and it's a shame that this book's wondrous editor, Ellen Kadin, wasn't born 30 years earlier. The book world of that time would have been privileged. The same thought extends to Ms. Kadin's editorial colleague Christina McLaughlin, who, in just one reading of an earlier manuscript, gave a trenchant and helpful critique. Likewise, I am particularly grateful for development editor Barry Richardson's sensitivity, keen eye, and wonderful touch. The woman who connected me to these people is my agent, Denise Marcil, whose attention to artistic and business detail make her another throwback to that Golden Age.

I am also indebted to my friend John Shostrom of *Sports Illustrated* for his adroit copyediting and excellent advice over the long course of writing this book. Erika Spelman, as well, kept everything together and on course during the book's production, and Georgia Maas did a fine job of vetting the final-final manuscript.

These acknowledgments do not include the many people who are mentioned in the book's introduction or who appear in its text. So this paragraph is about the others who consistently surprised me with their amiable generosity as mentors, conduits, or willing sources of information—when, often as not, I just appeared out of the blue by mail, e-mail, fax, or phone line. Just listing them here can hardly begin to express my gratitude: Laura Castoro, Bill Conlin, Gordon Curry, Jim Davis, Mark Donald, Terry Eckert, John Hare, Dr. Marcia Kropf, James MacLean, John Mersereau, Joe Murphy, Jeff Pirtle, Ann Rule, and Richard Whittingham. Also—for their patience and professionalism—Kevin O'Sullivan of AP/Wide World and David Woo of *The Dallas Morning News*.

Finally, there were valuable contributions from other Penney people who are still employed by the company and wished to remain anonymous.

index

Ackerman, Bruce, 153, 176–178, 180–182, 185–187
Albright, Mark, 258, 259, 276
Alcorn, Bill, 256
Allen, Ted, 110–111
anchor stores, 100, 113, 146
anti-chain movement, 73–74
Arthur Andersen, 265
AT&T, 121
Autenrieth, Caroline, 42n.3
automated warehouses, 126

Baker, Kay, 174
Bass, Paul, 99–100
Batten, Kathryn, 66, 89
Batten, William M. (Mil), 92, 158n.2
    on change, 1
    on conventions, 131
    criticisms of, 160
    and dealing with stockholders, 9–10
    early career of, 63–75
    expert opinions sought by, 162
    and headquartering in New York, 268
    on insularity, 163
    Johnson's criticism of, 13–15
    at Lansing store, 66–75
    and lessons learned from Penney, 16–19
    and management training program, 88–90
    and Maynard's tension over economy, 79–80

"The Memo" of, 112–114, 119
military service of, 96
and move to Dallas, 150
on move to New York, 149
move to New York by, 90
and Penney's formality, 15–16
and Penney's judgment of character, 15–19
and promotion to first man, 76–79
on reactions to power, 1
and rehabilitation of Penney's reputation, 10–11
and rose bush sales, 81–84
Seibert recommendation by, 127
and transaction recorder development, 119–126
as visionary, 128
Binzen, Bill, 82–83
Binzen, Dave, 2, 268
"The Blue Blazer Convention," 133
board of directors, 267–270
The Body of Doctrine, 36–37, 112
    see also The Penney Idea
"The Book," 119
Borch, Fred, 123, 124
brown goods, 129, 255
"Building for the Future" video, 165–166
bureaucracy, 148, 239–243
buying function
    centralization of, 87n.1, 283
    competition between retailing and, 145–148

buying function (*continued*)
  for early Golden Rule stores, 23, 24
  managers' involvement in, 30–31
  New York office for, 31–32
  and open-to-buy agreement for fashions, 85–87
  for Penney's Golden Rule stores, 30–31
  unethical business practices in, 146–147
  see also merchandising

C. J. Rouser Drug Store, 74
Caldwell, Robin, 216–217
Callahan, Tom, 22, 24, 29
Carlson, Kris, 250
Carson, Johnny, 149
cash sales concept, 23, 24, 113
Castagna, Vanessa, 264–267, 269–270, 279, 282
catalog operations, 113, 126, 257, 259
Catalyst, 128n.3
Catalyst Award, 211–214, 238
centralized buying, 87n.1, 283
CEOs, 92–93, *see also specific names*
chain stores, 73–74
character judgment (by Penney), 15–19
Citibank, 124
City National Bank, 53–54
civic involvement, *see* community service
Cody, John, 235, 251
Coleman, C. W., 63–65
Collins, Charlie, 203–204, 216, 234
communications to outsiders, 2
community service, 17, 46, 73–74
confidence, 37
conformity among managers, 133–139
consensus management style, 139n.7
consumer credit, 113–114
conventions
  district managers' meeting of 1980, 131–134

national, 41
regional, 41
  in Sale Lake City (1913), 36–37
Convery, Jerry, on Howell's favorite music, 159
cooperation, 37
Creating an American Institution (Mary Elizabeth Curry), 2
credit ratings (of stores), 24
credit sales, 113–114
Curry, Gordon, 167–173
Curry, Mary Elizabeth, 2
customer value, profit vs., 230–231

Dallas
  headquarters facilities in, 165–172, 197, 199–200, 210, 229–230
  move to, 149–158, 268–269
The Dallas Morning News, 191
data recovery, 113, 119, *see also* transaction recorder
Davis, Gary, 250, 261–262
death
  of Berta Penney, 33–34
  of James Penney, 20
  of Earl Sams, 91
  of Don Seibert, 280
Department Store of the '80s concept, 143
Derby, Earl, 99
designer clothing
  foreign, 148
  by Hankins, 175–182, 184–188
Diana, Princess of England, 149
direct marketing insurance, 255n.1
district managers' meeting of 1980, 131–134
diversity, 128–129, 233–234, *see also* inclusion
drugstore retailing, 255
Duff-Bloom, Gale, 8, 197–207
  advancement of, 208–210
  and announcement of retirement, 261–264
  on career at Penney's, 278–279
  and Catalyst Award, 238

and concern about Oesterreicher's
    abilities, 244
on Dallas facilities, 157–158
and Department Store of the '80s
    concept, 143
and Eckerd Drug deal, 256–257
financial expertise of, 208
and Hankins as designer, 177–182
and Howell's LPGA speech, 189–
    190, 192–193
and ideas for changing bureau-
    cracy, 240–243
and inclusion programs, 212–216
and Lenexa shareholders meeting,
    271
and loss of Penney Idea, 260
marketing changes made by, 260
on responsibility for company's
    fall, 159–160
and San Francisco retail confer-
    ence, 235–237
and sponsorships of St. James,
    174–175
Warrington College speech of,
    231–235
Dunn, J. C., 131–134

Eckerd Corporation, 255–259
Eddins, Hal, on Seibert's challenges
    as CEO, 127–128
Edwards, Carol, 190–196, 219–224,
    228
Eggleston, Elmer, 58–60
Elsie, Mrs., 69–70, 82
employee complaints, Maynard's
    handling of, 66–67
esprit de corps, 44, 45
ethics, 37, 146–147, 268
executives
    emphasis on breadth of experi-
        ence for, 161
    financial assistance from, 43
    see also managers

Farley, Steve, 264
fashion, 31
    credibility of, 148–149
    expansion of lines in, 143–144

foreign designers for, 148
and Hankins as designer, 175–
    182, 184–188
open-to-buy agreement for,
    85–87
as store emphasis, 130–131
and young men's apparel line, 134
Federated Department Stores,
    123–124
Fickert, Mark, 253
financing (of early J. C. Penney
    stores), 34–35
first man position, 76–78
Fitzgerald, F. Scott, 38
five-year plan, 117
Flynn, Rita, 259, 276, 277
Fulcomer, Dave, 2, 151–153
fund-raising campaign (for Penney),
    49–58

General Electric (GE), 123–125
generosity (of Penney), 15
Gill, Bob, 138, 209, 274–275, 277
Gillam, Carey, 276
Golden Rule stores
    of Johnson and Callahan, 21–27
    Penney's early ownership of,
        27–29
    Penney's start in, 21–27
    renaming of, 34
Gosnell, Joan, 231
Gottl, Marti, 165–166
Graham, Kerry, 94, 191, 195, 196,
    220–221
Great Depression, 51–55, 79
Grove, Andy, 161

Haake, Tony, 177, 178, 181
Hailey, Jim, 176
Halkias, Maria, 276
Halston, 143
Hankins, Anthony Mark, 175–182,
    184–188, 229
HCSC, 37, 163–165, 284
Henderson, Ralph, 126
Herbert, J. I. H., 34
Hess, Mrs., 105–106
Hicks, Tom, 257

Hitchcock, Mrs., 105–106
honor, 37
Hooper, H. B., 45
Hovey, Bill, 204–206
Howell, William (W. R., Bill), 127
    boards under, 268
    and career of Duff-Bloom, 204,
        210–212
    and Catalyst Award, 238
    as CEO, 158–162, 230
    as CEO choice, 138
    and Duff-Bloom's comments on
        bureaucracy, 240–243
    and inclusion policy, 209,
        211–213
    and LPGA convention speech,
        194–196, 201, 219–228
    and merchandising divisions cre-
        ation, 144–145, 148
    and move to Dallas, 150–158,
        163–164
    name change by, 158
    and name of Dallas headquarters,
        168–169
    and Oesterreicher's promotion,
        251
    and Penney's view of financial
        community, 208
    self-reliance of, 281
    and sponsorships of St. James,
        174–175
Hughes, Al, 38, 79, 112
    Batten as assistant to, 16
    and Batten's potential in com-
        pany, 90
    criticisms of, 160
    and rose bush sales, 83
    and "too much" profit, 231
Hutchens, Tom, 181, 182, 235, 236,
        251, 256
Hyer, Wilk, 45, 46, 92

IBM, 121–123
inclusion, 128–129, 193–194, 209,
        211–216
    LPGA convention speech on,
        189–196, 211, 219–228

    Warrington College speech on,
        231–235
incorporation of stores, 34
individualism, lack of, 133–139
inflexibility of management,
        239–240
insularity, 2–3, 161
internal truth, 89
Isaacs, Moe, 35

J. C. Penney Company (JCPenney),
        35
    business credo of, 37
    decline and fall of, 159–160, 259,
        270–271
    and financing of early stores,
        34–35
    and growth of chain, 38
    and names of company, 128n.3
    New York City office of, 35–36
    present makeover of, 282–284
    and responsibility for company's
        fall, 159–160
    sidelines of, 255n.1
    store configurations of, 100
Jackson, Jack, 127
JCPenney Classic, 213
JCPenney Eminent Scholar honora-
        ria, 216
Johnson, Guy, 22–25
Johnson, Roy, on Batten's running of
        company, 12–14
Jordan, Ray, 9–12, 14–15
Jordan, Vernon, 269
judgment of character (by Penney),
        15–19

Kellogg Sanitarium, 58–60
Kennedy, Jim, 152, 167, 173
Keys, John, 65–66
Kimball, Mary, 42n.3
Klein, Lucille, on changes in com-
        pany, 163
Klepper, Mr., 104–106
KPMG, 265
Kreps, Juanita, 128
Kudsk, Sören, 97, 98

Lakers, Pete, 98, 99
Lang, Kim, 94, 190–191, 195, 196,
    219–224, 227, 228
Lansing J. C. Penney store
    Batten's early career at, 66–75
    and Depression economy, 79–80
    first man coholder concept at,
        77–78
    management training program at,
        89
    Maynard's appointment to, 46–47
    and open-to-buy agreement,
        85–87
    rose bush sale at, 81–84
    sales per square foot at, 87
Lansing State Journal, 47–48
LaRovere, Ralph, 182–184, 187–188
Lazarus, Ralph, 123–124
Lenexa shareholders meeting,
    271–276
Levi Strauss, 44, 235, 236
Lites, Jim, 257
Litwak, Debbie, 215
Lotter, Charlie, 261–262
LPGA convention speech, 189–196,
    211, 219–228
luck, 92

Macy's, 143
Maher, Marian, 97
Main Street stores, 100
management style
    consensus, 139n.7
    of Maynard, 66–69, 108
    of Neppl, 108
    of Oesterreicher, 139n.7
    of Seibert, 108–109
Management Training Program,
    88–90
managers
    backgrounds of, 38–39
    community service by, 17
    early buying trips of, 30–31
    of early stores, 38–41
    financial assistance to Penney
        from, 43
    lack of original thinking by,
        133–139

and open-to-buy agreement,
    85–87
and partnership concept, 32
tension between buyers and, 31,
    145
The Man with 1,000 Partners, 41
marketing, 144, *see also* merchandising
Marshall, Bill, 116–117
Maynard, Irene, 49, 50, 69–70
Maynard, Jack, 92
    and Batten's early career, 66–75
    and Batten's promotion to first
        man, 76–79
    community service of, 73–74
    and fund-raising for Penney,
        44–51
    lifestyle of, 70
    management style of, 66–69, 108
    and management training program, 87–89
    merchandising style of, 71–73, 81,
        82
    and rose bush sales, 81–84
    and tension over economy, 79–80
McCaffrey-McCall, 130–131
McKay, Don, 261
McKinsey Company, 265
McMahon, Peggy, 130–131
Mechem, Charlie, 201, 211, 221
"The Memo," 112–114
merchandising
    and creation of "merchandising
        divisions," 144–145, 147–148
    and fashion credibility, 148–149
    lack of emphasis on, 241
    Maynard's style of, 71–73, 81, 82
    and open-to-buy agreement for
        fashions, 85–87
    Seibert's style of, 105, 106, 130
    Torrey's style of, 39n.2
    and uniformity of merchandise,
        81
    see also buying function
"merchandising divisions," 144–145,
    147–148
micromanagement, 167n.2
Miller, Dave, 134, 151, 209

Miller, Roy, 97, 98
minorities in workforce, 128–129
money, James Penney's attitude
    toward, 7–9
Morath, Kathy, 253
Morris, Trudy, 210
Mowry, Virginia, 20
Muir, Duncan, 261
    and concerns for changes in com-
        pany, 238–240
    on Dallas buildings, 166
    and Duff-Bloom's announced re-
        tirement, 263–264
    on Duff-Bloom's effectiveness,
        208
    on move to Dallas, 154–155

National Cash Register (NCR), 120–
    122, 124–125
Neppl, Marian, 101, 102
Neppl, Walter J., 15, 92–102
    "The Book" created by, 119
    on centralized buying, 283
    early career of, 97–102, 115–118
    and lack of managers' individual-
        ism, 136, 138, 139
    and Lenexa shareholder's meeting,
        274–275, 277
    management style of, 108
    military background of, 93–97
    and need for expertise, 254
    as president, 127
    and return to soft lines sales,
        129–130
    and Seibert's death, 280, 282
Newman, Frank, 256
Nigh, George, 269
no-haggle pricing, 24
Nystrom, Dee, 272, 273, 276–277
Nystrom, Gary, 272–277

Oelman, Bob, 120–122, 124–125
Oesterreicher, James E., 92
    and announcement of Duff-
        Bloom's retirement, 261–264
    background of, 247
    as CEO, 247–253

consensus management style
    under, 139n.7
Duff-Bloom's opinion of, 244
and Eckerd Drug deal, 255–259
and hiring of outside consultants,
    264–265
lack of charisma in, 266
leadership mistakes of, 254–257
and Lenexa shareholders meeting,
    271–276
personal attributes of, 251–252,
    266
and responsibility for company's
    fall, 159–160
retirement of, 279, 280
and San Francisco retail confer-
    ence, 235, 236
as script doctor, 252–253
and Seibert's funeral, 281
shortcomings of, 248–251
and sponsorships of St. James,
    174–175
Oesterreicher, Pat, 248, 280
open-to-buy agreement, 85–87
"Oral History" program, 2
ownership of stores, 32, see also part-
    nership concept

Parker, John, 82, 83
parochialism, 161
partnership concept, 30
    and buying function, 145
    fortunes made by, 41
    and growth of company, 32
Pasch, Bob, 2
Patman, Wright, 73, 74
Penney, Berta Hess, 2, 21–23, 25–26,
    32–34, 55
Penney, James Cash, 2
    adaptation/execution of ideas by,
        29
    and attitude toward money, 7–9
    and Berta's death, 34, 37
    breakdown of, 55–60
    buying expertise of, 31
    cattle breeding by, 42
    crisis of faith in, 59
    criticisms of, 160

death of, 20
employees' fund-raising for,
    49–58
and failure of butcher shop, 24
formality of, 15–16, 21
as good judge of character, 15–19
and growth of chain, 38
in-company reputation of, 10
issues and ideas focus of, 34
at Johnson and Callahan's Golden
    Rule stores, 21–27
marriages of, 26, 42n.3
and Maynard, 46
money borrowed by, 43
and move to New York City, 35
1920s lifestyle of, 42, 44
and partnership concept, 32
and The Penney Idea, 36–37
personality of, 28, 50
personnel choices of, 92–93
popularity of, 41
post-crash financial problems of,
    51–53
reaction to credit issue by,
    113–114
reputation of, 54 55
and retirees' criticism of Batten,
    13–15
and rose bush sale, 83
in Salt Lake City, 32
and Sams's death, 91
self-doubt of, 21–23, 25
spending by, 41, 42
statue of, 229–230
and stock market crash, 42–44
suits tailor-made for, 19
as teacher by example, 16–19
and tipping, 8–12
and Torrey's advancement in
    company, 40–41
working hours of, 33
the Penney formula, 29
The Penney Idea, 36–37, 112
    under Howell, 230–231
    under Oesterreicher, 259–260
Peterson, Coleman, 234, 242
Pfeiffer, Jane, 128–129
philanthropy, 43, 54, 216

point-of-sale data, 113, 119, see also
    transaction recorder
Ponder, Michael, 3
Potts, Carl, 106, 107
Powell, Colin, 265
PriceWaterhouseCoopers, 265
Prindiville, Terry, 165
private brands/labels, 32, 42, 144
profit, customer value vs., 230–231
profit sharing, 15, 32
public stock, 42

Questrom, Allen, 248, 255n.2, 259,
    270, 279, 280, 282
Questrom, Kelli, 279

Reagan, Nancy, 149
regional conventions, 41
Restaino, Mike, 167, 170–172
retailing function, 145, 255, see also
    managers; specific topics
Rhiel, Jack, 130–131
Rittenour, Lloyd, 67–68
rose bush sales, 81–84
Rouser, C. J., 73–75
Rozelle, Cathy, 197, 198, 217–218
Rozen, Miriam, 266n.5
Rushin, Steve, 3, 4

Sams, Earl Corder, 2, 43
    and Berta's illness/death, 33–34
    criticisms of, 160
    and customer-first precepts, 231
    death of, 91
    early responsibilities of, 34
    and fund-raising for Penney, 44,
        49–51, 55–56
    and management training pro-
        gram, 87–89
    and Penney's breakdown, 58
    on Penney's reaction to Berta's
        death, 37
    Penney's recruitment of, 27–29
    and Penney's working hours, 33
    and public shares in company, 42
    and rose bush sale, 83
    and Torrey's merchandising style,
        39n.2

Sams, Lula, 28, 29, 33
Scaccia, Don, 176, 180, 182, 185–187
Schwamb, Herb, 88–90
Sears, Chris, 210
Seibert, Don, 92, 93
    and catalog warehouse, 126
    early career of, 103–111
    funeral of, 280–282
    Howell monitored by, 149
    management style of, 108–109
    merchandising style of, 130
    and move to Dallas, 150
    on Neppl's move to New York,
        118
    and second thoughts about How-
        ell, 160n.3
Seibert, Verna, 103, 107, 128
self-improvement correspondence
    course, 10–11
service, 37
shareholders meeting (Lenexa),
    271–276
Shoener, Mark, 190–191, 194–195,
    219–221, 227, 228
shopping-center stores, 100, 113
Singer, 121
The Skins Game, 213
speaking engagements, rationale for,
    214
Spirit of the American Woman cam-
    paign, 174–175
sponsorships, 214–215
    of Lyn St. James, 174–175
    of women's golf events, 192
St. James, Lyn, 174–175, 182
St. Petersburg Times, 258
Steinmetz, Herb, 68

stock market crash, 42–43, 51–54
strip-center full-line stores, 100
suburban stores, 100
Sullivan, Kathleen, 195, 223
synergism, 256–257

Taj MaHowell, 169
Thomas, John, 263
thrift, 15
tipping, 8–12
Torrey, Homer, 39–41, 81, 99
transaction recorder, 119–126
tris-treated merchandise, 138
truth, internal, 89
Tygart, Barger, 235–236, 250

uniformity of merchandise, 81
Unitas, Johnny, 3
United Way drives, 216

Wal-Mart, 234, 242, 243
Wanda Wonder, 259
warehouses, 126, 271
Warrington College speech, 231–235
Wayne, John, 42–43
Weitz, Bart, 217, 232
White, Bob, 239–240
women
    and inclusion program, see inclu-
        sion
    in Penney workforce, 128–129
    and Spirit of the American
        Woman campaign, 174–175
working hours, 32, 33
World War II, 95–96
Wright, Cece, 101, 102, 110, 111, 116
Wright, Lee, 134, 143